POOLE
PRIVATE PILOTS GUIDE

Part-FCL PPL

Principles of Flight & Aircraft General (Aeroplane)

David Cockburn

Nothing in this manual supersedes any EU legislation or European Aviation Safety Agency (EASA) Regulations or procedures; or any operational documents issued by any United Kingdom Government Department, the Civil Aviation Authority, National Aviation Authorities, the manufacturers of aircraft, engines and systems, or by the operators of aircraft throughout the world. As maps and charts are changed regularly, any extracts reproduced in this book must not be used for flight planning purposes.

Principles of Flight & Aircraft General (Aeroplane) for the Private Pilot - David Cockburn
Copyright 2022 © Pooleys Flight Equipment Ltd

ISBN 978-1-84336-111-4

First Edition 2007
Second Edition May 2022

All rights reserved. No part of this publication may be reproduced in any material form (including photocopying or storing it in any medium by electronic means and whether or not transiently or incidentally to some of the use of this publication (without the written permissions of the copyright owner) except in accordance with the provisions of the Copyright, Designs and Patent Act 1988 or under the terms of a licence issued by the Copyright Licensing Agency Limited, 90 Tottenham Court Road, London, England W1P 0LP. Applications for the copyright owner's written permission to reproduce any part of this publication should be addressed to the publisher.

The information contained in this publication is for instructional use only, and must not be used in place of official publications. The Author will not be held responsible for any inaccuracies or omissions contained in the text or diagrams in this publication.

Warning: The doing of an unauthorised act in relation to a copyright work may result in both a civil claim for damages and criminal prosecution.

Pooleys Flight Equipment Ltd
Elstree Aerodrome
Hertfordshire
WD6 3AW England, UK

Tel: +44 (0) 208 953 4870
Email: **sales@pooleys.com**
Website: **www.pooleys.com**

Preface

This addition to the Pooley's Part-FCL PPL guides is designed to provide the necessary information for a student to pass the two ground examinations on the subjects of aeroplane principles of flight and aircraft general, without going into the amount of detail required by commercial licence examinations. Like the others in the series it contains the essential facts in a easy to read and understand style which not only helps to retain the important parts of the syllabus for that examination but can be used as a refresher for qualified pilots. It also contains additional material to help with differences training for more complex aeroplane types.

Chapters 1 to 5 of the book provide all necessary material for the Principles of Flight examination. Chapter 6 to 14, together with Chapter 4, cover the Aircraft General syllabus. Chapter 7 is not currently required for PPL theory exams, but contains essential information for certain differences training.

While updating this edition, the author has taken the opportunity to revise and increase the number of specimen questions, including general revision questions at the ends of Chapters 5 and 14. There is also a new chapter on propulsion systems which for the first time includes descriptions of turbine and electric engines.

The most important parts, especially those relating directly to safety, are covered in detail. However, the coverage of parts which the author considers less vital is only sufficient to give a basic understanding of general structure. It is always advisable to improve one's knowledge, and pilots should strive to learn as much about their aircraft and its environment as possible. Pilots must refer to the Flight Manual and other official documents for accuracy and confirmation before flight.

This is especially true because this document is not amended as legislation changes.

In this document, the male pronoun 'he' is often used to refer to both genders. This is no slight on the ladies who fly, merely a space saving and readability measure.

The author would like to thank friends who assisted in this publication and to Diamond UK and Garmin UK for permission to use promotional material.

Comments or suggestions on this or any other guides in this series are welcomed.

Editorial Team

Author David Cockburn

David Cockburn served for many years in the Royal Air Force as a pilot and flying instructor, amassing nearly 6000 flying hours including over 1000 hours instructing on jet trainers and 1000 hours on light piston aeroplanes. During that time he specialised in teaching mainly visual navigation techniques to pilots and navigators in the air and on the ground. He holds a UK Airline Transport Pilots Licence, and since leaving the RAF has worked as a ground instructor in professional flying training schools in this country and abroad, and is the author of several professional training books and manuals. He holds a Master Air Pilot Certificate and is a Fellow of the Royal institute of Navigation, and continues to give flying instruction at flying clubs to PPL and IMC rating students.

Having decided to concentrate on private pilot training, it became apparent that students and private pilots found it difficult to find the practical and important information they needed from the detailed descriptions in the available textbooks. He has therefore produced these guides to provide this practical and important information.

Daljeet Gill

Daljeet is Head of Design & Development for Pooleys Flight Equipment and editor of the Pooleys Private Pilots Guides, Pre-flight Briefings, R/T Communications, Pooleys Air Pilot Manuals Manuals and Air Presentations plus many others. Daljeet has been involved with editing, typesetting and design for all these publications. Graduated in 1999 with a BA (hons) in Graphic Design, she deals with marketing, advertising & design of our new products. She maintains our website and produces our Pooleys Catalogue annually.

Contents

Chapter 1	How an Aeroplane Flies	1
Chapter 2	Aeroplane Controls	21
Chapter 3	Manoeuvring	39
Chapter 4	Pressure Instruments	53
Chapter 5	Stalling and Spinning	67
Chapter 6	Piston Engines	83
Chapter 7	Other Engine Types	105
Chapter 8	Propellers	115
Chapter 9	Engine Instruments & Health	125
Chapter 10	The Airframe	131
Chapter 11	Aircraft Systems	143
Chapter 12	Other Flight Instruments	163
Chapter 13	Other Equipment and Flight Safety	181
Chapter 14	Airworthiness	193
	Answers to Exercises	207
	Index	211

Intentionally Left Blank

Chapter 1

How an Aeroplane Flies

1.1 Introduction

Aeroplanes are heavier than air aircraft. They are flying machines with fixed wings. The basic principles of flight apply to all heavier than air aircraft, but this book is concerned with aeroplanes only.

1.2 The Structure

The structure of an aeroplane (the airframe) consists of several parts. The **fuselage** contains most of the load, including the pilot and the engine of a single-engined aeroplane. The flow of air over the **wings** provides the force to keep the aeroplane flying. Other parts of the airframe will be discussed as the book progresses.

■ *Figure 1.1* **A Typical Light Aeroplane**

1.3 Forces

The airframe has mass. The earth's gravity exerts a force on the airframe, attempting to move it in the direction of the centre of the earth. This force is called 'weight'. When the aeroplane is parked on the aerodrome surface, that balancing force is provided by a reaction through the aircraft tyres and undercarriage structure. Once the aeroplane is in the air, however, another force must be provided to balance the weight and keep the aeroplane in flight. That force is called lift, and is provided by the wings deflecting the air through which they are moving.

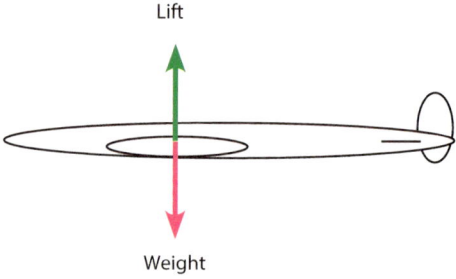

■ *Figure 1.2* **Lift and Weight**

Looking at a wing from the side, the wing "section" is a specific shape, similar to that in figure 1.3. If the wing is moved towards the left, the air through which it is moving will be pushed out of the way by its movement. Although the wing is moving and the air is static, the effects are the same as if the wing were static and the air (the "relative airflow") moving. This is the way we shall describe most "aerodynamic" effects.

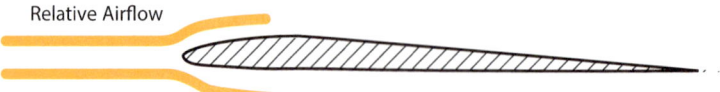

■ *Figure 1.3* **Airflow round a Wing Section**

The shape of the wing section deflects the relative airflow a certain amount. However, if the wing section is angled to the relative airflow, the effect is to deflect the air even more. The deflection of the air by this combination of the shape and the "angle of attack" produces a reaction on the wing itself, pushing it upwards as in figure 1.4. The faster the air flows relative to the wing, the greater the mass of air is deflected in a given time, and the greater the reaction. The greater the angle of attack, the greater the reaction (but only up to a certain "critical" angle).

■ *Figure 1.4* **Airflow Deflection**

As can be seen in figure 1.5, the "total reaction" force produced by the deflection of the airflow does not act in exactly the opposite direction to the weight. It points slightly rearwards. The total reaction provides not only lift in an upwards direction at 90 degrees to the relative airflow, but also a component acting in the same direction as the relative airflow. This component, attempting to slow the aeroplane down, is called "drag". Fig 1.5 also shows the "chord line" of the wing (a straight line between the "leading" edge and the "trailing" edge). The angle of attack is the angle between the chord line and the relative airflow.

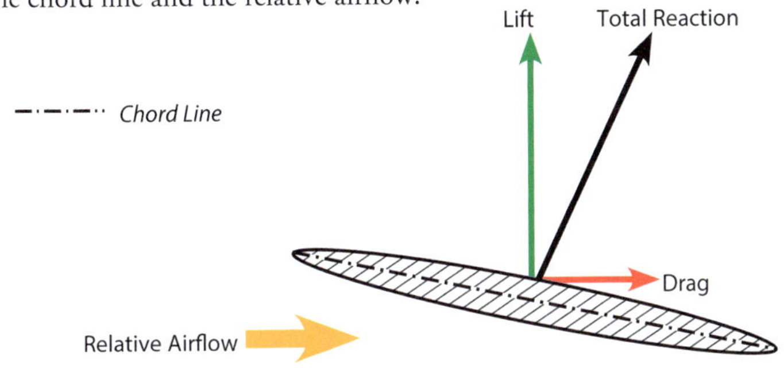

■   *Figure 1.5* **Lift and Drag**

In fact, the drag component from the flow deflection is only part of the total drag from an aircraft (the "induced" or "lift-dependent" drag). Further drag ("profile" or "parasite" drag) is produced by the movement of all parts of the aircraft structure through the air, and the faster that structure moves the more profile drag is produced. Weight, lift and drag are the only forces acting on a glider, as we shall see later. However, a powered aeroplane has an engine, and the engine produces another force which can counter that drag, called "thrust", which acts along the aeroplane centreline. For the aeroplane to maintain straight and level flight without accelerating in any direction, the horizontal forces [thrust (**T**) and drag(**D**)] must balance, and so must the vertical forces [lift (**L**) and weight (**W**)], as in figure 1.6.

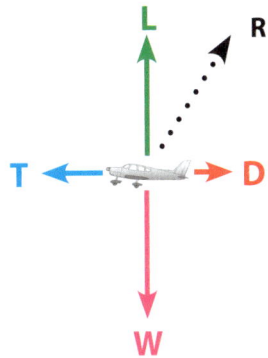

■   *Figure 1.6* **Forces in Equilibrium - Straight & Level**

3

1.4 The Air

As seen in the volume on Meteorology, the earth's atmosphere is composed of a mixture of gases, mainly Nitrogen (78%) and Oxygen (21%), in almost constant proportions at all altitudes. The molecules (the tiny basic components) of these gases have mass. The earth's gravity affects all of them, and the molecules at the 'top' of the atmosphere push down on those below them, which in turn push down on those below, progressively compressing the air (increasing its "pressure") as it becomes closer to the earth's surface. The high molecules are far apart, but the compressed molecules at lower altitudes are closer together, or 'denser'. The density of a gas is defined as mass per unit of volume, and is affected by its temperature as well as its pressure. Density increases as pressure increases, but decreases as temperature increases ($\rho\alpha$ [is proportional to] P/t).

The density of the air affects the forces produced by air deflection. Dense air produces a greater total reaction, and also more thrust from the engine. However, since weight is not affected by air density, an aeroplane performs better when the air is dense. Density is affected by temperature; cold air is denser than warm air. Air with low humidity (the proportion of water vapour molecules in the atmosphere) is denser than 'humid' air.

The fact that pressure reduces with altitude can be and is used to indicate the altitude of an aircraft. An 'altimeter' measures the pressure of the air around that aircraft but is marked to indicate altitude (see chapter 4). The actual density and pressure of the atmosphere is neither constant nor varies consistently. Nevertheless, ICAO (the International Civil Aviation Organisation) has agreed that a "International Standard Atmosphere (ISA)" with an assumed constant temperature, density and pressure at sea level, and an assumed consistent variation with height, gives an acceptable approximation to average conditions at and above the earth' surface. This standard atmosphere is used to calibrate instruments, and to compare performances of aircraft and engines.

At sea level, the ISA density, temperature and pressure is 1225 grams per cubic metre, +15 degrees Celsius, and 1013.2 hectoPascals (hPa) [or millibars (mb) which are exactly the same unit]. The temperature is assumed to reduce by 1.98 degrees with every thousand feet of altitude above sea level, up to an altitude of 36090 feet (think of it as 2 degrees per thousand feet). Pressure reduces by a complex formula, but on average by 1 hectoPascal per 30 feet of altitude close to sea level, and 1 hPa per 100 feet at 10,000 feet above sea level. Examination questions may require you to calculate the temperature or pressure at different altitudes in the ISA, but you should not have to make density calculations.

1.5 Level Flight

We have seen that for level flight at a constant speed, thrust and drag must balance each other, and so must weight and lift. At any time, the weight is fixed, and the lift generated by the wings must exactly equal that weight. The lift from a particular shape and size of wing depends on density, true airspeed and the angle of attack - there is a recognised formula "**Lift = $C_L \frac{1}{2}\rho V^2 S$**" where V is the true airspeed, ρ is the air density, S is the wing area, and C_L (the "coefficient of lift") depends on both the shape of the wing section (its 'camber') and its angle of attack. It may be useful to remember the formula for exam purposes, but it is more important to remember the actual factors. The combination of "$\frac{1}{2}\rho V^2$" is the "dynamic pressure" felt on a moving aircraft and actually equates to the "indicated airspeed" we see on an airspeed indicator. Co-efficients are used in aerodynamics to compare different wing "sections" at varying dynamic pressures. The lift of a given wing therefore depends on the indicated airspeed and the angle of attack.

To fly level at a particular speed, the pilot adjusts the attitude of the aircraft so that the air hits the wing at the correct angle of attack for that speed. If the angle is too great, lift will be more than weight and the aircraft will accelerate upwards in a climb; at too small an angle, it will descend. If the airspeed increases, perhaps by increasing thrust to be greater than drag, the angle of attack required for level flight becomes less. At a lower airspeed, the angle required increases (until the "critical angle" is reached, when the lift actually starts to reduce - we call this point the "stall" and the corresponding airspeed the "stalling speed").

1.6 Drag

"Profile" or "parasite" drag is the "air resistance" experienced by any object moving through air. It depends on the area exposed to the air and also on the density of that air, as well as the relative speed between the object and the air. Profile drag depends on the same aerodynamic factors as lift (which we have seen as the dynamic pressure), and also on the way the air flows over the object. Sometimes called 'zero-lift drag', it is usually considered to be a combination of 3 separate components.

"Skin friction" can be considered to be the 'stickiness' of the air to the object's surface. In very simple terms, a smooth highly polished surface will allow the air in contact with it (the "boundary layer") to flow relatively easily over it (referred to as "laminar" flow), while a rough surface (perhaps covered in dead insects) will create "turbulent" flow and more drag. Laminar flow is usually only achieved close to the leading edge.

"Form drag" is caused by the object's shape relative to the direction of the airflow, and streamlining is normally considered as being the way to minimise it at the design stage, while the pilot can also reduce it by accurate flying (into the airflow). However, an aeroplane has many parts, and the airflows over these parts interact with each other to cause turbulence. This "interference drag" is a major component of profile drag, and designers make considerable efforts to smooth out the flow at interference points such as where the wing joins the fuselage.

Therefore, in addition to the aerodynamic factors, the amount of profile drag depends on the aircraft's shape, surface and the fit of its parts, as well as the "frontal area" exposed to the flow. All these can be combined in a coefficient of drag "C_D" so that we can arrive at a formula for profile drag which is very similar to the lift formula - $\mathbf{D = C_D \tfrac{1}{2} \rho V^2 S}$

'Induced drag' is the unwanted result of the airflow being altered by a wing to produce lift and we shall consider it further later, but a similar formula can be produced with the coefficient of induced drag depending on the angle of attack. Induced drag increases with the angle of attack (and does not reduce at the critical angle!), and therefore reduces with airspeed in level flight. Profile drag, as we have seen, increases with speed, and the total drag is the sum of these two.

The graph at figure 1.7 represents the variation in the types of drag with airspeed. Adding them together gives a curve as shown, and there is a speed where the total drag is at a minimum. This speed is called the "minimum drag indicated airspeed" or "V_{IMD}" and as described in another volume is important in aeroplane performance. The 'coefficient of total drag' mentioned in most textbooks has to take into account all the factors affecting both induced drag and profile drag, and can be plotted for individual aircraft.

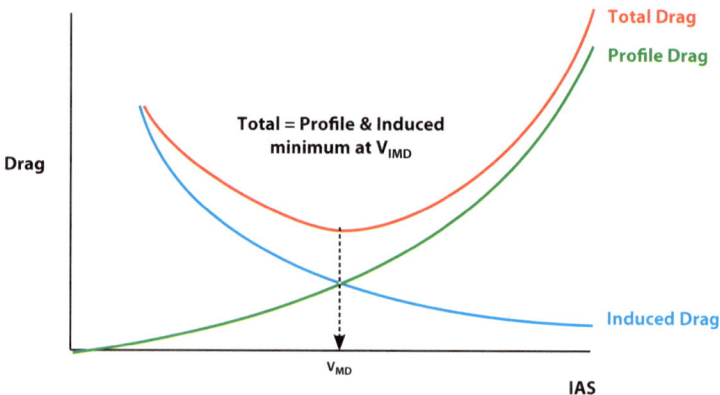

■ *Figure 1.7* **Drag Against Indicated Airspeed**

Minimum drag speed is important for another reason. At an airspeed <u>above</u> V_{IMD}, if the aircraft slows down because of turbulence, total drag decreases. Provided the thrust from the engine remains the same, there will be more thrust than drag so the aircraft will accelerate again to its original speed. The same would happen in reverse; - if the speed increased, the increased drag would slow it down again. We say its airspeed is "stable", because if its speed changes the aeroplane tries to return to its original speed.

However, if the airspeed is <u>below</u> V_{IMD}, any reduction in that airspeed will produce an increase in the total drag. If thrust remains the same, drag will be more than thrust and the aircraft will continue to slow down. The airspeed is "unstable" and the aeroplane requires more care to fly.

1.7   The Tailplane

Unfortunately, the forces on the aircraft do not all act in the same place. Weight is said to act through the "centre of gravity". Lift acts through a "centre of lift" which moves forward as the angle of attack increases. Drag and thrust do not act through the same point either, in fact the average aeroplane forces act rather as in figure 1.8. In this case the "couples" formed by the two pairs of forces act in different directions - the lift/weight couple tends to "pitch" the nose of the aeroplane upwards, while the thrust/drag couple tends to pitch the nose down. The amount of drag and the positions of the centres of lift and gravity will determine the overall "pitching moment" (a moment is a force multiplied by the distance from whatever pivot we measure it around). The aeroplane illustrated in fig 1.1 would probably have a considerable nose down pitching moment at most speeds.

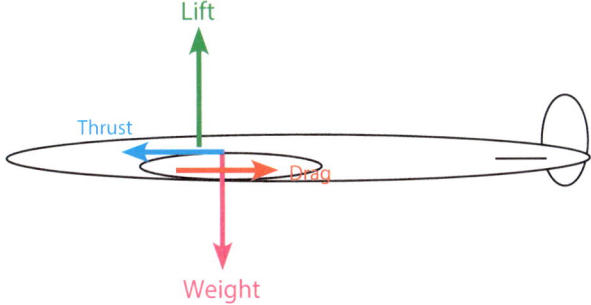

■   *Figure 1.8* **Pitching Moments**

Whatever final pitching moment results must be compensated by a lift force on the **tailplane**, as shown in fig 1.9, although in different aircraft (as in fig 1.1) or at different speeds the tailplane lift may have to act downwards. The tailplane of course produces profile drag, and any lift force also produces induced drag from the tailplane (this is often called "trim drag").

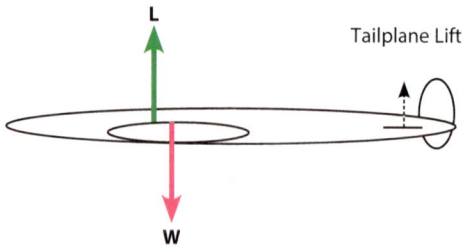

■ *Figure 1.9* **Tailplane Lift**

1.8 Stability

The tailplane is also an important means of stabilising the aircraft in the pitching plane (nose up and down). The tailplane produces a "restoring moment" if the aircraft pitches in turbulence. If the nose is pitched upwards, the angle of attack of the tailplane will increase, and there will be more lift upwards (or less lift downwards) at the tailplane. Because the tailplane is a long way from the centres of gravity and lift, that small upwards force at the tailplane will be strong enough to pitch the nose down again, bringing the aircraft back to the pitch attitude from which it started. This means the aircraft is "stable" in pitch. It also means that if the centre of gravity is too far aft (to the rear of the aircraft), the restoring moment, and therefore stability, reduces.

An object is "statically stable" if it returns towards its original position after being disturbed. If it were to continue to move in the direction it was disturbed, it would be "unstable", and if it were to stay in the same position that it had been left in, we would say it was "neutrally stable".

However, just because an aeroplane is statically stable and returns to its original position after being disturbed, that is not the end of the story. For example, we could expect the tailplane to pitch the aircraft back down again after a nose-up disturbance. However that downwards restoring pitch would not stop at the exact original position - its "inertia" makes it continue past the original position until the restoring force in the other direction took effect and brought the nose back up again. The nose would continue for some time pitching up and down, hopefully pitching progressively less every time until eventually stopping. If that happens, we say the aircraft is "dynamically stable" in pitch also. However, if this "phugoid" motion up and down were to become progressively worse, the aircraft would be "dynamically unstable", even though it was statically stable. Dynamic stability is affected by whether the pilot holds the control column steady (stick-fixed) after the disturbance, or lets it go (stick-free). Training aeroplanes will be dynamically stable in pitch with the stick fixed, although few aircraft have stick-free stability - the pilot is expected to exercise some control over the situation.

1.9 Lift

Light aeroplane wing sections are curved. This is not only to reduce the profile drag by streamlining, but also to produce a certain amount of lift. What happens is that as the air flows over a curved surface, its speed, and therefore its pressure, changes. This book does not propose to try to explain why, but others will refer to "Bernouilli's Theory" which is the accepted explanation. Basically, if we restrict the flow of air by making it flow towards itself over a curved surface, we increase its speed and reduce its pressure. The greater the curvature, the lower the pressure. So if a wing section is more curved at the top than at the bottom, like the section in figure 1.10, the pressure above the wing will be lower than at the bottom (although in both cases the pressure will be less than the "free stream" pressure away from the wing). The lower pressure effectively 'sucks' the wing upwards, which adds to the lift produced by physically deflecting the airflow downwards (the "flat plate" lift effect). The Bernoulli effect is more pronounced in aerofoils designed for fairly low speed flight.

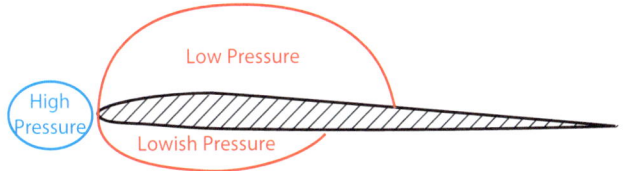

■   *Figure 1.10* **Pressure around a Wing Section**

The pressure pattern around a wing resulting from a combination of aerofoil shape and angle of attack varies not only from front to rear, but also from fuselage to tip, as in fig 1.11, where we are looking at a wing from the front (with the "leading edge" towards us). Around the wing tips, air tries to flow from the relatively higher pressure below the wing to the lower pressure above it, and although it cannot actually do that because of the speed of the wing's movement, it produces a twist to the flow behind the wing. This twist continues and a "vortex" is formed behind each wingtip. Inside the vortex the air pressure is reduced, which tends to suck the wing backwards. This is a major part of the induced drag we have already discussed.

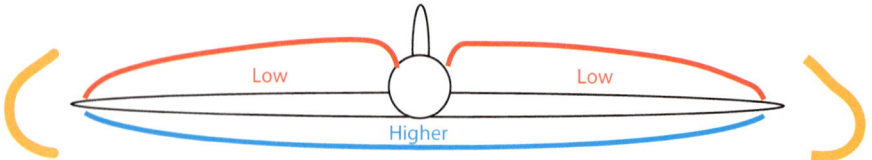

■ *Figure 1.11* **From the Leading Edge**

We have said that lift increases with an increase in the angle of attack, but only up to a certain "critical" angle. For most light aeroplane aerofoils (wing section shapes) this critical angle is approximately 15 degrees. A graph illustrating the change in CL (lift "coefficient" - the factor we include to take account of angle of attack and camber) with angle of attack is at figure 1.12. This graph is for a symmetrical aerofoil (one whose curvature is the same top and bottom so there is no pressure difference or lift at zero angle of attack). Notice that even though CL decreases as the angle increases beyond the critical angle, it does not fall to zero, and neither does the amount of lift produced by the wing! The actual shape of the graph depends on the wing section, which may not be the same all the way along the wing (in fact there is usually a twist called "washout" towards the tip).

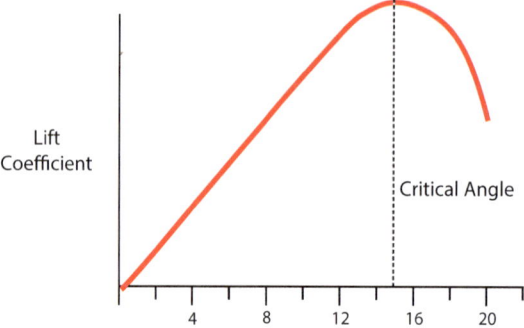

■ *Figure 1.12* **CL Changing with Angle Of Attack**

The shape of the graph in fig 1.12, and therefore the amount of lift produced by a given wing, also depends to some extent on the shape of the wing "planform" - what it looks like from above, although the planform's effect on drag is more significant.

1.10 Aspect Ratio and Induced Drag

The wing "span" is the total distance from the wing "tip" on one side to the wing tip on the other side. We saw in fig 1.5 that the chord is a line joining the leading edge of the wing section with the trailing edge. Dividing the span of a wing by its chord (or usually the average chord - few wings are rectangular) gives us a number called the "aspect ratio". Fig 1.13 shows wing planforms with the same area (S) but different aspect ratios.

We saw in fig 1.11 that the air tries to flow around the wing tips from below to above. That attempt does actually move the air around the tips inwards above the wing and outwards below it, forming vortices (plural of vortex) at each tip. That movement also induces some general "spanwise flow" further inboard, all along the trailing edge, so induced drag is a combination of wingtip vortices and smaller trailing edge vortices.

Over a wing with a high aspect ratio, as the left one in fig 1.13, less air has to be moved over each metre of wing span for the same lift to be generated than over a low aspect ratio wing. In addition, the air moves over a shorter distance along the wing section, giving less time for spanwise flow to form. A wing with a high aspect ratio therefore produces smaller vortices for the same amount of lift than a low aspect ratio wing. That means it has less induced drag, although its greater frontal area will produce more profile drag. For this reason, gliders and sailplanes, which spend a lot of time at low speeds, use wings with a higher aspect ratio than most light aeroplanes, which in turn have a higher aspect ratio than jet fighters.

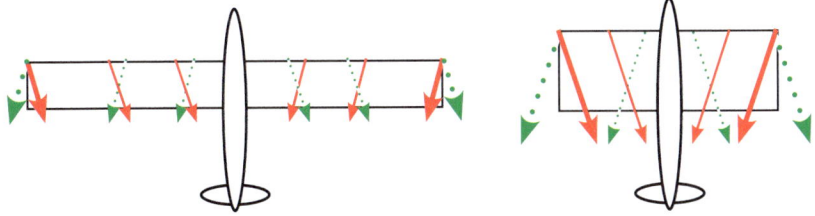

■   Figure 1.13 **Aspect Ratio & Spanwise Flow**

The flow through these vortices generates low pressure inside them, which effectively 'sucks' the aircraft backwards in a similar way that the low pressure caused by the flow over the curved wing surface 'sucks' the wing upwards. This is induced drag. The air flow is deflected downwards by the wing, and the vortices travel with that flow. This "downwash" is the reaction to the lift produced.

The wing moving through the air affects the air around it, and indeed ahead of it. The downwash causes a slight increase in the pressure of the deflected air. Unless the aircraft is flying at supersonic speeds, that downstream increase in pressure is 'felt' by the air ahead of the wing. In order to conserve energy and momentum, the air ahead of the oncoming wing attempts to minimise the overall change in pressure by moving upwards before it contacts the wing. This directs the relative airflow upwards toward the leading edge and moves the 'stagnation point' (where the air does not flow either over or under the wing but impacts it) downwards as angle of attack increases. The angle of attack effectively increases without the aircraft's pitch attitude appearing unduly high.

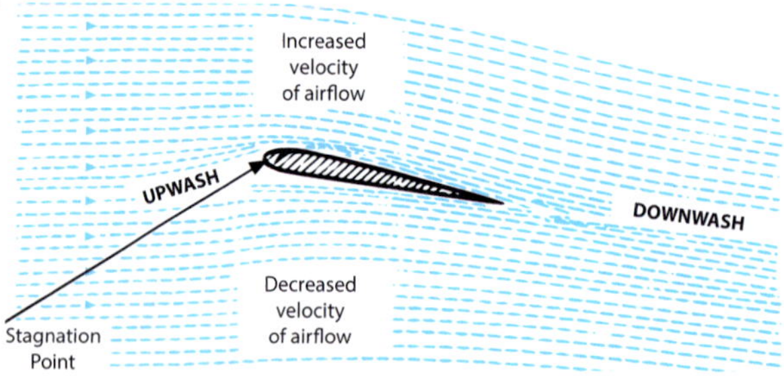

■ Figure 1.14 **Downwash altering relative airflow**

This early deflection can have an effect on landing. As an aeroplane with a low wing approaches the runway (usually at a high angle of attack and therefore a high "downwash angle"), the ground prevents the air ahead of the wing from arriving from below. This 'ground effect' reduces the angle of attack just as the aircraft is landing, and will encourage the aircraft to sink onto the runway. The reverse happens on take-off, when the angle of attack increases immediately after lift-off. The effect is of course less on an aeroplane with a high wing.

The vortices, especially the wing tip vortices, tend to stay in the air deflected by the aircraft which has made them, moving slowly downwards and outwards, slowly becoming weaker. The twisting motion they impart to the air is greatest at low speeds, when the wing has to produce a large coefficient of lift. A heavy aeroplane such as a commercial 'jumbo jet' produces tip vortices on take-off and on the approach to land which, if a light aircraft pilot were to fly through them, would turn the light aircraft upside down even if the pilot used all his controls to stop it. Light aircraft pilots must stay well away from any vortices which may have been left by a large aeroplane, for perhaps five minutes. The greater the aircraft weight and the slower it is flying, the stronger the vortex. The CAA has produced an aeronautical information circular (AIC) and a General Aviation Safety Sense leaflet on the subject of wake vortex, which list recommended distances and times of separation from large aircraft. If forced to follow or cross behind a large aircraft, especially at a distance less than that recommended in the AIC, stay above its flight path, never below it.

1.11 Aircraft Axes

We have already talked about "pitching" being movement of the aircraft's nose up and down in relation to the pilot. Rather than use these long descriptions of direction, it is common to refer to movement around one or other **axis** of the aircraft. An axis (plural=axes) is an imaginary line around which an object can rotate, rather as a car wheel rotates around an 'axle' in real life. **Pitching** is rotation *around* (sometimes the word "about" is used) the aircraft's "lateral" (side to side = wingtip to wingtip) axis. **Rolling** is rotation *around* (about) the aircraft's "longitudinal" (nose to tail = along the aircraft) axis. **Yawing** is rotation *around* (about) the aircraft's "normal" (at 90 degrees to both of the others = up & down) axis. The axes are shown in figure 1.15.

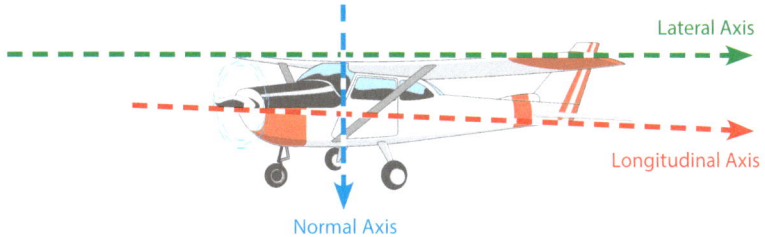

■   *Figure 1.15* **The Axes of an Aircraft**

A problem with the names of these axes is that *directions of movement* can also be described in books as being longitudinal or lateral, if the movement is either along the aircraft or from side to side. We shall not use the terms in this book.

1.12 Directional Stability

Light aeroplanes are designed to be stable if disturbed in any direction. We have already looked at stability in the pitching plane (nose going up and down around the lateral axis). However, the aircraft can move in other directions. If the nose goes from side to side (around the normal axis), that is called "yawing", and if one wing goes down and the other goes up (rotating around the longitudinal axis), that is "rolling".

To provide stability in yaw, an aeroplane has at least one vertical aerofoil, or **fin**, usually above the tailplane. Any yaw, whether caused deliberately by the pilot or by turbulence, will produce an angle of attack at the fin and generate sideways lift to return the nose of the aeroplane to its original direction, as in fig 1.16. The long fuselage behind the centre of gravity also produces sideways lift and a restoring moment, and the further forward the centre of gravity the more stable the aircraft.

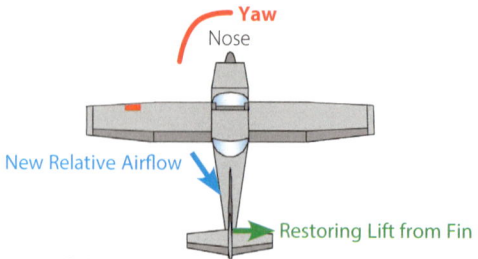

■ *Figure 1.16* **Yaw Stability**

If the aeroplane rolls, as in figure 1.17, whichever wing goes downwards will automatically have a greater angle of attack than the upgoing wing, so at normal speeds a certain amount of roll stability is naturally present. However, the restoring moments in roll (and yaw) tend to be weak, and the result of a disturbance in one or the other produces a change in the aircraft's direction.

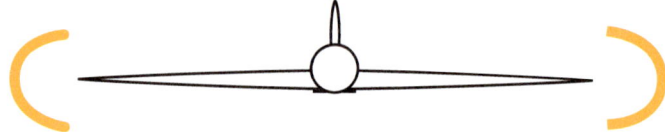

■ *Figure 1.17* **Rolling**

For this reason, designers include features to increase the lateral stability. For example, an aeroplane with the wings above the fuselage such as the one in figure 1.15 has a natural tendency to roll back once disturbed, rather like a pendulum. A high fin will also increase lateral stability. Most light aeroplanes, especially those with low wings, often have the wings placed at an angle of "dihedral", as in fig 1.18, which increases stability by reducing the vertical component of lift from the high wing while increasing it from the low wing.

■ *Figure 1.18* **Dihedral**

We shall look at the interaction between directional and lateral stability in chapter 3.

1.13 Exercise

1. What forces act on a powered aeroplane in flight?
   (a) Lift, thrust, and weight
   (b) Thrust, weight and total reaction
   (c) Lift, thrust and total reaction
   (d) Drag, lift and thrust

2. In a powered aeroplane, which of the following is true concerning the aerodynamic forces in level flight at a constant speed?
   (a) Lift balances Drag and Thrust balances Weight
   (b) Thrust is always more than Drag and Lift is always less than Weight
   (c) Lift balances Weight and Thrust balances Drag
   (d) Thrust is always less than Drag and Lift always more than Weight

3. At which point of a aeroplane is lift said to act?
   (a) Where the wing trailing edge meets the fuselage
   (b) At the centre of gravity
   (c) Where the wing leading edge meets the fuselage
   (d) At the centre of lift

4. The angle of attack of an aeroplane is the angle between:
   (a) The mean camber line of the aerofoil and the relative airflow
   (b) The chord line of the aerofoil and the angle of incidence
   (c) The chord line of the aerofoil and the relative airflow
   (d) The chord line of the aerofoil and the horizontal

5. When describing aerodynamic forces, which of the following statements is completely correct:
   (a) Weight acts at 90 degrees to the relative airflow, Thrust acts in the direction the aircraft is pointing
   (b) Lift acts vertically upwards from the centre of the earth, Drag acts directly against the direction the aircraft is pointing
   (c) Lift acts at 90 degrees to the relative airflow, Drag acts directly against the aircraft's flight path
   (d) Weight acts towards the centre of the earth, Thrust always acts at 90° to Weight

6. The density of a gas is:
   (a) Directly proportional to pressure and inversely proportional to temperature
   (b) Directly proportional to both pressure and temperature
   (c) Directly proportional to temperature and inversely proportional to pressure
   (d) Inversely proportional to both temperature and pressure

7. In conditions of constant temperature and pressure, moist air compared with dry air has:
   (a) Higher density
   (b) Unchanged density
   (c) Variable density
   (d) Lower density

8. The International Standard Atmosphere:
   (a) Details actual conditions of temperature and pressure at the aircraft's altitude
   (b) Details standard conditions of temperature and pressure at all altitudes
   (c) Details actual conditions of temperature and pressure at all altitudes
   (d) Is restricted to standard conditions of temperature and pressure at sea level

9. The air temperature at 11000 feet is −5 degrees C. The approximate temperature deviation from ISA is:
   (a) −2 degrees C
   (b) +2 degrees C
   (c) −9 degrees C
   (d) +9 degrees C

10. What effect does a reduction in air density have on an aeroplane in flight?
    (a) Lift increases and drag increases
    (b) Lift increases and drag reduces
    (c) Lift reduces and drag increases
    (d) Lift reduces and drag reduces

11. As the speed of an aeroplane increases:
    (a) Induced drag decreases and parasite drag increases
    (b) Both induced drag and parasite drag decrease
    (c) Both induced drag and parasite drag increase
    (d) Induced drag increases and parasite drag decreases

12. If an aeroplane has a low wing, and its lift acts behind the centre of gravity, which way will the lift force from the tailplane act?
    (a) Downwards
    (b) Upwards
    (c) Backwards
    (d) Forwards

13. At what angle of attack would you expect the coefficient of lift of a light aeroplane's wing to be greatest?

(a) 0 degrees
(b) 4 degrees
(c) 15 degrees
(d) 30 degrees

14. What is the critical angle?

(a) The dihedral angle at which the wings are attached to the fuselage
(b) The angle of attack of the wing when the aeroplane is on the ground
(c) The angle of attack of the wing above which the lift coefficient reduces
(d) The angle of attack of the tailplane when the angle of attack of the wing is zero

15. Which of the following is most likely to be the critical angle of a light aeroplane?

(a) -5 degrees
(b) 0 degrees
(c) 5 degrees
(d) 14 degrees

16. If an aeroplane's wing has a high aspect ratio, which of the following is untrue in comparison with a low aspect ratio wing of the same area at the same airspeed?

(a) It will have smaller wingtip vortices
(b) It will produce less induced drag
(c) The pressure difference between top and bottom surfaces will be the same
(d) It will have less profile drag

17. In normal flight, the airflow over the upper and lower surfaces of the wing will have:

(a) The same speed and surface pressure over both surfaces
(b) A higher speed and lower pressure over the upper surface
(c) A lower speed and higher pressure over the upper surface
(d) A higher speed and higher pressure over the upper surface

18. If you have to pass behind an aircraft whose wake vortex may hazard you, where would it be safest to pass?

(a) At the same altitude
(b) Above its flight path
(c) Below its flight path
(d) None of the above would be safe

19. Which part of an aeroplane's structure provides stability in pitch?
   (a) The wing
   (b) The fuselage
   (c) The fin
   (d) The tailplane

20. What is roll?
   (a) Rotation about the lateral axis
   (b) Rotation about the normal axis
   (c) Movement of the nose up and down
   (d) Rotation about the longitudinal axis

21. Which of the following will not assist in providing directional stability?
   (a) A large fin
   (b) Dihedral
   (c) A short fuselage
   (d) A high wing

22. If an aeroplane is disturbed in pitch by turbulence pushing the nose upwards, then when the turbulence force is removed the nose returns to its original position, what can we say about its stability?
   (a) The aircraft is laterally stable
   (b) The aircraft is laterally unstable
   (c) The aircraft is longitudinally neutral
   (d) The aircraft is longitudinally stable

23. The .... (i) .... the aircraft and the .... (ii) .... it is flying, the .... (iii) .. .. its wake vortex.

	(i)	(ii)	(iii)
(a)	heavier	slower	stronger
(b)	lighter	faster	stronger
(c)	lighter	slower	weaker
(d)	heavier	slower	weaker

24. In normal flight, the air flowing under the wing, compared to the air above it, will be at:
   (a) The same pressure
   (b) Variable pressure depending on airspeed
   (c) A higher pressure
   (d) A lower pressure

25. Angular movement of an aeroplane around its normal axis is:
   (a) Side-slipping
   (b) Yawing
   (c) Rolling
   (d) Pitching

26. We refer to the 'coefficient of lift'. What factors are included in that coefficient?
   (a) Wing camber and angle of attack
   (b) Wing area and air density
   (c) Air density and angle of attack
   (d) Wing area and air density

27. What effect does the position of the aeroplane's centre of gravity have on its directional stability?
   (a) The closer the C of G to the nose, the more directionally stable the aircraft
   (b) The closer the C of G to the fin, the more directionally stable the aircraft
   (c) The position of the C of G has no effect on directional stability
   (d) The closer the C of G to the tailplane, the more directionally stable the aircraft

28. If an aeroplane increases speed above the speed for minimum drag, which of the following is incorrect?
   (a) Induced drag decreases
   (b) Profile drag increases
   (c) Total drag increases
   (d) The aircraft becomes unstable with regard to speed

29. In order to maintain level flight while accelerating, what changes are required in aerodynamic forces and/or angle of attack?
   (a) Thrust must be greater than Drag and the angle of attack must progressively increase
   (b) Drag must be less than Thrust and the angle of attack must progressively reduce
   (c) Thrust must be less than Drag and the angle of attack must progressively reduce
   (d) Drag must be greater than Thrust and the angle of attack must progressively increase

Intentionally Left Blank

Chapter 2

Aeroplane Controls

2.1 Introduction

We have seen that an aeroplane is stable. A mathematician might say that it demonstrates Newton's first law, in that it remains in a state of steady motion unless acted upon by an external force (there are actually four forces acting on it. As we have seen, but if they are in balance the overall effect is as if no force were there). In order to make the aircraft change its flight path in the manner and direction he wants, then pilot must apply an extra force, or change the ones already acting on it. The more stable the aircraft, the less effect that force will have.

To do this, the pilot moves the "flight controls" in the cockpit. These flight controls are connected by linkages to parts of the aircraft structure, the "control surfaces", and the control surfaces move to bring about the desired effect.

2.2 Control Surfaces

Control surfaces are fitted at the trailing edge of various parts of the aircraft. As air flows over them, they produce forces which cause the rear of the aeroplane to move in a particular direction. Because the aircraft is moving forward when these forces are produced, a movement at the rear of the aeroplane produces a reaction at the front which moves the nose of the aircraft in the opposite direction to the force at the rear. Again, mathematicians might say this demonstrates Newton's third law, because to any action (at the tail) there is an equal and opposite reaction (at the nose).

Although some early controls actually bent the structure itself, most control surfaces are now individual aerofoil shapes attached by hinges, as the surface in fig 2.1. If the flight control in the cockpit is moved, the control linkage (usually either rods or cables) pushes the surface to one side. In many cases the linkage is contained within the structure to minimise profile drag, but we have shown an external linkage in fig 2.1.

If the airflow comes from the left in this particular example and the pilot's control in the cockpit pulls on the linkage, the linkage in turn will make the surface move downwards around the hinge. That movement will push the airflow further downwards (it is effectively changing the shape of the main aerofoil and increasing its angle of attack), to produce a total reaction including a lift force upwards, moving the rear of the aircraft upwards and the nose downwards.

The more the control surface is deflected, the greater the angle of attack change and the more rapidly the aircraft will change its direction. The higher the airspeed, the greater the effect that control deflection will have on the aircraft, and the 'firmer' the control will feel to the pilot. The other factors involved are the area of the control surface, and the distance (the "moment arm") between the control surface and the centre of gravity (to be precise the "aerodynamic centre", which is the centre of the lift/weight couple).

■ *Figure 2.1* **Control Surface**

2.3   Elevators

Elevators in buildings go up and down. Elevators in an aircraft make the nose go up and down (in other words they cause 'rotation around the lateral axis'). They are attached to the rear of the tailplane. If we consider that the main aerofoil shown in figure 2.1 represents a tailplane (or "horizontal stabilizer"), the control surface illustrated would be the elevator. In order to move the linkage and the surface in the desired direction, the pilot would move the control column in the cockpit forward. The effect would be as shown in fig 2.2, pitching the nose down. A similar effect would be caused by the control moving the whole tailplane, as is the case of an "all-moving tailplane" or by US manufacturers "stabilators", but we shall refer to elevators in this book.

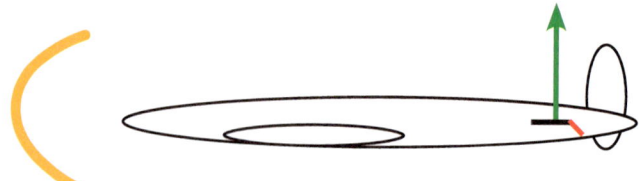

■ *Figure 2.2* **Elevator Down**

All the time the control surface is deflected in relation to the main aerofoil, that reaction will be taking place, and the aircraft in this case would continue to pitch (although the stability we saw in chapter 1 will normally reduce and probably eventually stop the pitch rate). In order to stop the aircraft rotating, the pilot must return his flight control to the neutral position (where the surface is no longer deflected), when stability will slow the movement down to a stop.

2.4   Ailerons

Ailerons are designed to make an aeroplane roll (about the longitudinal axis). To achieve that, each wing has a control surface at the trailing edge towards the tip. These are connected to the pilot's control column so that when he rotates the top of the control column (which may be a wheel or just a hinged stick), the aircraft rotates in the same way.

If we consider Fig 2.1 as representing a section of the left (or "port") wing close to the wingtip, the control surface shown is the left (port) aileron. If the pilot rotates the control column clockwise (top towards his right), the aileron shown will move down, increasing the angle of attack and therefore the lift on the outboard part of the port wing. At the same time, the linkage is connected to the aileron on the right (starboard) wing, but in the opposite direction, so that when the port aileron moves down, the starboard aileron moves up. That upgoing aileron reduces the lift from the outboard part of the starboard wing. The combined effect of the increased lift on the left and reduced lift on the right wings is to produce a "rolling moment" to roll the aircraft to the right (clockwise around the nose as the pilot sees it). In fig 2.3 we illustrate that movement, again as seen from the rear.

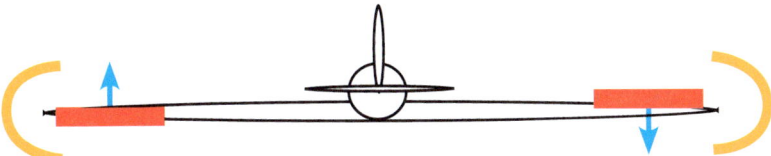

■   Figure 2.3 **Effect of Ailerons**

As before, the further the pilot moves the flight control, the more the aileron surface is deflected, the greater the changes in lift on each wing, and the more rapidly the aircraft will roll. Again it will continue to roll until the pilot returns the control column to the neutral position.

2.5 The Rudder

The rudder is the control surface found at the rear of the fin (or "vertical stabilizer"), which we can imagine as the main aerofoil on which we are looking down in fig 2.1. This surface is controlled by pedals in the cockpit which are connected to each other. If the pilot pushes on the left pedal, the linkage will move the rudder to the left, causing lift to move the fin to the right, and the nose of the aircraft to the left, as in fig 2.4.

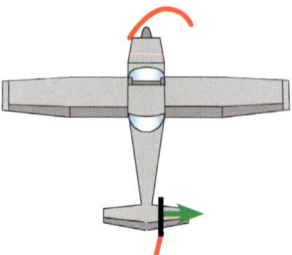

■ *Figure 2.4* **Rudder Effect**

However, we have seen in chapter 1 that there are many design features to maintain an aircraft's directional stability. These strongly oppose the yaw force generated by the rudder. The aeroplane will indeed yaw as the rudder is applied (the rate of yaw depends on the amount of pedal movement). However, once the nose has moved to one side, the airflow against the side of the fuselage and the fin, and over the wings, will produce so much stabilising force that the rate of yaw slows considerably. Once the pedals are returned to neutral and the rudder deflection is removed, the stabilising force may yaw the aircraft back to almost its original direction again. Although the rudder is the only aerodynamic control which can turn an aeroplane on the ground, it is of little use for actually changing direction in the air. Its main purpose in the air is to prevent unwanted yaw, reducing drag by keeping the aircraft "balanced" with the air flowing straight along the fuselage.

2.6 Primary Effects of Controls

We have seen that the elevators pitch the aeroplane, the ailerons roll it, and the rudder yaws it. The rate at which the aeroplane responds depends on the speed of the airflow and the amount the pilot moves the flight controls. In general if the control is returned to neutral, the rotation will stop, although stability may be attempting to return the aircraft to its original position.

All of these movements are in relation to the aircraft axes, or for practical purposes to the pilot's eyes as he sits upright in the aircraft. For example, if the aeroplane has already rolled into a position where the port wing is pointing upwards, away from the earth as we look from the rear of the aeroplane in fig 2.5, moving the elevator up by pulling the control column backwards will still pitch the aircraft, but in this case along the horizon rather than away from the earth.

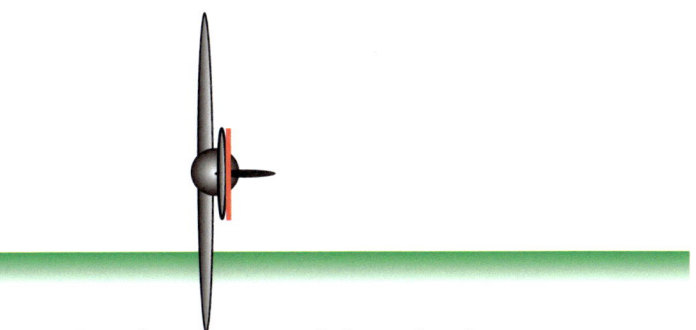

■ *Figure 2.5* **Controls produce movement relative to aircraft axes**

2.7   Aileron Drag

Any control surface deflection produces not only a change in lift, but also a corresponding change in drag. Since the movement of the surface usually produces lift, in general every time a control is deflected, the aircraft will slow down slightly unless more power is produced from the engine. A minimum of small, smooth control movements is therefore the ideal to achieve the maximum performance from each litre of fuel.

However, the drag changes have another effect specific to the ailerons. Consider fig 2.3 again. The increased lift on the port wing will also increase its induced drag, and the reduced lift on the starboard wing will reduce its induced drag. These aileron drag changes will produce a moment attempting to yaw the aircraft to the left, as in fig 2.6, at the same time as the aircraft is rolling right. This "adverse yaw" is worst at low speeds where induced drag is at its greatest, and on aeroplanes with long wings such as gliders.

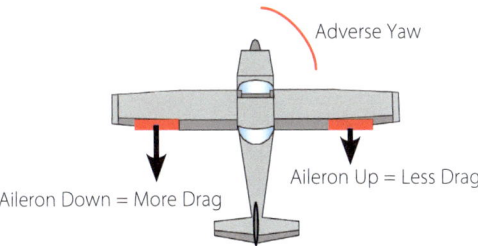

■ *Figure 2.6* **Aileron Drag**

Since a pilot seldom wants to yaw in the opposite direction to the direction of roll, he must counter this adverse yaw by applying rudder to prevent it every time he moves the ailerons. The greater the aileron deflection and the slower the airspeed, the more rudder required. However, designers have means of reducing the rudder movement required from the pilot.

One way is for the downgoing aileron to move much less than the one which is going upwards. These "differential ailerons" are found on many light aeroplanes. Another way is to shape the control surface in such a way that the leading edge of the upgoing aileron pushes down into the airflow below the wing, increasing the profile drag to compensate for the increased induced drag from the other aileron. The hinge is usually positioned to achieve the effect, as in fig 2.7. These shaped control surfaces are called "frise" ailerons.

■ *Figure 2.7* **Frise Aileron**

Another method of reducing aileron drag is to use "lift spoilers" on the wing either on their own or in conjunction with conventional ailerons. If the control column is moved to the right, for example, a flap hinged at the front (the "spoiler") on the top of the starboard wing would operate, reducing the lift on that wing (and increasing profile drag).

A third way is for the controls to be actually linked together in such a way that when the pilot applies aileron, the rudder controls are moved in the same direction. This linkage would only be correct at a particular airspeed and power setting, however, so unless fairly advanced computer technology were involved, the pilot's skill would still be required.

2.8   Trimming

While an aeroplane is designed to be stable, the pilot may not want it to stay in the position (the "attitude") it wants to all the time. To fly level at a certain speed with a certain loading requires the aircraft's nose to be in a certain pitch attitude in relation to the horizon. Unless the pilot is exceptionally lucky, the aircraft's stability will attempt to put it in a different attitude, perhaps with the nose lower than he wants. In that case, the pilot will be always pulling back on the control column to hold the correct pitch attitude, and that pulling can be tiring. An additional small control surface (a "tab") can be fitted to assist him in this, by using aerodynamic forces to hold the elevator where the pilot wants it.

A small trim tab is fitted to an elevator just as the elevator is fitted to the tailplane. In fig 2.8, the trim tab has been moved (usually by a wheel in the cockpit) to exert a force downwards on the elevator. This might be the result of the pilot finding himself constantly pushing forwards on the control column, so he has moved the top of the trim wheel similarly forwards in the cockpit. The elevator being pushed downwards will produce more lift from the tailplane and provide a small downwards pitching moment, which will counter the aircraft's stability trying to push the nose back up again. Depending on the linkage, the "simple" trim tab may move a fixed amount when the wheel is moved, or more commonly the more the elevator moves, the more the "geared" tab moves. This provides an extra stabilising force towards the desired pitch attitude.

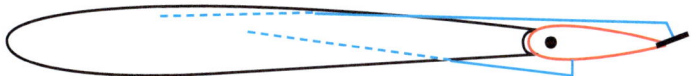

■ *Figure 2.8* **Elevator Trim Tab**

The trim control should only be used to remove the force remaining after the pilot has selected the pitch attitude he wants. If a pilot attempts to move the trim control before he has selected the attitude, he will find himself working at least twice as hard thereafter!

Similar trim tabs may be fitted to the rudder (especially in multi-engined aircraft) or even the ailerons. However, in most light aeroplanes these tabs are not controlled by the pilot, but are "fixed tabs", metal plates which are fitted and adjusted by engineers after flight testing, to hold the rolling and yawing attitudes constant. If you find that you constantly need to hold a force on the rudder or aileron controls, you should advise an engineer accordingly.

Other tabs are sometimes fitted for specific reasons. A geared tab which is not connected to the trim control may be fitted as an "anti-balance" tab to increase stability. Similarly, if an aeroplane has too much stability, a "balance" tab may be fitted to make the movement of the control surface easier by moving the opposite way from the elevator to assist in its movement. A "servo" tab is one step further. The control column is not connected directly to the elevator at all, but to a tab which moves (for example upwards) pushing the elevator (downwards) to provide the desired (downwards) pitching movement.

Trim may be achieved by different means. Sometimes there is no tab, but a system of springs in the linkage physically holds the control surface in the desired position. Electrical trimming systems allow electric motors to drive either a tab or a spring datum, and these sometimes form part of an autopilot. If your aircraft has either an electric trim or an autopilot, make sure you have read the Flight Manual and understand the system, especially every possible way to disconnect it!

2.9 Control Balancing

Any control surface, whether a primary control or a tab, revolves around its hinge system. If the hinge is right at the front of the control, we can imagine that the force required to move it would be considerable, especially if the aircraft were moving at high speed. The hinge is therefore "inset" to allow easier movement.

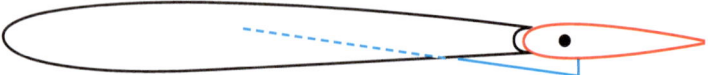

■ *Figure 2.9* **Inset hinge**

Another way of achieving some "aerodynamic balance" of the control is to build the surface in such a way that part of it extends forward of the hinge, as the elevators seen from above in figure 2.10. As the elevators move down, the "horn" at the front of the tips moves up, reducing the control force required overall. As with an inset hinge, however, the surface must not "overbalance" at any time, or the pilot will find difficulty in controlling the aeroplane.

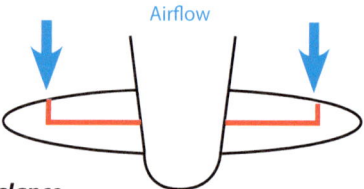

■ *Figure 2.10* **Horn Balance**

This aerodynamic balance helps the pilot to control the aircraft. There is another form of balance which is important in control systems, that of **mass balancing**. If the centre of gravity of the control surface itself lies a long way behind the hinge as in figure 2.11, every time the control surface moves the inertia of the surface will encourage it to continue moving beyond the position intended. The airflow acting against the deflection then tries to make it move in the reverse direction and the reversing control surface deflection in turn reverses the aircraft's movement.

■ *Figure 2.11* **Control Surface Centre of Gravity**

This overbalancing would make control rather difficult, and the control reversals (called "Flutter") put considerable strain on the structure, which increases significantly with airspeed. For this reason, designers attempt to reduce the effect by moving the control surface centre of gravity as close to the hinge as practicable. This is done by placing extra mass in positions forward of the hinge, for example inside a horn balance or along the leading edge of the control surface. The aircraft's maximum permitted airspeed (V_{NE}) is often dictated by flutter considerations.

2.10 Flaps

An aeroplane landing has a considerable amount of energy, which must be absorbed by friction, either by the brakes or by dragging some form of skid across the ground (as in a Tiger Moth). The slower the aircraft can land, the less energy has to be absorbed (and the longer the brakes last!), and the shorter distance is needed to absorb it. It is usually an advantage to make the landing at as low a speed as possible. This can be achieved by making landings into wind, to produce a lower groundspeed than the indicated airspeed, but there are other ways to reduce the landing speed safely.

One of these is to produce a higher lift coefficient at low speeds, so that the total lift needed to balance weight can be provided at a lower airspeed. The shape of the wing section can be changed mechanically by adding "flaps" at either the leading or trailing edges. Leading edge flaps are usually found on large aeroplanes, so we shall consider only trailing edge flaps here.

■ *Figure 2.12* **Slotted Flap**

A flap acts rather like an elevator, at the inboard end of the wings. It increases the angle of attack and therefore the lift coefficient at that point, so more lift is available at the same airspeed. This on its own would not allow the aircraft to approach to land at a slower speed, because the critical angle would occur at the same speed.

However, lowering the flaps also changes the curved shape of the wing section (the camber), and that does affect the speed at which the critical angle (the stall) occurs. In addition, in what is referred to as a "slotted" flap, a small gap opens in front of the flap itself (as seen above in fig 2.12) which allows air to flow through it from the higher pressure below the wing and create more flow over the flap which actually increases the lift coefficient (you may remember from fig 1.9 that there is normally little pressure difference between the surfaces at the rear of the wing).

The other change which occurs is that the aircraft pitch attitude for a given speed becomes more nose-down when the flaps are lowered. This means that the pilot has a better view of the runway as he approaches it. This better view is also available in poor visibility. If a pilot flies level with the flaps down, he has a better view over the nose at the lower speed at which he would prefer to fly in order to give himself more time to see an approaching hazard such as another aircraft.

The use of a small amount of flap can be advantageous on take-off, allowing the aircraft to leave the ground at a slower speed and after a shorter ground roll. However the angle of climb usually reduces with flaps deployed, and the total distance required to clear an obstacle may increase with flap selected.

The benefits we have considered so far are achieved at a fairly shallow angle of flap "setting" (typically between 10 and 15 degrees from the wing chord line). However, many aeroplanes provide flap settings at greater angles, as in figure 2.13. These larger angles give almost no further lift advantage, but do increase drag. The increased drag at a "landing flap" setting allows a pilot to make a steeper approach over obstacles, and assists in slowing the aeroplane down after touchdown.

■ *Figure 2.13* **Landing Flap**

Because profile drag is increased most, the speed for minimum total drag (V_{IMD}) reduces, giving greater speed stability on the approach. The increased drag may also allow the pilot to approach with a higher power setting, which may provide more rapid engine acceleration in the event of abandoning the approach. However, more thrust is required to overcome that drag if the aircraft is to accelerate, so if the pilot wishes to go around from his approach, he should raise the flaps to a setting which reduces drag as soon as he has applied full power. Because raising the flaps completely would produce a reduction in lift, he must keep a certain amount of flap selected until the aircraft has reached a safe airspeed and height above the ground.

There are different types of flap. In a "simple flap", the whole trailing edge moves around a simple hinge, as in the "slotted flap" we have seen. A "split flap", as its name suggests and as shown in figure 2.14, effectively splits the trailing edge and is favoured by some designers. Its effects are similar to those of the simple flap.

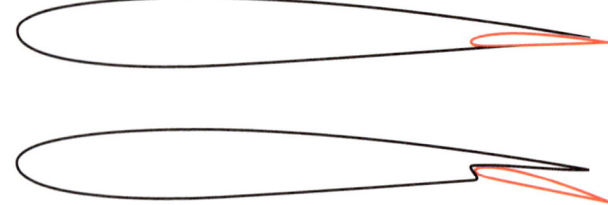

■ *Figure 2.14* **Split Flap**

A particular combination of split and slotted flap favoured by some designers is the **Fowler flap**. As shown in figure 2.15, the Fowler flap not only lowers, but moves backwards to the trailing edge when selected. This not only increases the coefficient of lift over the portion of the wing containing the flap, but also increases its area at the same time, giving a further increase in lift.

■ *Figure 2.15* **Fowler Flap**

We need to mention here that selection of flap affects not only lift and drag of the whole wing, but has further effects. The selection of flaps moves the centre of pressure backwards (more lift comes from the rear part of the wing than before). This produces a change in trim force for the pilot, although if the increase in drag is allowed to slow the aircraft down, he may find that the aeroplane returns to a trimmed condition at the lower speed.

We have considered the increase in speed stability already, but because the total reaction is now concentrated closer to the fuselage, lateral and directional stability are reduced when flaps are lowered.

The rearwards movement of the centre of pressure also produces a twisting moment on the wing, which may encourage flutter and lead to damage at speeds much lower than VNE. There are therefore limiting speeds for operating flaps and for flight with flaps selected, and these limiting speeds may be different for different flap settings.

2.11 Slats

Another means of increasing the lift coefficient at low speeds is to open a small slot just behind the wing leading edge. This is often done by fitting devices called "slats", which move forwards and upwards as in figure 2.16 automatically as the wing's angle of attack increases and the pressure above the leading edge becomes low enough to suck them open. The air flows through the slots as well as over the extended slats, increasing the speed of the flow over the middle of the wing upper surface and increasing the total lift. The slats can normally be locked closed if desired.

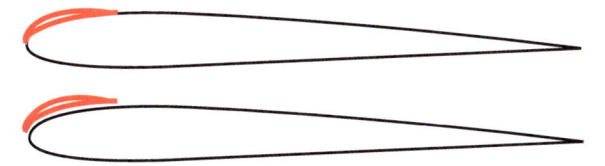

■ *Figure 2.16* **A Slat**

Although slats increase the lift coefficient, they do not give the pilot a better view of his approach, so are not common on modern light aeroplanes.

Large aeroplanes may also have leading edge flaps, which may also open a slot as well.

Figure 2.17 shows the effect of lowering flaps and opening slats on the graph of lift coefficient against angle of attack. Slats increase lift and increase the critical angle, flap produces increased lift at a lower angle of attack.

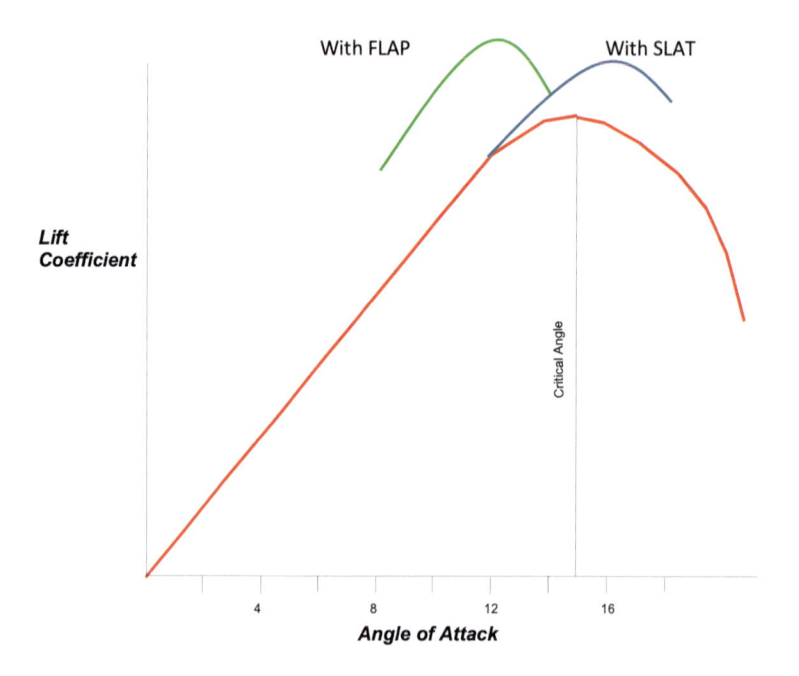

Figure 2.17 **Effect of flaps and slats on the lift coefficient**

2.12   Spoilers

Some light aeroplanes with wing sections designed for minimum drag, including gliders and most Touring Motor Gliders, have devices to increase their rate of descent and therefore their angle of approach at a fixed (often closed) throttle setting. Lift 'spoilers' are flaps rather like small solid doors which lie flush with the top surface of the wing, but when raised by the cockpit control generate turbulence in the low pressure airflow, reducing the lift available from that part of the wing. The amount of lift lost, and therefore the rate (and angle) of descent, depends on how far the spoiler is opened.

Operating spoilers usually produces a trim change, but the increase in drag is relatively small so little attitude change is required to maintain a constant airspeed. However, deploying spoilers does increase the stalling speed.

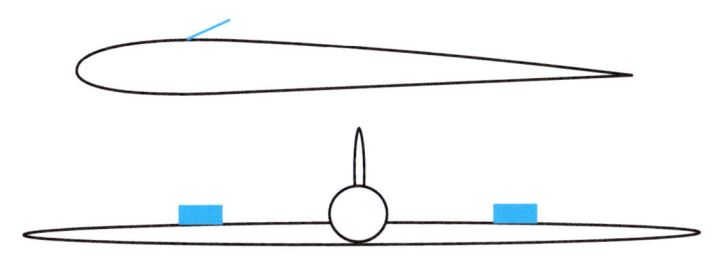

*Figure 2.18 **Spoilers deployed***

2.13 Airbrakes

Another means of increasing an aircraft's rate of descent is an airbrake, or usually a pair of airbrakes, one on each wing. Airbrakes primarily produce profile drag, although by interfering with the airflow over the wing they also reduce some of the lift available, and increase the stalling speed. They are, however, usually positioned behind the wing's maximum thickness to minimise that loss of lift.

Moving the cockpit control progressively opens the airbrakes and therefore the drag increase. To maintain airspeed the pilot must lower the nose, so approach control requires co-ordination between elevator and airbrake controls. Some sailplanes are fitted with a tail parachute which acts as a powerful airbrake with a fixed drag increase.

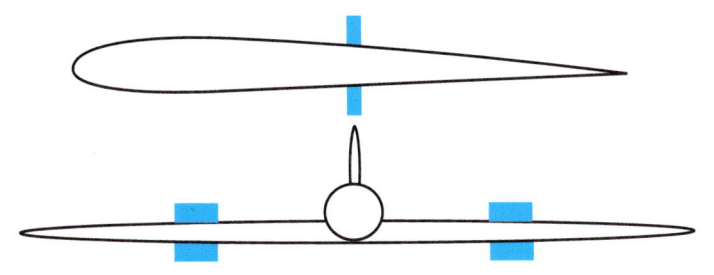

*Figure 2.18 **Airbrakes open***

Intentionally Left Blank

2.13 Exercise

1. Rotation of an aircraft around its longitudinal axis is called:
   (a) Pitch
   (b) Roll
   (c) Trim
   (d) Yaw

2. If a pilot moves his control column backwards towards himself in normal flight, which of the following will happen?
   (a) The aircraft nose will drop
   (b) The ailerons will move upwards
   (c) The aircraft will rotate about its lateral axis
   (d) The aircraft will pitch downwards

3. What is the main purpose of the rudder in an aeroplane in flight?
   (a) To turn the aircraft
   (b) To move the aircraft about its longitudinal axis
   (c) To yaw the aircraft
   (d) To keep the aeroplane in balance

4. If the pilot moves only his control column to the left, which of the following is unlikely to occur?
   (a) The aeroplane will roll left
   (b) The aeroplane will yaw left
   (c) The right aileron will move downwards
   (d) The angle of attack of part of the left wing will reduce

5. If a pilot moves the top of his trim wheel backwards, which of the following will not happen?
   (a) He will feel an increased nose down force at the control column
   (b) The trim tab will move downwards
   (c) The trim tab will attempt to move the elevator upwards
   (d) The aircraft will attempt to pitch upwards

6. To trim an aeroplane correctly, which is the correct initial order of the following actions?
1. Move the trim wheel
2. Select the correct pitch attitude for level flight
3. Check for force at the control column

(a) 3-1-2
(b) 1-2-3
(c) 2-3-1
(d) 1-3-2

7. With a balance tab assisted rudder, moving the rudder bar to yaw the aircraft right will move:
(a) The rudder left and the tab right
(b) The rudder right and the tab left
(c) The rudder left and the tab left
(d) The rudder right and the tab right

8. Which of the following is not a usual effect of lowering flap to 15 degrees?
(a) The aircraft will pitch down
(b) The lift will increase
(c) The drag will increase
(d) The aircraft will become more directionally stable

9. Which of the following is an effect of lowering flap to 15 degrees?
(a) Drag will increase proportionately more than lift
(b) The pitch attitude for level flight will be more nose-down
(c) The aircraft will be less speed stable at low speed
(d) The maximum permitted airspeed will increase

10. Which of the following flap types increase the wing area when selected?
(a) Simple flap
(b) Split flap
(c) Fowler flap
(d) All of the above

11. Flying controls have their effects:
(a) Relative to the pilot's head
(b) Relative to the aircraft's axes
(c) Relative to the direction of the airflow
(d) Relative to the horizon

12. Which of the following will not reduce aileron drag?
   (a) Increasing airspeed
   (b) Frise ailerons
   (c) Increasing angle of attack
   (d) Differential ailerons

13. Which of the following statements is correct about frise ailerons?
   (a) They reduce adverse yaw and increase total drag
   (b) They increase adverse yaw and increase total drag
   (c) They reduce adverse yaw and reduce total drag
   (d) They increase adverse yaw and reduce total drag

14. Which advantages are available when slats are fitted?
   (a) Increased lift coefficient at low speeds
   (b) Better view at low speed in poor visibility
   (c) Both (a) and (b)
   (d) Neither (a) nor (b)

15. What is the main reason for mass balancing flying controls?
   (a) To assist the pilot in maintaining a constant attitude
   (b) To reduce control forces
   (c) To reduce the danger of flutter
   (d) To keep the aircraft's centre of gravity within limits

16. Which of these is a means of achieving aerodynamic balance of a flying control surface?
   (a) A horn balance
   (b) An inset hinge
   (c) Both (a) and (b)
   (d) Neither (a) nor (b)

17. Slots increase the stalling angle of attack by:
   (a) Maintaining the smooth airflow and delaying separation
   (b) Increasing the camber
   (c) Providing an extra lifting surface in front of the wing
   (d) Increasing the effective wing area

18. During the preflight check the pilot notices the mass balance weight is missing from one of the ailerons. What should he do before the aircraft next flies?
   (a) Remove the equivalent balance weight from the other aileron
   (b) Have the aircraft repaired by an appropriately qualified engineer before it next flies
   (c) Fly to a repair facility using normal limiting speeds
   (d) Fly to a repair facility limiting airspeed to 10% below normal V_{NE}

19. A stabilator is another name for:
   (a) A type of flap
   (b) An all-moving tailplane
   (c) A tailplane with dihedral
   (d) A control column

20. The effect of a control column movement on the aircraft depends on:
   (a) The moment arm of the control surface from the centre of gravity
   (b) The amount of deflection of the control column
   (c) The aircraft's airspeed
   (d) All of the above

21. A force applied to an object:
   (a) Will produce an equal force reacting against the original force
   (b) Will produce an equal force acting in the same direction as the original force
   (c) Will only cause movement if the object is already moving
   (d) Will only cause movement if the object is stationary

22. Compared to an aeroplane without flap selected, selecting flap is likely to:
   (a) Reduce lateral stability
   (b) Increase directional stability
   (c) Increase stalling speed
   (d) Increase the critical angle

23. What is the function of the pitch trim control in the cockpit?
   (a) To adjust the aircraft's pitch attitude by small increments
   (b) To remove or reduce elevator control loads while maintaining a constant pitch attitude
   (c) To vary the aircraft's stability in pitch
   (d) To remove or reduce elevator control loads while manoeuvring

24. Some light aeroplanes and most Touring Motor Gliders may be fitted with airbrakes or spoilers to increase their angle of approach. Spoilers are designed to (i) .... and airbrakes are designed to (ii) ....

   (a) (i) reduce lift   (ii) increase induced drag
   (b) (i) increase profile drag   (ii) reduce lift
   (c) (i) increase induced drag   (ii) increase profile drag
   (d) (i) reduce lift   (ii) increase profile drag

CHAPTER 3

Manoeuvring

3.1 Introduction

For much of the time, a pilot uses his controls to maintain the aeroplane at a desired attitude in the sky. That means most control movements are made to counter the effects of turbulence (or the pilot's own wrong inputs - it is very easy when looking at something other than the horizon in front of the aircraft to allow one's hands to move with the controls in them!).

However, the pilot will at some time want the aircraft to do something other than fly straight and level. For example, the aircraft must climb to a safe altitude after take-off, and descend again for landing. It is unlikely that the pilot will want to continue pointing (heading) in the same direction, so he will want to turn. For these and other more advanced manoeuvres he must use the controls in a co-ordinated fashion.

3.2 "Secondary Effects" of the Controls

Flying training books occasionally refer to the "secondary effects of controls". These are actually a result of the aeroplane's stability acting in combination with the primary effects seen in the last chapter.

If the pilot deliberately yaws the aircraft without applying any other control force, the inside wing (the one towards which he is yawing) will slow down relative to the outside wing. This differential in speed will cause a differential in lift produced by the two wings, and the aircraft will roll towards the inside wing. The "secondary effect" of yaw is roll, and will occur whenever the aircraft yaws, and not only after the pilot has applied rudder. It is not a secondary effect of the control, but of the aircraft movement.

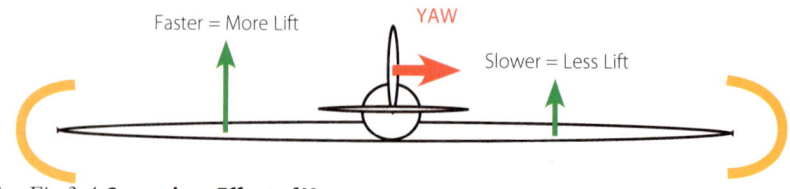

Fig 3.1 **Secondary Effect of Yaw**

If the aeroplane is rolled to any "angle of bank", the lift from the wing will no longer be directly opposing the weight, as in figure 3.2. Weight will be greater than the opposing component of lift, and the aircraft will start to accelerate downwards. In addition, because the lift is now directed at an angle to the original direction of flight the aircraft will also accelerate ("slip") towards the lower wing.

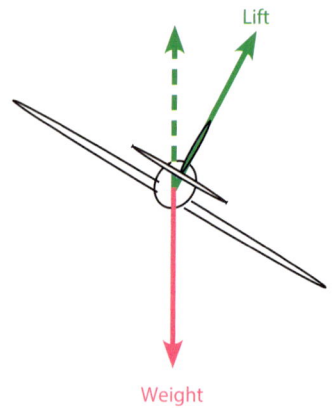

Fig 3.2 **Lift at an Angle of Bank**

If the pilot does nothing else, the aircraft's directional stability will now attempt to bring it into line with the relative airflow, and encourage the nose of the aircraft to yaw towards the low wing and downwards. The "secondary effect" of roll is yaw (the adverse yaw we saw in the last chapter is caused by the aileron movement, not the roll).

Because yaw and roll induce each other as secondary effects, we can see that any disturbance in roll or yaw will produce a combination of both. If allowed to develop by the pilot continuing to apply aileron or rudder, that combination would result in a tightening spiral descent as the nose pointed progressively downwards, the vertical component of lift reduced, and roll and yaw continued to induce each other. This spiral is also often described as a further effect of both aileron and rudder.

3.3 Dynamic Directional and Lateral Stability

We have seen in Chapter 1 that the aircraft is designed with both lateral and directional stability. We would expect this stability to slow down and eventually stop the spiral unless the pilot holds the controls away from the neutral position. Unfortunately, matters are not simple. If in a particular aeroplane at a particular speed the directional (yaw) static stability is stronger than lateral (roll) stability, the yaw induced as a counter to the initial disturbance may induce a greater rate of roll than the lateral static stability can restore. The resulting spiral dynamic instability would require opposing control movement (roll then pitch) to stop it.

If lateral stability is stronger than directional stability, the aircraft will tend to develop an out-of phase movement, yawing in one direction while rolling in the other. This oscillatory dynamic instability is usually only met in high speed aeroplanes, and may be referred to as 'snaking' or 'dutch rolling', depending on whether the yaw or the roll is most obvious.

3.4 Turning

Let us assume that in figure 3.2 the pilot deliberately selected the aircraft's banked attitude by rolling with the ailerons (balancing adverse yaw with rudder) and returned the controls to neutral when he had reached the angle of bank he wanted. He could stop the aircraft descending by increasing the angle of attack (preventing the nose dropping by holding the nose in the same apparent pitch attitude is usually sufficient to achieve that in practice). Lift would increase to maintain the aircraft level (as in fig 3.3). Now the only out of balance force would be the sideways component of the lift from the wings, accelerating the aircraft sideways around a circle.

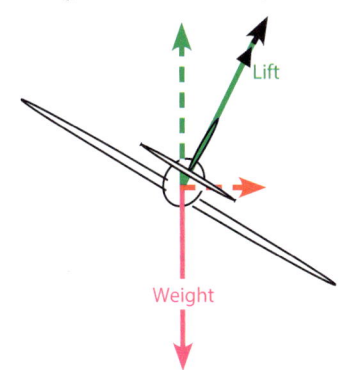

■ *Fig 3.3* **Turning**

The aircraft will now turn, and continue turning for as long as it is banked. The controls, including the rudder, are used to maintain the aircraft's attitude in balance. To stop the turn, the pilot uses aileron and balancing rudder to roll the wings level again until there is no bank, progressively reducing the angle of attack as he does so to maintain level flight.

In fact, the controls do not act or stop acting instantly. Because of its mass, the aircraft possesses a certain amount of **inertia** (reluctance to change a rate of movement), and the pilot must anticipate slightly with his control movements to select exactly the angle of bank or pitch that he wants. He may even have to move the controls the other way to stop the movement.

The greater the angle of bank in a level turn, the more rapidly the aircraft will change its direction around the horizon (the greater the **rate of turn**). However there is a limit to the amount of bank that can be achieved. Once the critical angle is reached, no more lift can be obtained at that speed, and any further bank increase will result in a descent.

In the turn, as lift increases to maintain level flight, induced drag also increases, so to maintain speed the pilot must increase power (not usually a concern at small bank angles but important in a steep turn). Even before the critical angle is reached, the drag will usually start to slow the aircraft down. This in turn means that the critical angle is reached even quicker as the pilot increases the angle of attack further to compensate for that reducing speed.

If the pilot allows the bank angle to increase without maintaining height, as speed increases, any up elevator deflection will pitch the nose up, but at a steep bank angle that may only tighten the turn and increase the rate of descent. To recover from this "spiral dive", or indeed to prevent it, a pilot must roll the aircraft wings level before attempting to raise the nose with the elevators.

3.5 Climbing

In order to climb, the pilot must pitch the aircraft upwards. However, the increased drag from the increased angle of attack would slow the aircraft down and reduce lift, so at the same time there must be an increase in thrust to overcome that drag. Once that has been done, and when the aeroplane settles down in a steady climb, the forces will balance. However, unlike straight and level, where each pair of forces balances, the situation is more complex, as shown in an exaggerated form in fig 3.4. Weight must be balanced by the vertical components of both lift and thrust, which also have to compensate for the vertical component of drag (albeit a very small amount) which acts downwards.

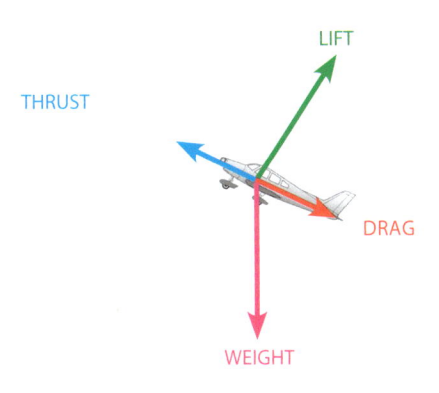

■   *Fig 3.4* **Forces in a Climb**

The vertical component of thrust means that slightly less lift is required than in level flight. However, some of that lift is acting rearwards, and must be overcome, together with the drag, by the increased horizontal component of the thrust.

As seen the volume on 'Aeroplane Flight Performance and Planning', a light aircraft has usually little power to spare from the engine, so climbs relatively slowly. Any turning should be done at small angles of bank.

We could geometrically prove that the angle of climb in figure 3.4 depends on the lift and the drag forces. The vertical distance covered for each unit of horizontal distance (number of feet climbed per foot forward, for example) is equivalent to the amount of drag divided by the amount of lift (D/L). Since the lift required varies very little with the small angles of climb achieved by light aeroplanes, in order to achieve the steepest climb the pilot should fly at the speed for minimum drag (V_{IMD}), or in fact at a slightly higher speed (called V_x) to maintain speed stability. That steepest climb may be needed to climb above an obstruction shortly after take-off, for example.

However, in order to climb at the maximum rate (least time used to climb to a given height), the pilot needs to fly faster than that. He should fly at the speed nominated in the aircraft's Flight Manual as "V_y". This is slightly above the speed which gives the greatest excess of power available from the engine and propeller combination over the power required to maintain level flight at that speed, as shown in figure 3.5. Minimum power speed, which we shall discuss later, is shown at V_{MP}.

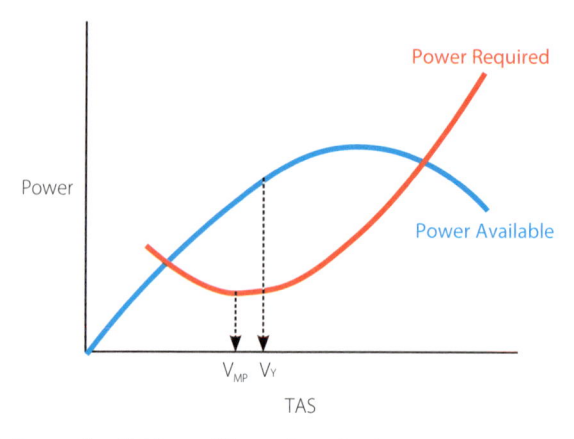

*Fig 3.5 **Power Available and Power Required***

3.6 Descending

When the aircraft is in a steady descent, the forces will again balance. In the case of a descent with power, all four forces will exist in balance. However, in a glide descent, whether deliberate or as a result of an engine failure, thrust will be non-existent, and the forces will appear as in the simplified but again rather extreme case shown in figure 3.6.

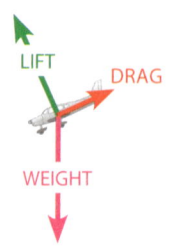

*Fig 3.6 **Forces in a Glide Descent***

Again it can be seen that lift is (slightly) less than in level flight, this time because the vertical component of drag is acting upwards.. The angle at which the aircraft is gliding downwards is the same as the angle at which the lift is pointing forwards. In fact, in still air the distance travelled in the glide before the aircraft hits the ground, divided by the height the aircraft is above that ground (D/H) is the same mathematical fraction as the lift divided by the drag (L/D, the "lift/drag ratio"). For example, if lift/drag ratio is 10 to 1, the gliding aircraft will travel 10 miles for every mile (approximately 6000 feet) of height. Since the vertical component of drag is actually very small, and varies little between "glide angles", the best angle of glide will be achieved when drag is least, usually at an angle of attack of about 4 degrees.

An increase in drag will steepen that descent angle. It follows that if a pilot wants to glide a long distance (for example after an engine failure) he should fly at the speed which gives him the minimum drag (V_{IMD}), and fly in balance (if the airflow comes from the side profile drag increases). Sideslipping, lowering flap, or flying at a higher or lower speed than V_{IMD} will all steepen the descent angle.

Turning requires an increase in lift, usually provided by increasing the angle of attack, which results in a speed reduction. To prevent the speed reducing below V_{IMD}, gliding turns should either be limited to small angles of bank or if a rapid turn is required the speed must be increased beforehand (the higher speed will increase lift for the same angle of attack).

If the engine is still giving power, we can consider whatever thrust is coming from it as being effectively a reduction in drag. If power is increased, the angle of descent will reduce for a given speed. This method is used to vary the descent angle on a powered approach to land. Of course, to maintain a steady speed while the angle is changing, the pitch attitude also needs to be adjusted. As power increases, the nose attitude must rise, and as power decreases, the nose must drop to maintain the airspeed. However, if the aircraft has been accurately trimmed to the desired speed, maintaining it should be relatively easy.

3.7 Aerobatics

The basic flying controls allow an aeroplane to manoeuvre in more exciting ways than just turning, climbing and descending, although most simple aerobatic manoeuvres are merely combinations of these. The forces involved in aerobatics are often more than a training aeroplane is designed for, so the aircraft's Certificate of Airworthiness may not permit more than simple turns, or may limit the weight or centre of gravity positions at which more advanced manoeuvres may be performed. However, performing aerobatics (like any other flying) is basically deciding what attitudes you want to select with the flying controls, climbing and accelerating until you have enough height and speed to perform the manoeuvre safely, and selecting the necessary attitudes in order.

For example, if the aeroplane is in the banked attitude shown in figure 3.2 or 3.3, the pilot would normally return it to the straight and level attitude by moving the ailerons to the left (the views are from the rear). However, if the aircraft is strong enough and "certificated" for such manoeuvres, there is nothing to prevent him rolling the aircraft the OTHER way by applying full right aileron until he returns to the straight attitude. (It would however be sensible to raise the nose first, because stability would progressively allow the nose of the aircraft to descend during the manoeuvre.) This manoeuvre is called an "aileron roll".

Similarly, if the aeroplane were flying fast enough, the pilot could move the elevator to pitch the aircraft upwards all the way over the top of a loop and back to the normal pitch attitude again.

3.8 Load Factor

Any looping manoeuvre is achieved by increasing the lift from the wings to several times more than the weight (the ratio is known as the "load factor" or "g"). This produces a bending force where the wings join the fuselage, and that bending force must not be allowed to be too great.

This load factor also appears in a level turn, because lift exceeds weight. In a gentle turn, the load factor is small, very little above "1g". However, if the pilot were to fly a level turn at 60 degrees of bank, the load factor would be "2g", (the lift force would be twice the weight).

There is a limit to the "g" which an aeroplane is allowed to experience. If that "g" limit has been exceeded, even though there is no apparent damage, it will have weakened the structure and may have caused internal damage so the aircraft must be examined by a qualified engineer. At load factors above the published g limit, the damage becomes progressively more critical, until at about one and a half times that published limit, instant structural failure is likely.

3.9 The Manoeuvre Envelope

At low speeds, the lift available from the wing at the critical angle is insufficient to reach the maximum permitted load factor or g limit. As speed increases, so does the possible load factor. Above a certain airspeed, called "maximum manoeuvring speed" or "V_A", it would be possible for the g limit to be exceeded. Pilots are therefore advised not to manoeuvre the aeroplane at airspeeds above V_A. That is not to say that below V_A it is impossible to cause damage by manoeuvring the aeroplane. If the flying controls are moved violently at any time (especially in more than one plane), it is possible to produce loads on the control surfaces or other parts of the aircraft structure sufficient to cause damage or even failure. Damage is even more likely if the control inputs are reversed rapidly (for example, full left aileron then full right).

Graphs are drawn to illustrate the acceptable limits for a particular aircraft, such as the one in figure 3.7. A straight line at the top is drawn at the g limit. We saw in chapter 2 that there is a maximum speed which may not be exceeded at any time, the "never exceed speed" or "V_{NE}", usually dictated by flutter considerations. Above an airspeed referred to as "V_D" (approximately 10% more than V_{NE} and the maximum speed to which the aircraft has been tested) flutter is likely to cause structural damage and failure. V_{NE} forms the right hand border of the safe area, called the "manoeuvre envelope" or "flight envelope".

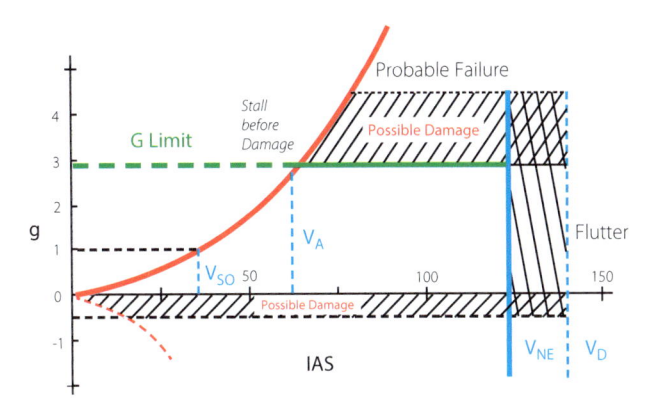

Fig 3.7 **Manoeuvre Envelope**

The flight envelope may provide an indication of the use for which the aircraft is likely to be certificated. For example, an aerobatic aeroplane will have higher load factor limits than a utility or normal category one.

The published flight envelope is not absolute. Safety factors are included, so that although the possibility of damage is marked, in still air there may be little immediate danger if V_{NE} for example is exceeded by a small amount. However, if the aircraft is subjected to turbulence, the forces produced by gusts of vertical air will add to the stresses on the airframe. Reversals of vertical movement will add to the danger of flutter, meaning a lower limiting speed is required in gusty conditions. Individual envelopes can be calculated for different gust strengths, which produce appropriately lower limiting speeds. In fact, V_D would be the limit in totally gust-free conditions, but these never exist, hence V_{NE} being the practical limit in conditions which the pilot feels are gust-free. Conditions of 'moderate' gusts provide a limiting maximum speed for 'normal operations;' or V_{NO}.

All limiting speeds and load factors are published in the Flight Manual which should be read as part of the aircraft's Certificate of Airworthiness (or "Permit to Fly" in certain cases if an aircraft is not eligible for a Certificate). We have already discussed V_A, V_{NE} and V_{NO}, and the maximum speed for flight with flaps extended, the "flap limiting speed" or "V_{FE}". There may also be published maximum speeds for lowering or raising a retractable undercarriage. In any case, if any limit has been exceeded the fact must be reported and the aircraft must be examined by a qualified engineer before it is flown again.

3.10 Centre of Gravity Position

As described in the volume on aeroplane performance, the position of the aircraft's centre of gravity has an effect on manoeuvring. The aircraft becomes more stable as the C of G moves forward, and may create problems raising the nose for the landing flare. With a rear C of G, the aircraft becomes more unstable, and the pilot may overstress or stall it during manoeuvres. Stall recoveries will also be more difficult, and spin recoveries may even become impossible (see chapter 5).

The same aircraft may be operated in different categories with different loads. The utility category, which permits bank angles greater than 60°, is likely to require a lower maximum weight and narrower C of G position limits.

3.11 Exercise

1. In which of these manoeuvres is lift more than in straight and level flight?
   (a) A level turn
   (b) A straight climb
   (c) A straight glide
   (d) All of the above

2. What is the effect of aileron drag?
   (a) Uncommanded roll towards the downgoing wing
   (b) Uncommanded roll towards the upgoing wing
   (c) Uncommanded yaw towards the downgoing wing
   (d) Uncommanded yaw towards the upgoing wing

3. At what speed should an aeroplane be flown in the event of engine failure to obtain maximum range in still air?
   (a) The indicated airspeed for minimum drag
   (b) Slightly more than the indicated airspeed for minimum drag
   (c) Slightly less than the indicated airspeed for minimum drag
   (d) The maximum permitted indicated airspeed

4. The aeroplane is at 1000 feet. The pilot wishes to reach an altitude of 5000 feet as quickly as possible. At what speed should he fly?
   (a) V_{NO}
   (b) V_y
   (c) V_x
   (d) V_A

5. At what speed should an aeroplane be flown to obtain the maximum climb angle?
   (a) V_{NO}
   (b) V_y
   (c) V_x
   (d) V_A

6. Which of the following will reduce an aeroplane's angle of descent at a constant speed?
   (a) Selecting landing flap
   (b) Sideslipping
   (c) Increasing engine power
   (d) All of the above

7. Which of the following is not a limiting speed?
   (a) V_{NO}
   (b) V_{NE}
   (c) V_A
   (d) All are limiting speeds

8. What will happen if the aeroplane exceeds its maximum load factor but is landed safely?
   (a) Nothing
   (b) The structure will be weakened
   (c) The structure will only be weakened if you can see external damage
   (d) The wings will fall off on the next flight

9. If an aeroplane exceeds V_{NE} in flight but there is no apparent damage, how soon must the aircraft be inspected by a qualified engineer?
   (a) Within 24 hours of the event
   (b) Within 7 days of the event
   (c) At the next scheduled maintenance inspection
   (d) Before it flies again

10. If the pilot needs to turn rapidly while gliding, what must he do?
   (a) Use as much bank as possible to minimise height loss
   (b) Increase speed before the turn
   (c) Both (a) and (b)
   (d) Neither (a) nor (b).

11. What load factor will an aeroplane experience in a level 60 degree bank turn?
   (a) 1g
   (b) 2g
   (c) 3g
   (d) 4g

12. Above what airspeed is it unsafe to apply full and/or rapid movement of the flying controls?
   (a) V_{NE}
   (b) V_{NO}
   (c) V_x
   (d) V_A

13. The initial secondary effects of (i) aileron and (ii) rudder are:

(a) (i) yaw   (ii) pitch
(b) (i) yaw   (ii) roll
(c) (i) roll   (ii) pitch
(d) (i) roll   (ii) yaw

14. At which of these speeds and altitudes should an aeroplane obtain the maximum rate of climb?

(a) V_X at low altitudes
(b) V_y at low altitudes
(c) V_x at high altitudes
(d) V_Y at high altitudes

15. An aeroplane with directional stability stronger than its lateral stability may develop an accelerating spiral as the secondary effect of aileron. What should the pilot do to recover to straight and level flight?

(a) Centralise both aileron and rudder
(b) Roll the wings level with aileron then pitch to level flight with elevator
(c) Yaw the aircraft the other way with rudder then pitch to level flight with elevator
(d) Pitch the aircraft to level flight then prevent yaw with rudder

16. An aeroplane is descending at a constant airspeed. What effect will a head wind have on the rate of descent and the descent angle?

(a) Rate of descent will increase and angle of descent will steepen
(b) Rate of descent will increase and angle of descent will be shallower
(c) Rate of descent will reduce and angle of descent will not change
(d) Rate of descent will not change and angle of descent will steepen"

17. If your aeroplane has a lift/drag ratio of 8 to 1, how far will it glide in still air from a height of 6000 feet?

(a) 6 nautical miles
(b) 6 kilometres
(c) 8 nautical miles
(d) 8 kilometres

Intentionally Left Blank

CHAPTER 4

Pressure Instruments

4.1 Introduction

Inside an enclosed cockpit, a pilot has little direct indication of what his aeroplane is doing. In good weather he can see what attitude it has adopted, but he needs assistance to know whether, for example, he is climbing or descending, or at a safe height above the terrain he is approaching. In order to navigate, he needs to know his speed. Over the course of many years, instruments have been designed to provide him with such information, and more.

4.2 Static Pressure

We have seen that the air pressure over the earth is not constant, but that it decreases as the aircraft's altitude increases. A barometer measures pressure, and an aircraft altimeter is such a barometer. The pilot can set the "datum pressure" of the point above which he wants to know his vertical distance, and the altimeter has been calibrated to indicate that vertical distance when it senses the "static" pressure outside the aircraft.

Unfortunately, air changes its pressure as it flows around an object. Finding a point at which the pressure of the flowing air is unchanged from the static pressure is quite difficult. In most aircraft, a correction factor must be applied to the indicated altitude at low speeds, especially when flaps are lowered and the relative airflow direction changes. However, the correction is usually quite small, and of little importance to a light aircraft whose pilot can see the ground ahead.

The static pressure is taken from a "static vent", often on the side of the fuselage. This is a small hole (usually two - one hole on each side to allow for unbalanced flight) which is kept unpainted. From these vents, tubes allow easy air flow in and out of the altimeter, so that the case of the instrument contains air at the same pressure as that outside the static vents.

In the event of a blockage in the main static system, most light aircraft have an "alternate static" source direct from the cockpit, controlled by a mechanical switch. This is much less accurate than the normal source, usually providing a higher altitude indication in flight because of the airflow round the outside of the cockpit and the airgaps around the doors. However, the indication are sufficient for emergency purposes.

4.3 Altimeter

As shown in figure 4.1, inside the case of the altimeter is a very thin sealed capsule (in fact several on top of each other). The air inside these capsules has been extracted, so that there is virtually no air inside them at all. They are therefore very flat when sea level air pressure is inside the case and outside the capsules. As static pressure inside the case reduces with altitude, the capsules expand slightly, and a linkage moves to indicate this expansion. [In fact the capsules are usually completely empty ("evacuated") and the expansion is felt against a spring.] The amount of expansion is calibrated to the ICAO standard atmosphere and indicates the correct pressure altitude above the datum selected.

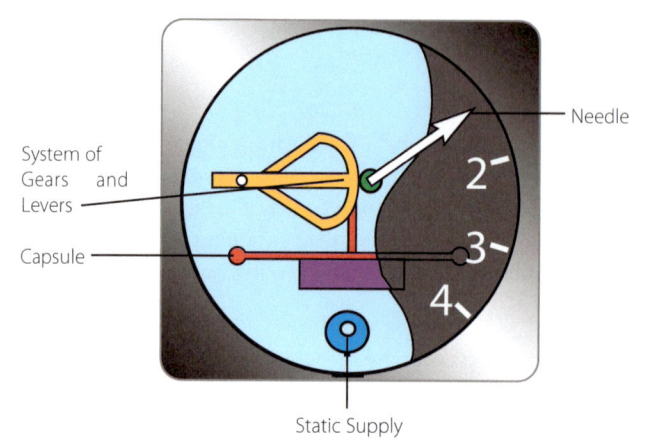

■ *Fig 4.1 **Altimeter Construction***

The linkage drives several pointers, like the hands of a clock. The longest pointer indicates vertical distance in hundreds of feet, the next longest moves at one tenth of the speed and indicates thousands of feet, and the shortest pointer indicates tens of thousands of feet. In figure 4.2, the altimeter is indicating 7,420 feet above the datum (set by the knob at the bottom and seen on the subscale) of 1004 hectoPascals.

■   *Fig 4.2* **Altimeter Face**

The pilot sets the datum (the "sub-scale") to the pressure of whatever point above which he requires to know his vertical distance. This is done by pressing in the setting knob and turning it until the correct numbers appear on the sub-scale (ensuring that the knob comes back out and is free to rotate). As shown in figure 4.3, setting the QFE (pressure at the aerodrome surface, obtainable from the aerodrome) will give an indication of height above that aerodrome. QNH (the pressure that shows the aerodrome elevation above sea level when the aircraft is standing on the aerodrome) will give an indication of the aircraft's altitude. A setting of 1013 will indicate the aircraft's pressure altitude, usually shortened to a series of numbers called flight levels (the number of hundreds of feet pressure altitude).

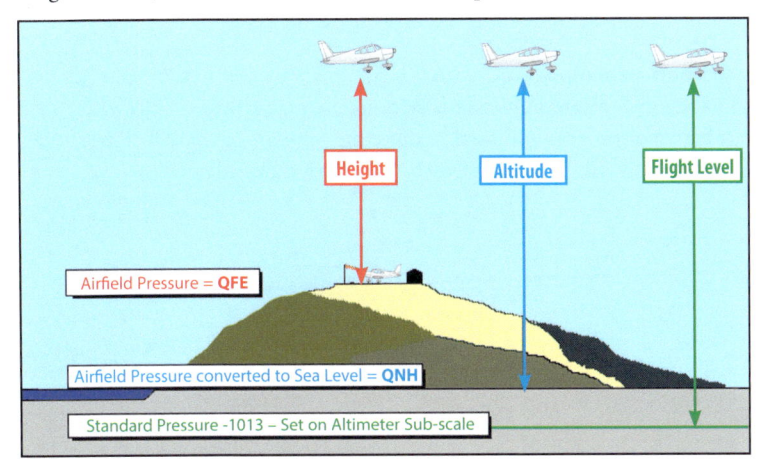

■   *Fig 4.3* **Altimeter Pressure Settings**

4.4 Altimeter Errors

An altimeter which is "approved" by an airworthiness authority for use as an aircraft part will have been tested to make sure that any "instrument error", caused by inaccuracies in manufacture or subsequent wear, is at a minimum (there will always be a little instrument error, which usually increases with altitude). However, most of the error in an aircraft's altimeter system comes from the difficulty in positioning the static vents to minimise the "position (or pressure) error", as we have already discussed. An aircraft's Flight Manual usually lists the position errors at various flap settings and indicated airspeeds.

Instrument error and pressure error are unique to an individual aircraft. However, other factors, often listed as "errors", mean that the indicated altitude may not be the true vertical distance which the pilot wishes to know. These are the result of the way in which the altimeter works and are the same for every aircraft.

The indications on the instrument assume that the atmosphere is the same as the ICAO standard. However, if the density of the air varies from that standard, either at the surface or at different levels, the instrument will not indicate true vertical distance. For example, different surface temperatures produce different air temperatures. Cold air is denser than hot air. In figure 4.4 we show cylinders of air at different temperatures with the same mass and the same area touching the earth's surface. The total air pressure (we can say the weight of the column above the point at which it is measured) on the surface is the same, so we can see that because the pressure at the top of each column (giving us an indicated altitude) is also the same, the actual height of the column (the true altitude) must be different. When flying towards low temperatures, a pilot should remember that his true altitude will be less than his indicated altitude ("high to low - look out below").

The variation in temperature with height is also seldom the same as the ICAO standard, so an indicated altitude is seldom the true altitude. However, since every aircraft has an altimeter calibrated to the same standard, they will all be subject to the same "error" and will be flying at the same <u>relative</u> altitude.

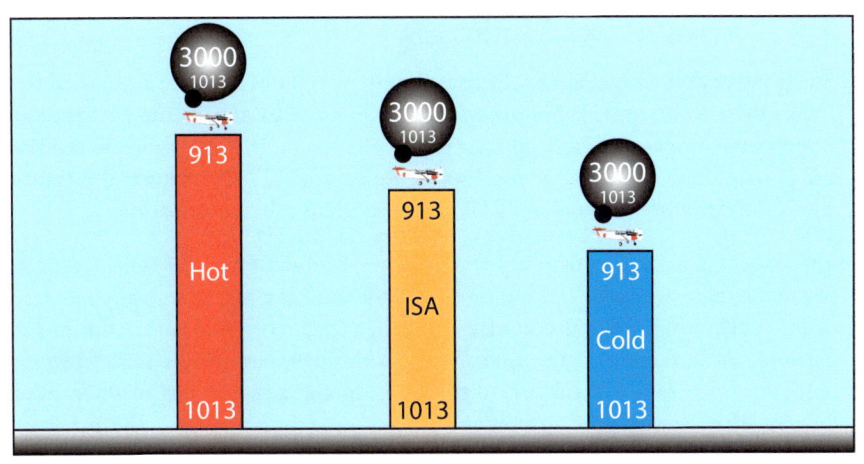

■ *Figure 4.4* **Temperature "Error"**

Similarly, if the surface pressure is different from that which the pilot has set on his altimeter sub-scale, the indicated altitude will be incorrect. Figure 4.5 shows this "barometric error". Again, the danger lies in flying towards an area of lower surface pressure than that set on the subscale ("high to low - look out below", or "high-low-high" meaning that the altimeter will over-read).

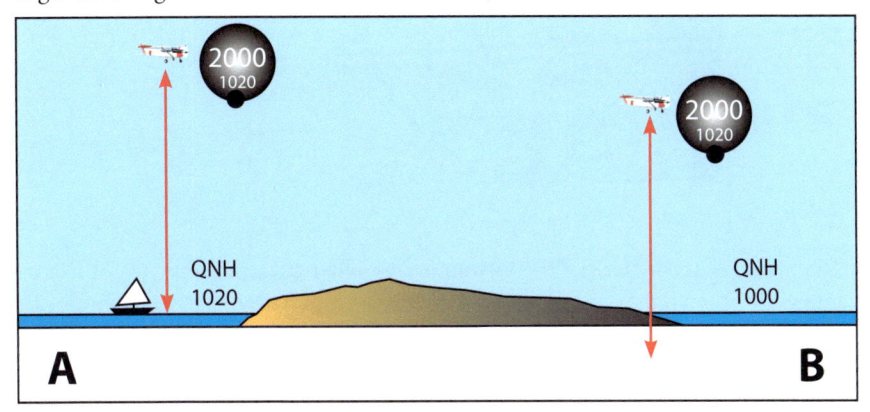

■ *Figure 4.5* **Incorrect Subscale Setting**

As explained in the Meteorology volume, every hectoPascal of pressure change will produce 30 feet of altitude error at low level.

4.5 Vertical Speed Indicator

An altimeter pointer moves very little as the aircraft climbs less than a hundred feet. In fact there is also some lag in the system, made worse by any instrument errors. It is sometimes important for a pilot to know whether he is climbing or descending, and perhaps how rapidly. A vertical speed indicator (VSI - also known as a "rate of climb and descent indicator" or "RCDI") can give him that information.

The VSI compares the static pressure at the time of reading the instrument with the pressure a short time ago, and indicates the difference as a rate of so many hundreds of feet per minute. A capsule inside the instrument contains air at the present pressure. As in figure 4.6, the same air passes through a delaying system (metering unit), so the capsule expands or contracts an amount proportional to the pressure difference between the pressure now and the pressure a short time ago. The movement of the capsule is transmitted to the indicating pointer on the face of the instrument.

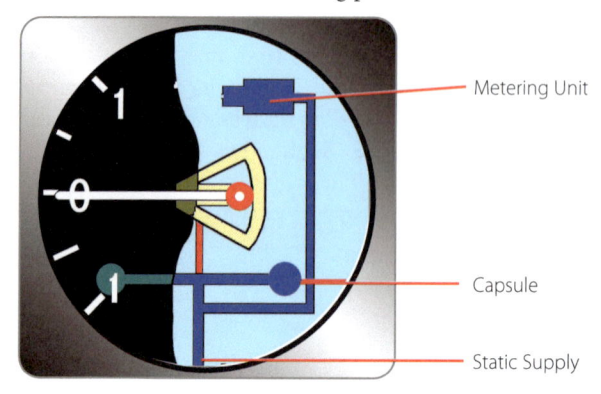

■ *Figure 4.6* **VSI**

The numbers on the face of the instrument usually represent thousands of feet per minute, with markings up and down representing hundreds of feet per minute. The indication in figure 4.6 shows level flight.

By comparing static pressure now with static pressure in the past, the instrument has an inherent lag. It will not indicate a rate of climb, for example, until the aircraft has actually climbed a certain amount. It may be necessary for a pilot to know his vertical speed more rapidly that the VSI allows. For that reason an "instantaneous VSI (IVSI)" has been developed. The IVSI uses the principle that a change of vertical speed is usually associated with a pitch change. A sprung ball in the linkage is affected by load factors, giving an instant climb indication when the aircraft pitches up, and a descent when it pitches down.

4.7 Airspeed Indicator

In chapter 1 we explained that the aerodynamic effects of the airflow around an aircraft depend on the dynamic pressure ½ρ V^2. The airspeed indicator (ASI) measures this dynamic pressure and indicates a speed which at the air density found at sea level in the ICAO standard atmosphere would be the aircraft's true air speed (V).

There is no direct means of measuring the actual dynamic pressure affecting the aircraft. The pressure felt at the front of a moving object such as an aeroplane (the "pitot pressure") is the sum of the dynamic pressure caused by the movement and the static pressure of the air itself. Inside an ASI, static pressure from the static vents is subtracted from the pitot pressure taken from a "pitot head" to provide an indication of the dynamic pressure - the "indicated airspeed" or "IAS".

The case of the airspeed indicator is filled with air at static pressure, and pitot pressure is fed into a capsule. The difference in pressure expands the capsule against a spring, which positions the pointer to indicate the airspeed corresponding to the dynamic pressure. Figure 4.7 illustrates the case of the aircraft accelerating from 70 knots towards 100.

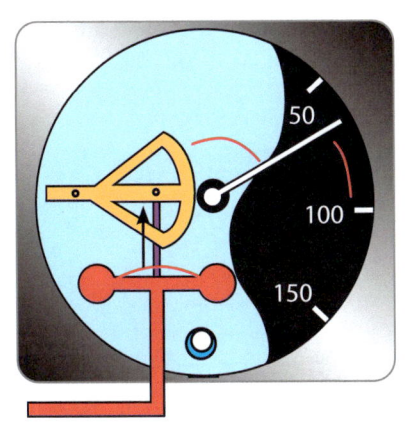

■   Figure 4.7 **Indicating airspeed**

The speed indicated is only "true airspeed" at sea level in ISA conditions, and with a perfect instrument and pitot/static system. In order to find the aircraft's true airspeed or TAS, required for navigation calculations, various corrections must be made. Any instrument error (caused by manufacturing imperfections) must be corrected. In fact, corrections are usually applied to take account of both instrument error and pressure/position errors in the pitot/static system to produce a "rectified airspeed (RAS)", also called "calibrated airspeed (CAS)". Finally (at the low speeds we are considering), corrections for the actual density of the air can be made to find true airspeed (TAS). At a density altitude of 5000 feet (5000 feet in the standard atmosphere), TAS is about 8% more than IAS.

Although we have considered the boundaries of the flight envelope as being indicated airspeeds, the 'flutter' described in Chapter 2 is a consequence of the inertia of the control surfaces, or actually the momentum the surfaces have gained when they move. Momentum is the product of mass and true velocity, so flutter occurs at a lower indicated airspeed as density reduces. Aeroplanes with powerful engines are usually limited to a maximum pressure altitude, and sailplanes must limit their IAS at high altitudes to remain within a safe TAS.

The numbers on most ASIs represent knots (nautical miles per hour), with marks at lesser intervals. Some instruments show two sets of numbers and the pointer goes round the instrument twice. Other instruments show the IAS in statute miles per hour (mph), or kilometres per hour (Km/h), or in some cases a double scale of knots and mph. On an aircraft with a certificate of airworthiness, the face of the ASI has several colour coded markings, unique to the individual aircraft type. As in figure 4.8, the green arc represents the speeds for normal operation, from the stalling speed at maximum mass to V_{NO}. The yellow arc continues to the aircraft's "never exceed speed" V_{NE}, marked with a red line. The white arc represents the flap operating range, between the stalling speed with full flap at maximum mass and the flap extended limiting speed V_{FE}.

■   Figure 4.8 **ASI**

4.8   Pitot/Static System

We have already considered the static vents. The pitot head must also be carefully placed to reduce position errors, although these are relatively low compared with those in the static system. Figure 4.9 represents a pitot head placed under a wing away from the propeller slipstream. It has a heating system (controlled by a switch in the cockpit) to prevent ice forming and causing blockage in the pitot line. To prevent water which enters the pitot head from causing similar blockage, a tiny drain hole is usually provided under the pitot head (the constant inflow of air keeps the pressure up in the line). If the head is fitted upside down the drain will not work!

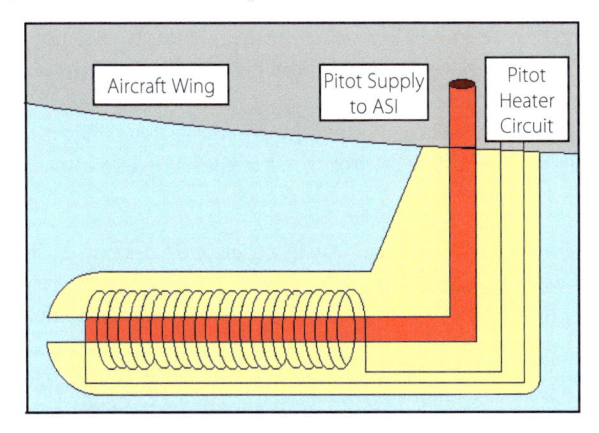

■   *Figure 4.9* **Pitot Head**

Other drains may be found in pitot and static lines. These usually take the form of water traps which can be drained as part of the pre-flight checks by depressing a lever to open them.

Some pitot heads are fitted with static vents around them, from where the air is taken either to just the ASI, or to all the instruments which require static pressure. Such a head is called a "pressure head".

4.9   Blockages and Leaks

We have mentioned blockages in the lines. Although such blockages are not common, it is important to understand what happens to the various instruments in the event of such a blockage, and how to get round the problem if it occurs.

If the pitot line becomes blocked, for example by an insect becoming lodged in the pitot head, the only instrument to be affected would be the ASI. The IAS would stay at the speed indicated when the blockage occurred, but would probably very slowly reduce as the drain hole allowed air to escape. If the blockage might be caused by ice, check the pitot heater is ON (and the fuse). If it is safe, descend to an altitude where the air temperature is above freezing. Otherwise, there is little the pilot can do, except fly the aeroplane by setting known powers and pitch attitudes. If the aircraft was carefully trimmed before the event, that eases the situation considerably. A satellite navigation system might give an indication of groundspeed, and if the wind is known (for example at the airfield of intended landing), the TAS can be deduced to give confidence that the power/attitude combination is working. However, it is advisable to make the approach and landing to an aerodrome with a long runway to add to the safety margins.

A blockage in the static line affects more instruments. It may not be noticed for a while, although a VSI giving a constant level flight indication is unlikely to be correct. The altimeter will also "freeze" at a constant altitude. We have seen that most aircraft have an alternate static source, so the pilot should switch to that for the rest of the flight, and advise Air Traffic Control that he will have difficulty flying an accurate altitude.

However, if there is no alternate static source, not only will the pilot have no indication of vertical distance or speed, but the airspeed indicator will also be incorrect. Assuming the pilot needs to descend below the altitude at which the blockage occurred, the ASI will be comparing an accurate pitot pressure with a lower than correct static pressure. The instrument will therefore be over-reading. However, if the pilot knows what IAS is normally achieved in level flight at a given power setting in the circuit, he may be able to calculate a correction to his indicated speed which he can use on the final approach.

Leaks in the static lines will be unlikely to create major problems, and will be almost impossible to detect anyway. However, a break or other major leak in the pitot line will cause the ASI to underread by an unknown amount.

4.10 Serviceability Checks

Pre-flight checks involve removal of pitot covers and static vent plugs if fitted. Operation of the pitot heater should be checked, but use the back of the hand - grasping a hot tube can cause serious burns. The altimeter setting knobs should be pushed in (if required) and turned until the instruments read zero or the aerodrome elevation. If there is more than one altimeter, the subscale readings should be within 2 hPa of each other. Pushed in setting knobs must come back out and be free to rotate after use. The pre-flight check on the VSI consists of checking the indication reads within 200 feet per minute of zero.

With QFE set before takeoff, altimeter readings should be within 50 feet of zero, or within 50 feet of the aerodrome or runway elevation with QNH set. Checks on the airspeed indicator are however normally limited to checking that the ASI gives normal indications during the take-off acceleration phase.

4.11 Exercise

1. Which of the following instruments uses both pitot and static pressure to function?
   (a) Airspeed indicator
   (b) Altimeter
   (c) Vertical speed indicator
   (d) All of the above

2. If an aircraft with its altimeter subscale set to the correct surface pressure of 1010 hPa flies through air which is warmer than the ICAO standard atmosphere, the altimeter will:
   (a) Read the correct altitude above sea level
   (b) Read higher than the correct altitude
   (c) Read less than the correct altitude
   (d) Read the correct pressure altitude, which will not be the true altitude

3. An aircraft with its subscale set to the correct QNH of 1010 hPa flies at a constant indicated altitude towards an area of low pressure. Which of the following is correct?
   (a) The aircraft will be higher than the altimeter indicates
   (b) The altimeter will under-read
   (c) The aircraft will descend
   (d) Both (a) and (b) are correct

4. Corrections for which of the following must be applied to IAS to find TAS?
   (a) Density error, position error and instrument error
   (b) Position error, barometric error, and instrument error
   (c) Pressure error, temperature error, and density error
   (d) Temperature error, position error and instrument error

5. At an altitude of 6000 feet, the ASI indicates 100 knots. What is the likely TAS?
   (a) 100 knots
   (b) 110 knots
   (c) 118 knots
   (d) 90 knots

6. If the aircraft's static vent becomes blocked, which of the following is incorrect?
   (a) The altimeter will freeze at the altitude when the blockage occurred
   (b) The ASI will over-read when the aircraft descends
   (c) The problem can be resolved by selecting "alternate static"
   (d) All the above are correct

7. The pitot line becomes blocked. There is no drain hole. Which of the following is correct?

   (a) The ASI indication will freeze
   (b) The altimeter will over-read when the aircraft descends
   (c) Both (a) and (b) are correct.
   (d) Neither (a) nor (b) are correct

8. What should an aircraft's altimeter which is set to the standard pressure setting indicate when it is on the surface of an aerodrome whose QFE is 993?

   (a) 60 feet
   (b) Minus 60 feet
   (c) 600 feet
   (d) Minus 600 feet

9. The highest speed in the white arc on an airspeed indicator indicates to the pilot:

   (a) The maximum speed for flight in normal operating conditions?
   (b) The maximum speed for flight with the flaps extended?
   (c) The speed which he must never exceed?
   (d) The stalling speed at maximum take-off mass?

10. The red line on an ASI indicates to the pilot:

   (a) The maximum speed for flight in normal operating conditions?
   (b) The maximum speed for flight with the flaps extended?
   (c) The speed which he must never exceed?
   (d) The stalling speed at maximum take-off mass?

11. How is the stalling speed with flaps extended at maximum take-off mass indicated on an ASI?

   (a) With a red line
   (b) It is the lower end of the green arc
   (c) It is the lower end of the white arc
   (d) It is not marked

12. What is the maximum error a pilot should accept during the pre-flight check of the altimeter?

   (a) 20 feet
   (b) 50 feet
   (c) 100 feet
   (d) None at all

13. The pressure entering the forward facing hole in a pitot tube in flight is:
   (a) Dynamic pressure only
   (b) Dynamic pressure plus static pressure
   (c) Pitot pressure plus dynamic pressure
   (d) Pitot pressure plus static pressure

14. If ice forms on the static vent when the aircraft is climbing, the altimeter indication will:
   (a) Always over-read the actual altitude
   (b) Gradually decrease to zero altitude
   (c) Always under-read the actual altitude
   (d) Continue to read the altitude at which the blockage occurred

15. In order to function, a vertical speed indicator has a metering unit. This:
   (a) Compares static pressure with pitot pressure
   (b) Causes a delay in dynamic pressure changes reaching the instrument case
   (c) Sends a proportion of the air at pitot pressure to an aneroid capsule
   (d) Restricts changes in static pressure being felt in the instrument case

16. What happens to the pressures being measured by the flight instruments as an aircraft climbs maintaining a constant indicated airspeed?
   (a) Dynamic pressure increases and static pressure reduces
   (b) Dynamic pressure reduces and static pressure reduces
   (c) Dynamic pressure reduces and static pressure remains constant
   (d) Dynamic pressure remains constant and static pressure reduces

Intentionally Left Blank

Chapter 5

Stalling and Spinning

5.1 Introduction

We mentioned "stalling" and "stalling speed" earlier. In this chapter we shall discover what a stall is and what a pilot must do to prevent the stall causing him problems in flight We shall also look at the aerodynamics involved in a spin, which may be the result of a stall from which the pilot does not correctly return to normal flight.

5.2 Stalling

If we look again at the graph showing the coefficient of lift changing with angle of attack, repeated at figure 5.1, we see that as the angle increases (either to compensate for speed reducing or to produce a higher load factor), the coefficient increases up to a maximum, then reduces as the angle continues to increase. Unless there is a corresponding increase in speed (unlikely, as the increasing angle will also increase induced drag) the total lift available above the critical angle will be less than the weight of the aircraft.

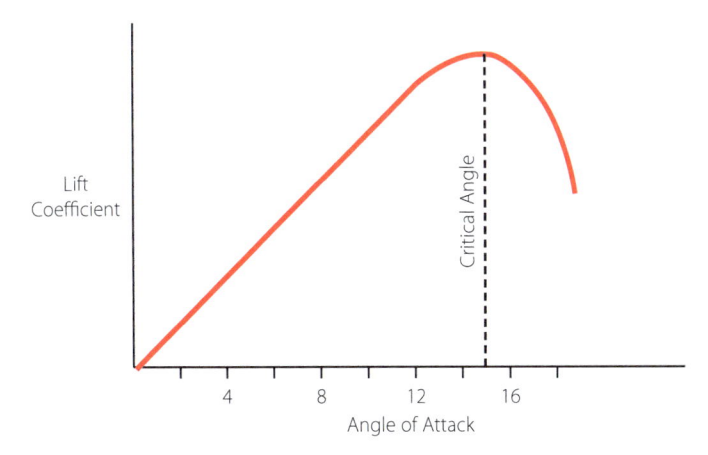

■ *Figure 5.1* **Lift Coefficient against Angle of Attack**

Weight being greater than lift will start to accelerate the aircraft downwards, although usually fairly gently to start with. This is the stall. Unless the angle of attack (now increased slightly by the flow from below as the aircraft sinks) is reduced below the critical angle, the aircraft will continue to accelerate downwards because of the imbalance of forces. However, design features in most aeroplanes will assist in recovering the situation, and if the pilot also reduces the angle of attack by moving the control column forward, the aircraft will "recover" from the stall. If he simultaneously applies power to help the aircraft to accelerate, the recovery will happen quicker and less height will be lost.

Air flowing over a wing never actually follows the wing shape exactly. It always seems to "separate" before it gets to the trailing edge, so there is little lift available from the rear of the wing. This is shown as a lack of low pressure above the rear of the wing in figure 1.9, and is illustrated in figure 5.2. As the angle of attack increases, the separation point moves forward slowly, increasing the turbulent flow at the rear of the wing (and of course the induced drag). However, the decreased pressure over the front of the wing compensates for the reduced working area of the wing which is still producing lift. At the critical angle, the working area has become too small for the decreasing pressure over the remaining portion of the wing to compensate for, and so lift actually reduces.

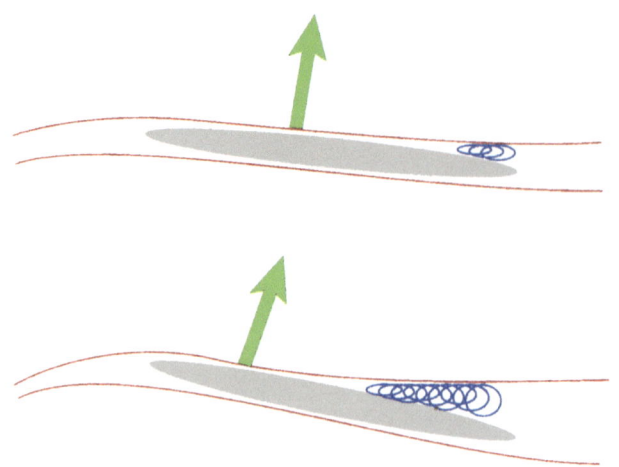

■ *Figure 5.2* **Separation**

This forward motion of the separation point produces a forward movement of the centre of pressure, which would suggest that before the stall the aircraft is pitching up. However, in most aeroplanes, the lift from the tailplane is also increasing, which produces an overall pitch down moment. The pilot usually has to deliberately increase the angle of attack to stall the aircraft.

At the critical angle, in addition to the effects above, the lift/weight couple will reduce, so the nose of the aircraft will pitch (usually designed to be downwards, but beware of any aeroplane which pitches up), and the angle of attack will change. The tailplane will be designed to have a lower angle of incidence (angle at which it is fixed to the fuselage) than the wing, so the tailplane angle of attack should be well below its critical angle when the wing stalls (this is assisted by the elevator or stabilator position normally required to produce the increased angle of attack). This not only means that the unstalled tailplane produces more lift than before so the aircraft again pitches downwards, but also that the pilot has control of the aircraft in pitch (well, downwards anyway - he will not be able to raise the nose!) even though the aeroplane is stalled.

The pilot should also have full rudder control (although a fin and rudder may stall at high sideslip angles). In most light aeroplanes he will also have control of the ailerons, because the wing section will be bent toward the tip (this is called "washout") so that the angle of attack is less than critical at the tip even though the inboard part of the wing is stalled.

However in some aeroplanes, if the pilot applies full aileron when the wing is at or close to the stall, the wingtip which he is attempting to raise may reach its critical angle as the aileron increases the effect in angle of attack of that part of the wing, and lift will reduce instead of increase. Since the other wingtip angle will be reduced below critical by the aileron application, the aeroplane will roll in the opposite direction to that intended! The increased induced drag, as pictured in figure 5.3, will yaw the aeroplane towards the stalling wingtip, and as we shall see shortly, this "autorotation" may lead to a spin. It is important that pilots should NOT attempt to pick up a wing which is dropping when the aircraft is close to the stall. Even though the aeroplane on which he is trained may be docile in this respect, he will probably fly something else later which is not!

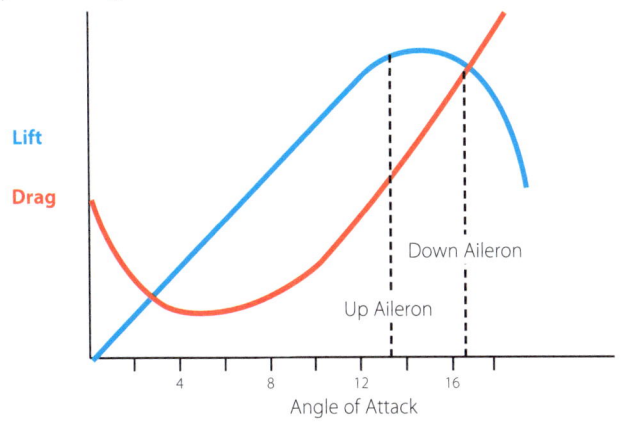

■   Figure 5.3 **Lift & Drag Coefficients**

Some books, and indeed some experienced pilots, suggest that a pilot can correct a dropping wing at the point of the stall by using the secondary effect of rudder. This may indeed succeed, but unless the exact amount of rudder is applied for exactly the correct amount of time, there is a serious risk of inducing a spin in the direction of the applied rudder. Unless the Flight Manual specifically recommends such a procedure, pilots should only apply the correct amount of rudder to compensate for the yaw resulting from any application of power. Once the aircraft has recovered from the stall, use controls as required to regain straight and level (or climbing) flight.

5.3　Stalling Speed

The stall comes at the critical angle. The actual airspeed at which the aircraft stalls is the speed at which that critical angle is reached. If the aircraft is in level flight when it stalls, that speed will depend on the weight (in fact the square root of the weight), since in level flight lift required equals weight, and Lift = $C_L \frac{1}{2} V^2 S$. If the stalling speed in level flight at a mass of for example 400 kilograms is 40 knots, at a weight of 324 kilograms the stalling speed would be $40 \times \sqrt{324} \div \sqrt{400}$ or $40 \times 18 \div 20 = 36$ knots.

If the aeroplane is manoeuvring, the speed will change with the load factor, or to be more precise again the square root of the load factor. At 4g the stalling speed will be twice that in level flight at 1g. If the aircraft is in a level turn, the load factor to maintain level flight increases as the angle of bank increases. Figure 5.4 shows that at 30° of bank, the load factor will be 1.155 and at 60° of bank the load factor to maintain level flight will be 2g. Stalling speed in a 60° level turn will therefore be $\sqrt{2}$ times the level flight stalling speed, or 1.4 times.

Because the condition of the wing surface affects the amount of lift generated, it also affects the stalling speed. Dirt, water droplets, and especially ice will increase the stalling speed and may also produce a more violent nose or wing drop at the stall.

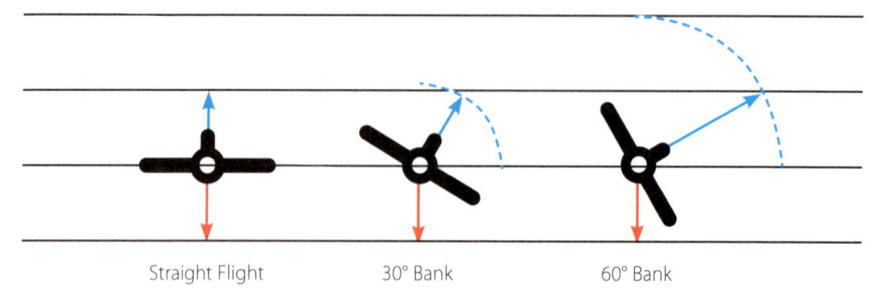

■　*Figure 5.4* ***Load Factors in Turns***

5.4 Symptoms of the Stall

The actual symptoms which a pilot may experience at the point of the stall will depend on the individual aeroplane and the conditions of flight at which it stalls. However, some or all of the following will be felt once the angle of attack becomes critical:

- Buffet as the separated air flows over the tailplane
- Undemanded roll if one wing stalls before the other
- Nose dropping despite the control column being fully back
- A high rate of descent for the pitch attitude

5.5 Standard Stall Recovery

Over the many years of flight, a standard technique has been developed for pilots to use to return their aeroplanes to normal flight if they reach the point of the stall. This "standard stall recovery" has been proved to minimise the amount of height lost during the return to unstalled flight.

As we have seen, the aircraft angle of attack must be reduced to below the critical angle and simultaneously the aircraft must be accelerated to a speed sufficient to provide enough lift to balance the weight at that less than critical angle. At the same time, no further yaw must be allowed to occur, and once the aeroplane is no longer stalled the descent must be stopped. The standard stall recovery is as follows:

Simultaneously -
 Move the **control column forward** to lower the nose until the stall symptoms disappear
 Centralise the ailerons
 Apply **full power** smoothly and rapidly, closing any airbrakes if selected
 Apply **only enough** rudder to prevent further yaw from the power application

Once the symptoms have disappeared, raise the nose into a pitch attitude just above that needed for level flight at that speed and climb away while accelerating. As soon as the power has been applied (full throttle selected and carburettor heat selected OFF), reduce drag by raising landing flap if it was selected. Once safely above ground and positively climbing at a safe speed, raise whatever flap may still be extended.

Care must be taken not to raise the nose too rapidly during the recovery. We have seen that the stalling speed depends on the square root of the load factor, but in addition the stall itself is more likely to produce a wing drop if entered while pitching.

5.6 Stall Prevention

Before the aircraft actually stalls, the pilot will notice certain symptoms of the approaching stall. If the aircraft was in level flight, the pilot would notice a high nose attitude and low airspeed. That low airspeed would provide another symptom - the controls would feel less effective and perhaps even 'sloppy'. However, an aeroplane can stall in any attitude and at any speed (the actual speed depends on the load factor), so these symptoms may not be apparent. Nevertheless, there is usually some indication that the aircraft is approaching a stalled condition; in many aeroplanes the separating flow affecting the tail produces a light buffet before the angle of attack reaches critical.

Every aeroplane with a Certificate of Airworthiness must provide some warning of the near critical angle of attack, either an obvious buffet or some artificial 'stall warning' device. Because the stagnation point moves downwards at the leading edge as the critical angle is approached, a device which senses the change in flow from under the wing to over it can trigger a buzzer or horn. In any event, if a pilot who does not intend deliberately stalling detects any of the symptoms of the approaching stall, he should take the standard stall recovery action immediately, although because the aircraft is not actually stalled, the control movements may only be those required to prevent pitch and yaw as the power takes effect.

5.7 Effect of flap

Selecting flap increases the lift available at a lower angle of attack and reduces the speed at which the aircraft will stall. However, the critical angle with flap selected is lower than that of the rest of the wing, so the effect of washout is reduced and a wing drop at the point of the stall becomes more likely. Recovery may require more time and more height because of the increased drag, hence the importance of raising landing flap early if it has been selected.

5.8 The Flight Envelope

We have seen in chapter 3 that every aircraft has a limiting speed V_{NE}. It must not be flown above that speed. Similarly, it cannot be flown in level flight below its stalling speed for the weight. There is also a limit to the maximum g force which it can withstand, but since stalling speed increases with applied g, the minimum possible flying speed varies with that g. As we saw in figure 3.6, designers can draw a graph to represent these limits pictorially, and that graph is called the 'flight envelope' since it encloses or 'envelopes' the possible flight conditions. If the aeroplane is capable of inverted flight, there will be a part of the flight envelope drawn around the limits for negative g also.

Figure 3.6 (repeated here as fig. 5.5) illustrates, in the area surrounded by the hatching and the red 'stall' line, a representative flight envelope for a typical light training aeroplane in the utility category (see volume 2). The g limit is 2.8g (with no negative g allowed), V_{NE} is 124 knots, and stalling speed in level flight (V_{SO}) is 36 knots.

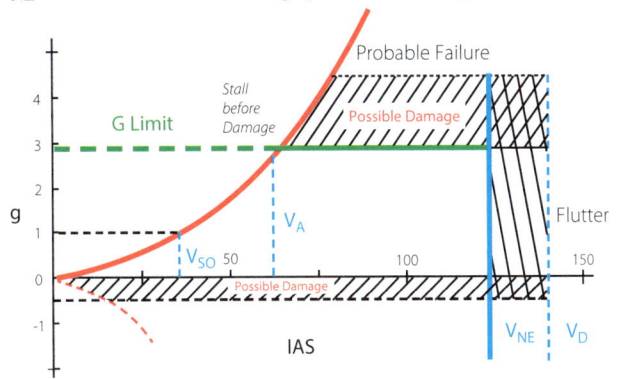

■ *Figure 5.5* **Flight Envelope**

5.9 Autorotation

In paragraph 5.2 we mentioned the consequences of inducing one wing to stall before the other. Such an asymmetric stall may be caused by a variety of situations. If the aeroplane yaws at the critical angle, the forward movement of the advancing wing increases the lift from that wing, moving it upwards and reducing the effective angle of attack of that wing and preventing the stall. Likewise the reduction in the lift from the retreating wing increases the effective angle of attack and inducing a stall on that wing only. Being stalled, the retreating, downgoing wing goes down faster, which again increases the angle of attack. The aircraft is rolling without any deliberate control input. It is sometimes said that it has "departed" from the control of the pilot.

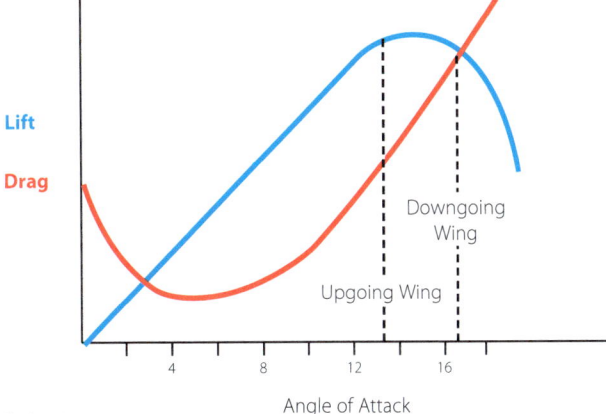

■ *Figure 5.6* **Autorotation**

After the point of "departure", as seen in fig. 5.6, the increased effective angle of attack of the downgoing wing increases the induced drag on that wing in relation to the upgoing wing. This emphasises the yaw in the original direction, which in turn continues to encourage the roll. This is called "autorotation", when the aeroplane is both yawing and rolling.

5.10 Spinning

If the aircraft is allowed to continue autorotation while holding the nose up with elevator, the overall increasing drag will cause the upgoing wing to stall also. The initial combination of rolling and yawing will change to a descending spiral type motion. Although the upgoing wing is stalled, the rolling motion maintains its angle of attack less than that of the downgoing wing, producing more lift and less drag and continuing the autorotation. At the same time, the rearward position of the control column combined with the forward centre of pressure overcomes the moment from the tailplane lift, and pitches the nose of the aircraft upwards relative to the pilot. The aeroplane is now pitching, rolling and yawing around all 3 axes, descending rapidly, but not accelerating. These facts are conclusive evidence that the aircraft is "spinning". In fact it is in what is called an "erect spin" - it is possible, especially if control is lost during advanced aerobatic manoeuvres, to enter an "inverted spin" where the aircraft is spinning while upside down. Each rotation around the horizon in the fully developed spin will lose a typical light aeroplane around two hundred feet.

To the pilot, the aeroplane seems to be spiralling downwards, so the natural reaction from someone who does not understand the situation may be to pull back on the control column in an attempt to raise the nose. Since the aircraft is stalled, **this will not produce the desired effect.**

5.11 Spin Recovery Actions

Different aircraft may require different actions from the pilot to recover from the spin in the most efficient manner, but in general the first requirement is to stop the yaw which is taking place and balance the angles of attack of the 2 wings. After that, moving the control column forward should unstall the wings and allow the aeroplane to accelerate. However, once the aeroplane has settled into the spin, the rotating motions build up a certain amount of inertia in all 3 planes, and this considerably affects what will happen as the controls move in the spin. The Flight Manual must be consulted (before it happens!) to learn the recommended technique for recovery for each individual aeroplane type.

Unfortunately, the recovery from the spin usually results in the aeroplane pointing very steeply towards the ground. Since drag has been reduced, it will accelerate rapidly, and lose a considerable amount of height very quickly. The pilot must therefore pull out of the dive (smoothly and without exceeding the g limits or V_{NE}) as soon as the aeroplane has recovered from the spin. He will know that this has occurred when the aeroplane stops rotating. To minimise the risk of overspeeding the engine or the airframe, the throttle should be closed as one of the initial actions. This will also reduce the height lost in the recovery, although losses of well over 1000 feet are typical during the pull out from the dive.

The spin recovery actions most commonly recommended in Flight Manuals are therefore as follows:

1. **Close the throttle.**
2. Identify the **direction of yaw** - the turn needle or, in an erect spin, co-ordinator indicates this.
3. Positively apply **FULL opposite rudder.**
4. Pause for one or two seconds.
5. Move the **control column centrally forward** until the spin stops.
6. **Centralise** the rudder and **ease out** of the dive.

5.12 Spin Prevention

The amount of height lost during a spin and recovery means that accidental spinning is highly dangerous and must be avoided. Maintaining balanced flight at all times will avoid autorotation and spinning but requires skill and practice. Avoiding the stall will also avoid spinning. However, if an accidental stall does occur, rapid and correct stall recovery action is the most efficient method of preventing a spin developing. As we saw in paragraph 5.2, it is important to ensure that the rudder and ailerons do not encourage further departure, so the rudder should only be used to balance the application of power, and the ailerons must be placed and kept in the neutral position until the aircraft has returned to normal flight.

5.13 Incipient Spin Recovery

Correct early stall recovery action will prevent an accidental stall developing into a spin. However, if autorotation starts, the pilot may become confused by the aircraft's motion. On average, a light aeroplane will descend through a few hundred feet during the autorotation or "incipient spin" stage, and if he recovers at this point the pilot will be able to return to level flight with the loss of only a few hundred feet more. We have referred to the large amount of height lost during a fully developed spin and recovery. Although most aircraft will recover from a fully developed spin if the correct action is taken as listed in the Flight Manual, an accidental autorotation (apparent when the aircraft does something the pilot has not moved the controls to induce) should not be allowed to develop to the full spin.

To prevent an incipient spin developing into a full spin, the pilot should attempt to recover by placing **all** the flight controls into the central (neutral) position immediately the aircraft "departs". The throttle position may be ignored, although less than full power is probably ideal. The aircraft may continue to autorotate for a short while, but stability should return it to normal, gently descending, flight, although the exact recovery attitude will vary. If not, full spin recovery action may be necessary.

It can be seen that this is effectively a version of the standard stall recovery, but greatly simplified to take account of the possible extreme attitudes the aeroplane may find itself in.

5.14 Principles of Flight Questions

1. Compared to a stall without flap, a stall in an aeroplane with flap selected:
   (a) occurs at a higher airspeed and a wing is less likely to drop at the stall
   (b) occurs at a lower airspeed and a wing is less likely to drop at the stall
   (c) occurs at a lower airspeed and a wing is more likely to drop at the stall
   (d) occurs at a higher airspeed and a wing is more likely to drop at the stall

2. An aeroplane has a stalling speed of 40 knots in level flight. What will be the approximate stalling speed during aerobatics when the pilot pulls 4 g?
   (a) 40 knots
   (b) 50 knots
   (c) 60 knots
   (d) 80 knots

3. An aeroplane has a stalling speed in level flight of 60 knots. What will be its approximate stalling speed in a 60° bank level turn?
   (a) 45 knots
   (b) 60 knots
   (c) 85 knots
   (d) 100 knots

4. An aeroplane has a stalling speed at a mass of 500 kilograms of 40 knots. What will be the approximate stalling speed in level flight at a mass of 750 kg?
   (a) 30 knots
   (b) 40 knots
   (c) 50 knots
   (d) 60 knots

5. Which of the following is not part of the initial actions in a standard stall recovery?
   (a) Move the control column centrally forward
   (b) Apply rudder to lift the falling wing
   (c) Apply full power
   (d) All are part of the standard stall recovery

6. In an erect fully developed spin, around which of its axes is the aeroplane not rotating?
   (a) Normal
   (b) Lateral
   (c) Longitudinal
   (d) It is rotating around them all

7. During normal spin recovery which of the following actions is not usually recommended?

(a) Apply full rudder in the same direction as the turn needle or turn co-ordinator
(b) Move the elevator control forward until the spin stops
(c) Close the throttle
(d) Keep the ailerons neutral

8. In straight and level flight at sea level, an aeroplane stalls at a certain angle of attack. If the aircraft stalls in a turn at a higher altitude, which of the following statements is true?

(a) The stalling angle of attack will increase because the aircraft is turning
(b) The stalling angle of attack will increase because the aircraft is at a higher altitude
(c) The stalling angle of attack will increase for both reasons
(d) There will be no change in the stalling angle of attack

9. At the onset of a stall in a typical training aeroplane:

(a) The aircraft pitches nose-down and loses height
(b) The aircraft pitches nose-up and loses height
(c) The airspeed continues to decrease
(d) The airspeed increases as the aircraft loses height

10. The stalling speed of a manoeuvring aeroplane at a given weight depends on:

(a) The square of the lift required
(b) The square root of the load factor
(c) The square of the load factor
(d) The square of the weight

11. Use of washout on an aeroplane wing will:

(a) Increase lateral stability
(b) Prevent the wing tips from stalling first
(c) Cause the outboard section of the wing to stall first
(d) Decrease the effectiveness of the ailerons

12. An aeroplane wing stalls at:

(a) A specific speed
(b) An angle of attack which varies inversely with the mass
(c) The stagnation point which may be visible
(d) A specific angle of attack

13. In order to recover from a fully developed spin, the recovery technique:

(a) Is standard for all aeroplane types
(b) Can be found in the aircraft's Certificate of Airworthiness
(c) Should be studied in the aircraft's Flight Manual
(d) Is unimportant, as every aeroplane will automatically recover

14. If a pilot hears a loud buzzing noise in his earphones when turning onto the final approach, what should his immediate action(s) be?
   (a) Raise the flap
   (b) Move the control column centrally forward and apply full power
   (c) Roll wings level then investigate the source of the noise
   (d) Apply into-turn rudder

15. What are the characteristics of a fully developed spin?
   (a) Low indicated airspeed, low rate of descent
   (b) High indicated airspeed, low rate of descent
   (c) High indicated airspeed, high rate of descent
   (d) Low indicated airspeed, high rate of descent

16. What is the most likely cause of an aeroplane entering an unintentional spin?
   (a) Lowering the nose at the stall
   (b) Yaw at the stall caused by out of balance flight
   (c) Roll at the stall caused by excessive elevator input
   (d) Reducing throttle setting at the stall

17. If the angle of attack increases above the critical angle, what happens to the coefficients of lift and drag?
   (a) The coefficient of lift increases and the coefficient of drag increases
   (b) The coefficient of lift reduces and the coefficient of drag increases
   (c) The coefficient of lift increases and the coefficient of drag reduces
   (d) The coefficient of lift reduces and the coefficient of drag reduces

18. Which of the following conditions will both increase the stalling speed of an aeroplane at the same mass and angle of bank?
   (a) Ice on the wings and increasing engine rpm
   (b) Ice on the wings and increasing the load factor
   (c) Reducing the load factor and increasing engine rpm
   (d) Increasing the load factor and increasing engine rpm

19. What generates the 'buffet' which may be felt as a pre-stall warning?
   (a) The separated airflow from the wing flows onto the ailerons
   (b) The high pressure air below the wing is allowed to flow around the wingtips and affect the ailerons
   (c) The separated airflow from the wing flows onto the tailplane and affects the elevators
   (d) The high pressure air below each wing flows inwards and mixes under the fuselage, and the turbulence affects the longitudinal stability

20. Which of the following is likely to cause an aeroplane to spin if it is already in a stalled condition?

(a) Torque from the propeller if full power is applied
(b) The secondary effect of ailerons if they are centralised
(c) Loss of lateral stability if rudders are centralised
(d) Gyroscopic precession from the effect of applying down elevator

21. What effect does the position of the aircraft's Centre of Gravity have on its directional and longitudinal stability?

(a) A forward CofG increases the directional stability but reduces the longitudinal stability
(b) A forward CofG increases the directional stability and increases the longitudinal stability
(c) A forward CofG reduces the directional stability but increases the longitudinal stability
(d) A forward CofG reduces the directional stability and reduces the longitudinal stability

22. At what angle of attack would you expect the coefficient of lift of a light aeroplane's wing to be greatest?

(a) 0 degrees
(b) 4 degrees
(c) 15 degrees
(d) 30 degrees

23. In normal flight, the airflow over the upper and lower surfaces of the wing will have:

(a) The same speed and surface pressure over both surfaces
(b) A higher speed and lower pressure over the upper surface
(c) A lower speed and higher pressure over the upper surface
(d) A higher speed and higher pressure over the upper surface

24. Where on an aeroplane wing in level flight would you expect pressure to be (i) highest and (ii) lowest?

(a) (i) at the stagnation point   (ii) on the top surface at the thickest point
(b) (i) at the stagnation point   (ii) at the separation point
(c) (i) on the bottom surface   (ii) on the top surface at the thickest point
(d) (i) on the bottom surface   (ii) at the separation point

25. Using a small amount of flap during take-off is likely to produce:

(a) An increase in ground run and an increase in take-off distance to 50 feet
(b) An increase in ground run and a reduction in take-off distance to 50 feet
(c) A reduction in ground run and a reduction in take-off distance to 50 feet
(d) A reduction in ground run and an increase in take-off distance to 50 feet

26. An aeroplane with a level flight stalling speed of 40 knots makes a level turn using 45 degrees of bank. Approximately what load factor will it experience and what will be its stalling speed?
   (a) It will experience 1.4g and will stall at 56 kt
   (b) It will experience 1.4g and will stall at 47 kt
   (c) It will experience 2g and will stall at 56 kt
   (d) It will experience 2g and will stall at 47 kt

27. Which of the following is an effect of lowering flap to 10 degrees?
   (a) Lift will increase proportionately more than drag
   (b) The pitch attitude for level flight will be more nose-up
   (c) The aircraft will be less speed stable at low speed
   (d) The maximum permitted airspeed will increase

28. If an aeroplane is disturbed in roll by turbulence pushing the left wing down, then when the turbulence force is removed the wing drops ever faster, what can we say about its stability:
   (a) The aircraft is laterally stable
   (b) The aircraft is laterally unstable
   (c) The aircraft is longitudinally neutral
   (d) The aircraft is longitudinally stable

29. As the speed of an aeroplane decreases:
   (a) Induced drag decreases and parasite drag increases
   (b) Both induced drag and parasite drag decrease
   (c) Both induced drag and parasite drag increase
   (d) Induced drag increases and parasite drag decreases

Intentionally Left Blank

Chapter 6

Piston Engines

6.1 Introduction

The thrust required to counter drag and allow an aeroplane to fly level and climb is provided by the combination of the engine and the propeller. Most piston engines burn petrol (aviation gasoline or AVGAS) in air with which it has been previously mixed in the correct ratio. The energy from that fuel is converted into rotational energy by turning a crankshaft, to which the propeller is attached. The speed of the crankshaft rotation in revolutions per minute is indicated on a "tachometer" or rpm gauge. The more rpm, the more power is available from the engine.

The ideal ratio of air to fuel for maximum power is approximately 12 to 1 by weight. If the ratio is greater than this (20 to 1 say), there is too much air for efficient burning (combustion) and the mixture is said to be 'weak', or 'lean'. If the ratio is less (10 to 1 say) it is 'rich', and some fuel remains unburnt. Excessively rich or weak mixtures may not ignite. Confusingly, many people refer to the mixture ratio as the "fuel/air" ratio, but continue to use the numbers with the greater first, as for example 12 to 1!

6.2 Cylinders

The burning of the fuel takes place in cylinders (usually of aluminium alloy). The cylinders are frequently arranged horizontally in pairs opposing each other around the crankshaft (a horizontally opposed engine), but occasionally in single lines along it (an in-line engine), and sometimes spread out all round it (a radial engine). As the fuel in each cylinder burns, the air in which it is burning expands with the heat. That expansion pushes a piston along the cylinder away from the burning. The far end of the piston is connected to the crankshaft in such a way that the linear movement of the piston is converted into rotational movement of the crankshaft. The volume of the cylinder with the piston at the bottom is the "total volume". The volume with the piston at the top is the "clearance volume". Total volume minus clearance volume is the "swept volume" (the piston face area multiplied by the distance moved by the piston).

Several pistons in several cylinders pushing the crankshaft in that rotational movement at different times provide a virtually continuous torque to rotate the crankshaft. Some of that torque drives the propeller, but some is required to push the pistons back up to their starting positions again, and also to compress the fuel/air mixture in those cylinders to make the next burning more efficient.

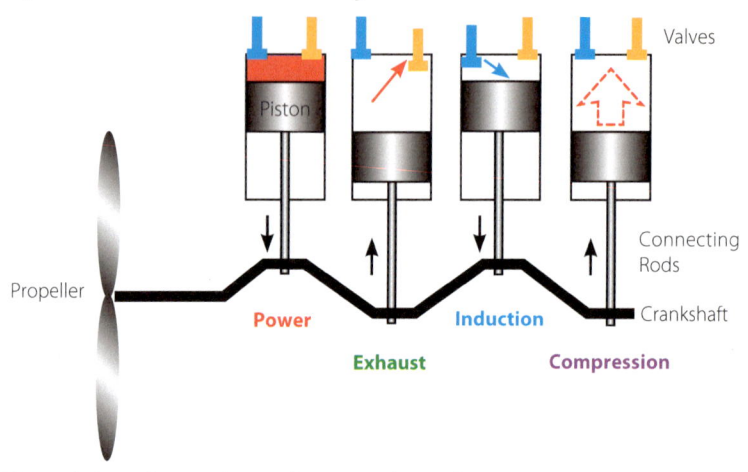

■ *Figure 6.1* **In Line Engine and Four Stroke Cycle**

6.3   The Four Stroke Cycle

Each piston moves (or "strokes") up and down (down being towards the crankshaft) in its cylinder twice for each expansion or "power" stroke. Once it has reached the bottom of its travel, the burnt gases are pushed out of an exhaust port (hole) by the piston moving back upwards. When the burnt gases have been exhausted, the exhaust port is closed by a valve and an "inlet" port is opened while the piston travels back down again. This "induction" stroke sucks in the fuel mixed with the air in which it will be burnt, and then when the piston moves up again it compresses the mixture to make the burning more efficient. When the piston is at the top of its travel, the fuel is ignited (usually by spark plugs) and burns very rapidly to drive the piston down again in another power stroke. Fig. 6.1 shows the piston positions just after starting each stroke.

Although there are such things as "rotary" engines available, and readers may also come across some "two stroke" engines, this four stroke or "Otto" cycle is the basis of most aeroplane piston engines. The four strokes are usually referred to as induction, compression, power and exhaust. In a four cylinder engine, each piston is at a similar stage in each of the individual strokes. A six cylinder engine provides a more continuous torque on the crankshaft and smoother running.

The position of the piston at the exact top of its travel, when the volume of the cylinder is at its smallest, is called "top dead centre" or "tdc". At the exact bottom of its travel, when the cylinder volume is at a maximum, the piston's position is referred to as "bottom dead centre" or "bdc". An engine may be described as having a certain "capacity", which is the total volume of gas in all the cylinders with the valves shut. The "compression ratio" is the volume of gas in the cylinder before compression (total volume - when the piston is at bdc) divided by the volume after compression (clearance volume - when the piston is at tdc).

6.4 Valves

The valves which operate the inlet and exhaust ports are kept closed by springs, and usually opened by a system of levers or "push rods" moved by "cams" which are egg-shaped lumps on a rotating "camshaft". The camshaft is driven by the crankshaft, but rotates at half the speed of that crankshaft so that the valves open only once every full cycle.

In order to allow efficient air flow in the cylinder, the valves actually open just before the piston reaches the end of its travel, and close just after. This is "valve timing", also called "valve lead" and "valve lag". The valves open just before the piston reaches tdc, and close just after bdc. This means, as in figure 6.2, that there is a period during which both exhaust and inlet valves are open, when the piston is around tdc at the end of the exhaust stroke.

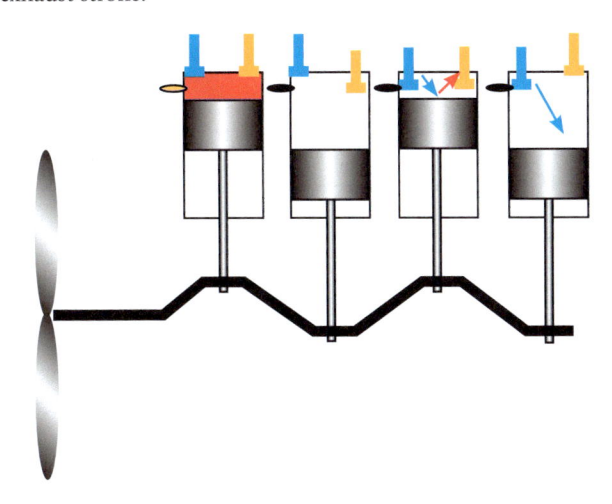

■ Figure 6.2 **Valve Timing**

6.5 Ignition

The mixture is ignited by sparks generated when a high voltage exists between two open electrodes inside "spark plugs", usually two in each cylinder. Each of these two plugs is supplied with electricity from a separate supply. This dual system produces not only rapid burning of the mixture (by igniting it in two places on opposite sides of the cylinder), but also provides redundancy by ensuring that the mixture burns even if one ignition system fails.

The electrical supply for ignition is produced in a "magneto" by induction from rotating magnetic fields, although several stages are required to produce the voltage required for ignition. Initially, a pair of permanent magnets are fixed together in such a way that their "poles" form a cross which is made to rotate inside a piece of soft (easily magnetised) iron. As one pole lies against one end of the soft iron bridge or "armature," an opposite pole lies against the other end. A magnetic field is set up, from the north pole to the south pole, through the iron. After a quarter turn of the rotor, the field runs in the opposite direction through the armature, so the field direction constantly changes from one direction to the other.

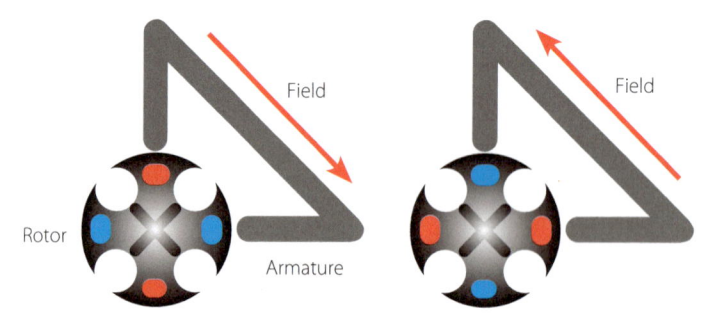

■ *Figure 6.3* **Magneto Rotor and Armature**

The armature is surrounded by a coil of wire (the "primary coil") connected to earth at both ends. The changing magnetic field induces a low voltage electrical current in the primary coil, which changes strength and direction as the magnetic field does. This part of the magneto is an alternating current generator.

To produce sufficient voltage for an ignition spark, the primary coil circuit is broken by contact breakers. The current only flows (to earth) when the contact breakers meet. The rotor drives a cam to open the breakers when the voltage in the primary coil is at its greatest. This produces a sudden collapse of current flow four times every rotation. A capacitor is also fitted to speed up this current collapse, and also to reduce wear on the contact breaker points. As a safety measure, a switch (the "ignition switch") when selected "OFF" provides an alternative route for the primary current to flow to earth and stops this collapse of the primary current.

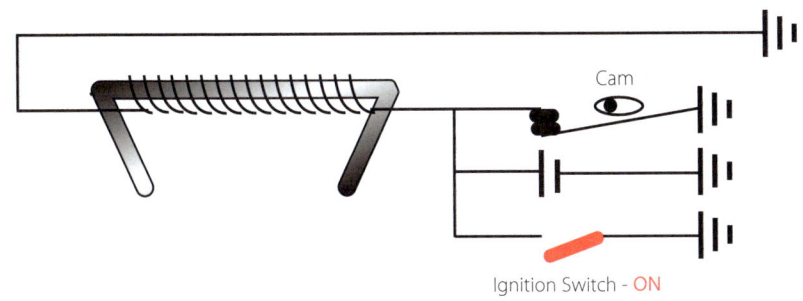

■ *Figure 6.4* **Primary Ignition Circuit**

A second coil of wires is wound around the primary coil in the opposite direction. The current flowing in the primary coil produces its own magnetic field, which in turn induces a voltage in this "secondary coil". Because there is such a rapid change in the current in the primary coil (it stops suddenly when the contact breakers open), the voltage induced in the secondary "windings" is high enough to produce a spark at a spark plug.

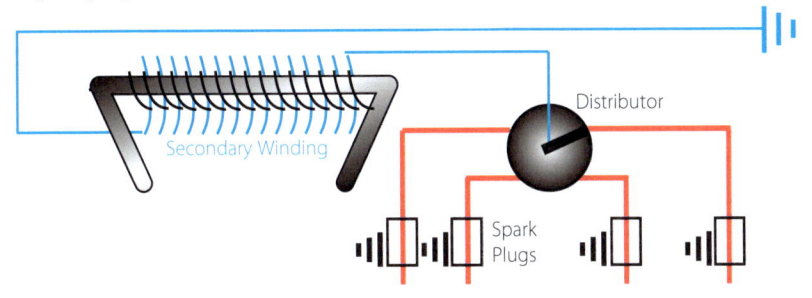

■ *Figure 6.5* **Ignition Secondary Circuit**

In some engines, the rotor of one magneto (the "impulse" magneto) is held back by a spring to increase the magneto rotor speed from the slow rotation produced by hand swinging the propeller. If hand swinging for starting, the other magneto switch must remain OFF until the engine has started.

The high voltage pulses induced in the secondary windings flow through a distributor. The distributor sends each pulse in order to the appropriate spark plug in whichever cylinder is starting its power stroke. The firing order is arranged for the smoothest possible running.

It should be noted that when the ignition switch is selected OFF in the cockpit, any current generated in the primary windings (as a result of for example the propeller being rotated) is allowed to flow to earth. Selecting "ignition ON" actually breaks the circuit. However, if the ignition switch wiring is broken, the current cannot flow to earth through the switch, and the ignition system will be permanently 'live', with the attendant danger of the engine bursting into life if the propeller is rotated. Propellers must always be regarded as 'live' and likely to cause serious injury; indeed they have been known to burst into life with all electrical power switched off and only a tiny disturbance to the propeller.

6.6 Carburettors

In most petrol burning piston engines, the fuel is mixed with air in a carburettor system, from where it is induced into the cylinders through the inlet valves. Although the carburettors in complex piston engines such as those fitted to second world war fighters contain a number of sophisticated devices, the carburettors in light aircraft are relatively simple.

The first part of a simple carburettor is a small tank, called the float chamber. Fuel flows into the float chamber until it is full and the float rises until a valve on the top blocks the inlet pipe. As the fuel level, and therefore the float, drops, the valve opens. This ensures that the head of fuel in the chamber, and therefore its pressure, is kept constant, and sufficient for sudden acceleration if needed. Fuel from the float chamber is fed to the engine "inlet manifold" which leads from the external engine air intake, where an air filter is usually situated, to the cylinder inlet valves.

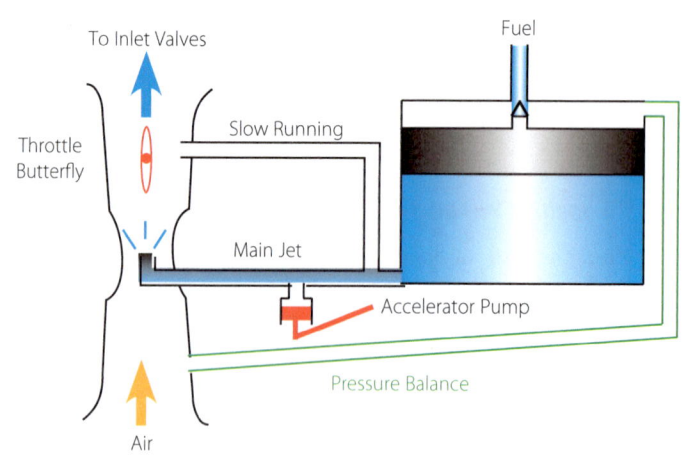

■ Figure 6.6 - **A Simple Carburettor**

The inlet manifold is shaped in the area where the fuel enters to form a "throat", "choke" or "venturi" (a narrow passage). The air flowing through that venturi from the intake is speeded up as it passes through, and therefore its pressure reduces, which sucks the fuel from the float chamber through a narrow aperture called the "main jet". The faster the air passes through, the lower the air pressure and the faster the fuel flows through the jet. This keeps the air to fuel mixture ratio relatively constant. The speed of the air flow is affected by the aircraft's airspeed, but more importantly by the suction generated in the cylinders by the induction strokes. This basically maintains a steady volume of mixture entering the cylinders.

Just after the venturi in the manifold is a butterfly valve connected to the pilot's throttle control lever. This is shown fully open in figure 6.6, but restricts the air flow when the pilot "closes the throttle", therefore also reducing the fuel flow. As the volume of mixture in the cylinders for each power stroke reduces, less expansion takes place within them, so the engine power reduces. The throttle valve itself never completely closes, but even so the slow flow through the venturi does not provide enough suction to maintain the mixture at low engine speeds, so a "slow-running jet" is fitted just where the very narrow remaining gap at the edge of the throttle valve is restricting the flow and providing an additional venturi.

Opening the throttle allows more air and therefore mixture to enter the cylinders, and increases the engine power. However, fuel is heavier than air, and changes its flow rate slower, weakening the mixture. A weak mixture would not increase the engine rpm, so unless the mixture is engineered to be already richer than ideal, an additional "acceleration pump" may be fitted in the line to the main jet. This may be compared to a syringe connected directly to the throttle lever. When the throttle is closed the "syringe" sucks excess fuel into itself; when the throttle is opened, the syringe pushes its contents into the manifold. However, the accelerator pump cannot always compensate for opening the throttle very rapidly.

In fact, despite the weakening mixture during acceleration, in general at wide throttle openings the amount of fuel sucked into the manifold is more than necessary to maintain the correct mixture ratio. To prevent this, either a diffuser (allowing air to leak into the main jet as speed increases) or a needle valve (to reduce the jet opening at large throttle settings) may be fitted to the jet itself. Other devices, such as an aneroid to reduce the fuel flow as atmospheric air pressure reduces with height, may also be found.

An addition to the carburettor is the priming pump, which provides a fine spray of fuel directly into the inlet manifold or valve ports for engine starting. The simple version is a hand pump operated by the pilot pushing and pulling like a bicycle pump, which is locked by pushing it home and rotating it. If not locked, however, an excess of fuel can find its way into the cylinder and cause a power reduction. It is vital to ensure the priming pump is locked before take-off.

6.7 Cooling

The heat generated by burning fuel in the cylinders is considerable, and although exhaust gases remove some of it, much is transferred to the pistons and walls of the cylinders. This has some benefits, in that the mixture is warmed during compression even more than the compression process itself provides. However, if metal becomes too hot it may distort, and even without that, hot spots in the cylinder could ignite the mixture before the ignition spark (this is called "pre-ignition"). It is therefore necessary to provide some means of cooling the engine.

Engines in most motor cars and some aircraft are cooled by surrounding the cylinders and other parts with a "jacket" of liquid, usually water containing chemicals to prevent freezing and corrosion. The liquid conducts heat away from the metal, and is pumped through a radiator where much of its heat is transferred to the outside air. All the metal parts in a liquid cooled engine are at approximately the same temperature, and temperature changes are slow.

Most aircraft engines are cooled directly by air flowing past the cylinders which have fins projecting into that air to conduct as much heat as possible. This is "air-cooling". Airflow resulting from an aeroplane's forward speed, coupled with the propeller slipstream, can absorb considerable heat. However, hot spots can only be prevented if the flow is directed carefully around the engine by means of engine cowling design and internal baffles. It is therefore important not to allow damage or removal of these cowlings and baffles.

One of the problems of an air-cooled engine is that the temperature may change rapidly with speed and power. If a large temperature difference is allowed to develop between adjacent engine parts, permanent distortion may result. Rapid closing of the throttle coupled with an increase in airspeed (and therefore cooling airflow) is a classic cause of this temperature difference, so care should be taken when starting a descent, especially for example immediately after a full-power climb.

The amount of cooling air passing the cylinders may be controlled on some aircraft by cowl flaps or other devices which cover the intake for the cooling air. The temperature of the cylinder head (where the valves are positioned) may be measured and indicated in the cockpit on a cylinder head temperature (CHT) gauge, and the pilot can adjust the opening of cowl flaps to maintain the CHT in the ideal sector as specified in the Flight Manual.

6.8 Lubrication

While the outside of the cylinder can be cooled by water or air, the internal workings cannot. Nevertheless, it is important to keep the temperature of individual internal parts of the engine as low, or at least as equal, as possible. Oil, which does not boil at engine operating temperatures, is used for this, and also to reduce friction and wear of the moving parts by lubricating them. For example, the piston connecting rods rotate around the crankshaft and the crankshaft itself rotates in the engine block. All these and other rotations are carried by roller, ball, or shell bearings, all of which must be lubricated.

The viscosity (thickness) of the oil dictates how easily it flows, and how well it lubricates. In simple terms, the viscosity of a particular oil increases as temperature reduces. In cold weather, a generally thinner oil will be needed to flow freely, although in hot temperatures such a thin oil may not lubricate well enough. Although "multigrade" oils are available, use only the ones recommended by the aircraft (or engine) manufacturer and approved in the Flight Manual for your aircraft.

The oil is contained, either always surrounding the moving parts (a wet-sump system) or in a separate tank (dry-sump). A rotary pump connected to the crankshaft pushes it around the moving parts of the engine components, which it lubricates by either surrounding the bearings, being sprayed onto them, or just splashing over them. During this process the oil absorbs heat. The hot oil then passes through a cooler (sometimes called a heat-exchanger) which is similar to the radiator in a liquid cooled engine, before returning to the sump, or being pumped to the tank by a 'scavenge pump'. On its way, it passes through at least one filter, which collects any metal which may have worn away and been flushed out by the hot oil. At intervals, the filter is removed and inspected, then replaced with a new one.

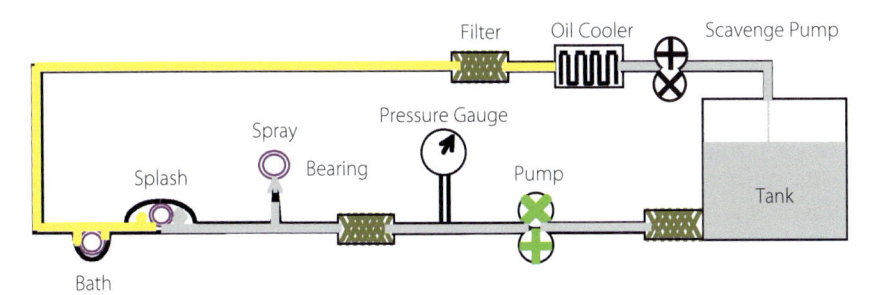

■ *Figure 6.7* **A Dry Sump Oil System**

New or replacement parts of an engine usually need to "bed in" or "run in" to wear off rough edges. "Straight" oil has reduced lubrication properties and is normally used for the first 50 hours running of new parts. Any pieces of metal which wear away are trapped in the filters. While these may be regarded as acceptable in straight oil, any metal found in the oil filter of a run-in engine is likely to be a symptom of a serious problem which must be investigated.

The pump must provide a certain minimum pressure to ensure that the oil reaches all parts of the engine. That minimum pressure must be reached within about 30 seconds of starting, otherwise damage may result. Similarly, unless the oil is warm enough (thin enough) to pass through all the filters and spray nozzles, damage may result at high power settings. For that reason, many engines are restricted to a maximum of about 1500 rpm until the oil has reached a minimum temperature indicated on an oil temperature gauge. Excessively high pressure in the system, which could damage the seals, is prevented by a relief valve which opens when pressure reaches the maximum limit, returning excess oil to the sump or tank. By-pass valves take the oil around any blockages in the filter or oil cooler to ensure the engine is still lubricated, and a further by-pass system keeps oil away from the cooler until it is above minimum temperature.

If the oil pressure reduces in flight, lubrication and cooling will reduce, so the pilot should prepare for a landing as soon as possible. If it falls to zero, expect the engine to seize very soon. However if the oil temperature remains normal, the pressure gauge may be faulty, and you may wish to fly towards an aerodrome at cruise power until certain of a safe landing, then close the throttle for a glide approach. If however the oil temperature increases, you may wish to shut down the engine (once certain of making a safe forced landing) before it seizes.

6.9 Mixture Control

Although the ideal mixture for maximum power is approximately 12 to 1, most simple aircraft engines actually provide a richer mixture under normal circumstances. This is mainly because too weak a mixture may cause detonation (a sudden explosion rather than a controlled burning) and damage. In addition, because a rich mixture leaves some fuel unburnt, the evaporation of that unburnt fuel acts as an additional means of cooling, so a rich mixture is an advantage at high power settings, especially when forward speed is low such as in a climb.

However, an over-rich mixture uses more fuel than necessary (sometimes considerably more), so there is a financial advantage in adjusting the mixture until the ratio is correct for the particular phase of flight. Moving the mixture control lever (coloured red) directly affects the fuel flow by inserting a needle valve into the main jet. When fully forward, the needle is kept away from the jet and the mixture is as rich as the carburettor provides. As the lever moves towards the lean position, the needle progressively closes the jet until when the lever is fully back no fuel can get through at all and the engine stops (idle cut-off or ICO).

Because air density reduces with altitude, the higher the aircraft is cruising the weaker the mixture setting should be, and the Flight Manual will give guidance. However, in general in UK conditions, the take-off and initial climb should be carried out with the mixture set fully rich. Except in hot weather or in a prolonged climb, the mixture should not normally be adjusted until cruising altitude is reached and power has been reduced for the cruise. Some aircraft may have instruments to assist the pilot. An exhaust gas temperature (EGT) gauge indicates the most efficient combustion at its maximum reading. However, any change in conditions may cause the mixture to become too weak, with possible over-heating, pre-ignition and damage, so most Flight Manuals recommend enriching the mixture until the EGT shows about 100°F less than maximum. A fuel flow meter indicates the rate of fuel being used, so a pilot can set the mixture to provide the minimum fuel flow or just above.

However, most simple aircraft have no such indication, and studying instruments prevents pilots seeing possible collision risks outside. A simpler means of adjusting the mixture is by ear. Slowly weaken the mixture until you hear the engine starting to run a little rough, then enrich it again until it runs smoothly. The more precise method is to lean the rpm until the rpm starts to decrease, then enrich it again until the rpm has recovered, but again it is inadvisable to spend time looking at instruments unnecessarily.

6.10   Carburettor Icing

As described in the volume on Meteorology, aeroplane engines in typical United Kingdom flying weather are liable to experience carburettor icing. Air entering the engine cools as the fuel mixing with it vaporises, and it cools even more as pressure is reduced at the venturi and throttle valve. If that air is moist, water condenses out of the air. If the air temperature in the venturi reduces to below freezing, ice forms, restricting the flow of air into the engine and consequently the power available, usually noticeable by a drop in engine rpm.

Most aeroplane engines fitted with a carburettor have a heating system for it. Selecting carburettor heat normally brings air from an alternate source in the area of the engine exhaust and by-passes the air filter. The hot air reduces engine power output and increases fuel consumption, so heating is usually applied (fully) for about 20 seconds at intervals of about 10 minutes in the cruise, as a precaution and also a check for the presence of ice. In a simple engine, rpm will drop as heat is applied.

When heat is removed, the rpm should rise again to its original level. If the rpm rises to a level greater than before the check, ice was present. In that case, the check should be repeated until it can be confirmed that it has melted.

Full carburettor heating should be always be applied if carburettor icing is noticed, suspected, or likely, and is a practical first action if the pilot considers the engine is running roughly or experiencing any power reduction. However, a consequence of the heating is that any ice which has formed will start to melt and be taken into the cylinders as water. The engine may run more roughly and lose even more power, until all the ice has melted and all the water has passed through. Full carburettor heating must be maintained throughout this possibly frightening period.

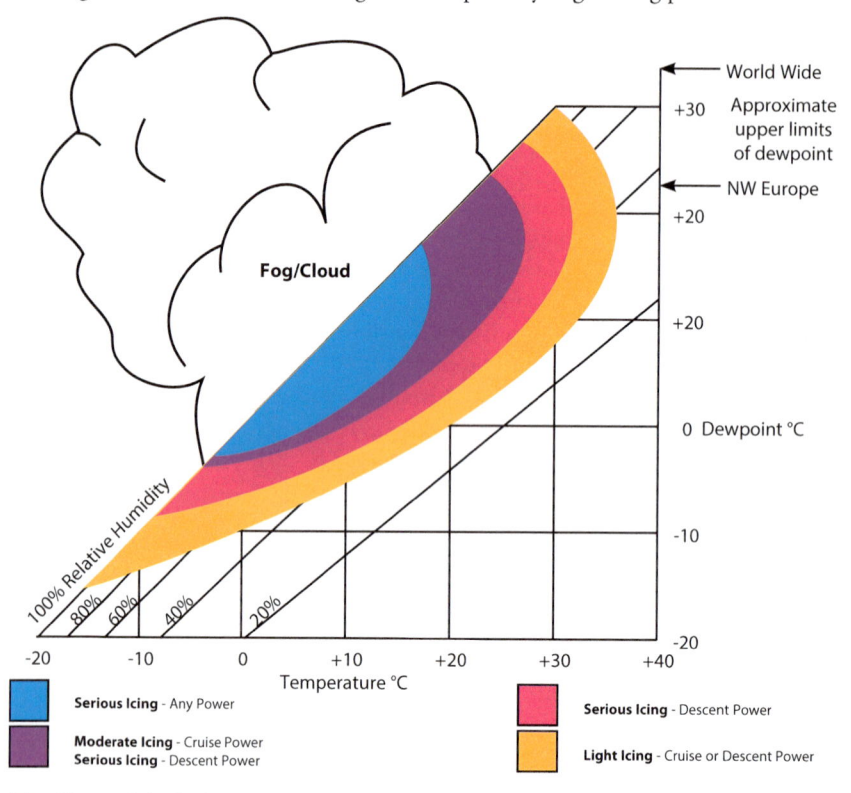

■ *Figure 6.8* **Carburettor Icing Hazard Graph**

The graph at figure 6.8 is taken from the CAA's Safety Sense Leaflet on Piston Engine Icing. It shows the temperatures and dew point bands (in the air, not at the surface) at which carburettor icing may be expected. The diagonal lines are drawn at percentages of air humidity. Note that cloud or fog gives 100% humidity, and so serious icing can be expected in either of these conditions. Use full heat whenever icing is likely.

94

At descent power settings, the temperature drop at the venturi may be well over 20 degrees C, so carburettor heating must be applied **before** reducing rpm for the descent. Warm air can hold more water vapour than cold air, so if the air temperature is around 20°C, severe carburettor icing is likely when the throttle butterfly is almost closed during a descent. A summer's day which combines such a temperature with moist air is the most dangerous time for the condition.

The speed of ice formation and the consequences of carburettor icing vary with different engines and installations. For example, if the carburettor venturi is situated in a warm area of the engine, the effect may be small. If, however, the venturi is in a cold part of the engine, the effect may be considerable and checking for ice should be done more frequently and for longer. The same should apply in obviously moist air.

Choke temperature gauges are available, which indicate the air temperature at the most likely icing area. When the gauge indicates in for example a yellow arc, carburettor icing is likely. Warning systems are also available which detect actual ice at the choke. Unfortunately, while both these devices may assist in the detection of carburettor icing, they are not foolproof.

6.11 Fuel injection

The problems with carburettors, especially icing, have encouraged their replacement in many engines with fuel injection systems. An injector pump supplies a fine spray of fuel either directly into the cylinder or into the inlet manifold immediately upstream of each inlet valve in turn. The amount of fuel injected is controlled by the mixture control and the throttle lever, and the excess is returned to the fuel tank.

The majority of fuel-injected engines use a fuel flowmeter in conjunction with the manual mixture control to set efficient cruising power. Although carburettor icing is prevented, impact ice or even fuel ice (from water contamination) may form inside the inlet manifold, perhaps on the air filter, so an unfiltered alternate air supply is usually provided.

6.12 Turbocharging

Air density reduces with altitude and temperature. To maintain an efficient mixture, as air density reduces the fuel supplied also reduces and the power available reduces in turn. Some piston engines use the power which is normally wasted in the hot gases pushed out by the pistons on their exhaust strokes to drive a turbine (a rotating wheel like a watermill which takes energy out of the exhaust and converts it into rotary motion). The turbine is connected to a compressor which increases the temperature and pressure of the air in the inlet manifold. When the required amount of increased manifold pressure or 'boost' is achieved (selected by the throttle control), oil pressure opens a 'waste gate' to allow the excess exhaust gases to bypass the turbine.

Although this turbo-charging is designed to maintain sea level mixture at higher altitudes, it can also provide increased power at sea level. However, in many cases, such increased power might overheat or otherwise damage the engine, so the waste gate is automatically opened by an 'overboost valve' when the maximum permitted inlet pressure is reached. However, it is not advisable to rely on such automatic devices during normal flight, and pilots should attempt to maintain the boost pressure and rpm within limits manually whenever possible.

6.13 Engine Starting and Checks

The checks and procedures for operating the aircraft listed in the manufacturer's Flight Manual or Pilots Operating handbook must be followed. In general, however, the pre-start checks include checking the controls for full and free movement, then setting them for the start. The fuel cock is switched on, mixture control set to rich, carburettor heat to cold, and variable propeller pitch to fine. Then the battery master switch, the anti-collision beacon, and the electric fuel pump (if fitted) are switched on and the priming pump operated for a few strokes if necessary depending on the engine temperature (the colder the more strokes). The area around the propeller is checked to ensure no-one will be endangered by the propeller (or the aircraft) moving, while the pilot calls "clear prop" loudly in warning. The magnetos are then switched on and the starter switch operated (often using an ignition key like a car) until the engine fires or it is obvious it will not start (after 30 seconds the motor is likely to overheat).

Throttle pumping may also prime an engine. However, this should only be attempted if the Flight Manual recommends it, because the accelerator pump may send too much fuel into the inlet manifold. This may run back, pool, and start a fire in the engine cowling. Too much priming may also cause over-fuelling on start-up, recognisable by the smell of fuel. Allow the fuel to evaporate before attempting another start (old engines may be turned backwards to "blow out" the fuel, but in most engines the suction pump drive is likely to shear).

After starting, it is important to check that the starter motor has disconnected and oil pressure is rising, within at least 30 seconds. If not, shut down immediately. Other services may then be switched on once the rpm has been set to a sufficient figure (perhaps 1200) to warm the engine without damage and allow the alternator to take on the electrical load. The ignition system is then checked by switching each magneto off and on in turn and checking that the engine does not stop but the rpm drops and then recovers when the magneto is switched back on.

After the engine has reached operating temperature, usually confirmed by the oil temperature gauge, the manufacturer usually requires its operation should be checked. Once the engine gauges are all indicating within limits, power should be increased to an intermediate figure and the gauges checked again. Selecting full carburettor heat should produce a drop in rpm, with a return to the original level but no higher after re-selecting cold air. Again the magnetos should be switched off and on again in turn, and this time the amount of rpm drop noted to check it is not excessive and that both systems produce similar drops. Variable pitch propellers should be exercised and feathering systems checked. The throttle should then be closed and the rpm at idle checked.

Finally the pre-take-off checks should be completed. These vital actions are the last opportunity to detect any defects or incorrect actions. The pilot should actually seek for faults while making a final check of engine instruments and setting the controls for take-off, usually including carburettor heat to cold, primer pump locked, propellers fine and mixture rich.

Intentionally Left Blank

6.14 Exercise

1. What is the ideal fuel to air ratio for maximum power?
   - (a) 12/1 by weight
   - (b) 12/1 by volume
   - (c) 1/12 by weight
   - (d) 1/12 by volume

2. At the end of the exhaust stroke, where is the piston?
   - (a) At top dead centre
   - (b) Just before top dead centre
   - (c) At bottom dead centre
   - (d) Just after bottom dead centre

3. What is the sequence of the four stroke cycle?
   - (a) Induction, exhaust, power, compression
   - (b) Compression, power, exhaust, induction
   - (c) Power, exhaust, compression, induction
   - (d) Exhaust, power, induction, compression

4. At what piston position does an inlet valve open?
   - (a) At top dead centre
   - (b) At bottom dead centre
   - (c) Just before bottom dead centre
   - (d) Just before top dead centre

5. What is the purpose of the camshaft and how fast does it turn?
   - (a) To control the ignition timing, at the same speed as the crankshaft
   - (b) To operate the inlet and exhaust valves at the correct time, at half the speed of the crankshaft.
   - (c) To operate the inlet and exhaust valves at the correct time, at twice the speed of the crankshaft
   - (d) To control the ignition timing, at twice the speed of the crankshaft

6. An air/fuel ratio of 20 to 1 is?
   - (a) Almost ideal for maximum power?
   - (b) Richer than ideal for maximum power?
   - (c) Leaner than ideal for maximum power but richer than ideal for cruise?
   - (d) Leaner than ideal for cruise?

7. The crankshaft in a piston engine:
   (a) Connects the piston to the camshaft
   (b) Adjusts the clearance of the valves
   (c) Reciprocates twice during a four stroke cycle
   (d) Converts reciprocating motion into rotary motion

8. The compression ratio is the ratio of the:
   (a) Clearance volume to total volume
   (b) Total volume to clearance volume
   (c) Swept volume to clearance volume
   (d) Clearance volume to swept volume

9. Pre-ignition in a four-stroke piston engine is:
   (a) The explosive combustion of the fuel-air mixture
   (b) The result of back-fire
   (c) An early burning of the fuel-air mixture
   (d) Caused by a rich mixture in a hot engine

10. The power of a simple four-stroke engine at a given altitude:
   (a) Increases as rpm increases
   (b) Increases with rpm then remains at a constant level
   (c) Increases then decreases as rpm increases
   (d) Remains constant as rpm increases

11. If a magneto switch is OFF, current in the primary windings:
   (a) Flows continually to earth
   (b) Induces a current in the secondary windings
   (c) Induces a current in the armature
   (d) Causes the magneto rotor to turn.

12. If a magneto switch is ON, current in the primary windings:
   (a) Flows continually to earth
   (b) Induces a current in the secondary windings
   (c) Induces a current in the armature
   (d) Causes the magneto rotor to turn.

13. If the wire through a magneto switch breaks during flight, which of the following will happen?
   (a) The engine will stop immediately
   (b) The engine will keep running if both switches are selected off
   (c) The engine will stop if only the other switch is selected off
   (d) The engine will stop if only the affected switch is selected off

14. A carburettor main jet provides fuel:
- (a) Directly into the cylinder?
- (b) Into the choke of the inlet manifold?
- (c) After the choke of the inlet manifold but before the throttle butterfly valve?
- (d) After the choke and the throttle butterfly valve?

15. If a complete blockage occurs in the carburettor main jet, what will happen?
- (a) The engine will accelerate to full power
- (b) The engine will stop instantly
- (c) The engine power will drop to idle
- (d) The engine will keep running normally

16. Airflow through the venturi of a carburettor causes:
- (a) A drop in pressure and a rise in velocity at the throat
- (b) A rise in pressure and a drop in velocity at the throat
- (c) A drop in pressure and a drop in velocity at the throat
- (d) A rise in pressure and a rise in velocity at the throat

17. What is the purpose of the oil system in a piston engine?
- (a) To cool the moving parts of the engine
- (b) To reduce wear in the engine
- (c) To reduce friction in the engine
- (d) All the above

18. In a 'wet sump' lubrication system:
- (a) Some of the oil is kept in a sump which is topped up from a tank as necessary
- (b) Scavenge oil is collected in a sump and returned to the tank
- (c) All the oil is contained in the engine and there is no extra tank
- (d) No oil is required for lubrication or cooling

19. Excessive oil pressure is prevented by:
- (a) A non-return valve
- (b) Providing a high capacity pump
- (c) A filter by-pass valve
- (d) An oil pressure relief valve

20. If metal is found in the filter of a lubrication system filled with straight oil:
- (a) The filter must be replaced
- (b) The engine must be replaced or stripped
- (c) Both (a) and (b)
- (d) Neither (a) nor (b)

21. The engine cowling is designed to:
   (a) Dissipate the heat from the cylinders to the cooling airflow
   (b) Form a tunnel around the engine, forcing air to flow around the cylinders
   (c) Control cylinder head temperature by regulating the airflow across the cylinders
   (d) Retain the lubrication oil for cooling purposes

22. Formation of carburettor ice may be indicated by:
   (a) A reduction in oil temperature?
   (b) An increase in carburettor temperature?
   (c) A reduction in cylinder head temperature?
   (d) A reduction in rpm?

23. Which of the following conditions is likely to produce serious carburettor icing?
   (a) Climbing in winter, clear air, temperature +2°C, humidity 90%
   (b) Descending through cloud in winter, air temperature +6°C
   (c) Descending in summer, clear air, temperature +15°C, humidity 70%
   (d) All of the above

24. Which of the following conditions are most likely to produce the most severe carburettor icing?
   (a) Climbing in winter, clear air, temperature -2°C
   (b) Descending in winter, clear air, temperature +4°C
   (c) Cruising in summer, clear air, temperature +10°C
   (d) Descending in summer, clear air, temperature +15°C

25. Which of the following is a consequence of an over-rich mixture?
   (a) Reduction in range
   (b) Overheating and possible detonation
   (c) Both (a) and (b)
   (d) Neither (a) nor (b)

26. If indicated oil pressure falls to zero, which instrument may assist you in deciding whether the gauge is faulty?
   (a) The EGT gauge
   (b) The oil temperature gauge
   (c) The CHT gauge
   (d) The tachometer

27. Which is the most likely consequence of removing a baffle from inside the engine cowling?
   (a) Reduced fuel consumption
   (b) Reduced engine cooling
   (c) Increased fuel consumption
   (d) Increased oil temperature

28. The pilot wishes to descend. Which actions should he take in which order?
   (a) Close the throttle rapidly, select full carburettor heat immediately
   (b) Close the throttle slowly, wait 10 - 20 seconds, select full carburettor heat
   (c) Select full carburettor heat, wait 10 - 20 seconds, close the throttle slowly
   (d) Select full carburettor heat at the same time as closing the throttle slowly

29. Why should a pilot select a rich mixture for climbing?
   (a) To compensate for the changing air density with height
   (b) To reduce the risk of overheating
   (c) To reduce fuel consumption
   (d) To improve lubrication of the main bearings

30. If an excessive cylinder head temperature is experienced in flight, engine cooling can be improved by:
   (a) Leaning the mixture with the mixture control
   (b) Enriching the mixture with the mixture control
   (c) Commencing a climb at reduced power
   (d) Closing the cowl flaps

31. Pumping the throttle before operating the starter is recommended in certain Flight Manuals. This procedure:
   (a) Should be adopted even if not specifically recommended
   (b) Should not be used unless recommended because it will result in over-revving when the engine starts
   (c) Should not be used even if recommended
   (d) Should not be used unless recommended because it may result in over-fuelling and possible fire

32. The pre-take off checks often include a check that the priming pump is locked closed. This is because otherwise:
   (a) Fuel may leak into the cylinders and cause a power reduction
   (b) Fuel may leak out of the carburettor into the exhaust system
   (c) Fuel may leak into the cabin from the pump
   (d) The throttle butterfly valve may not fully open

33. What is the purpose of an acceleration pump:
   (a) To increase the fuel flow during engine starting
   (b) To enrich the mixture when the throttle is opened
   (c) To remove excess fuel from the main jet when the throttle is opened
   (d) To increase the airflow to the inlet manifold when the throttle is opened

34. When hand swinging a propeller to start the engine:
   (a) The impulse magneto should be ON, and the other OFF until the engine starts
   (b) The impulse magneto should be OFF, and the other ON until the engine starts
   (c) Both magnetos should be OFF until the engine starts
   (d) Both magnetos should be ON all the time

35. A turbocharger:
   (a) directly increases the pressure of air within the inlet manifold
   (b) directly increases the pressure of air in the exhaust
   (c) directly increases the pressure of fuel in the cylinders
   (d) directly increases the voltage of the spark in the cylinders

36. A waste gate in a turbocharger:
   (a) maintains a set temperature of the exhaust gases
   (b) maintains a set air pressure in the inlet manifold
   (c) allows excessive oil to return to the oil tank
   (d) allows excessive air pressure to return to the air intake

37. A waste gate in a turbocharger is fitted:
   (a) between the air intake and the inlet manifold
   (b) between the inlet manifold and the cylinders
   (c) between the cylinders and the turbine
   (d) after the turbine

38. In a fuel injected engine, an injector pump supplies fuel:
   (a) into the inlet manifold by each inlet valve
   (b) into the main jet of the carburettor
   (c) into the carburettor slow running jet
   (d) onto the throttle valve

39. The carburettor's acceleration pump will always compensate for:
   (a) The additional fuel required as dynamic pressure increases with airspeed
   (b) The additional fuel required when the throttle is opened very rapidly from idle to full
   (c) The additional fuel required when the aircraft slows down with the throttle at idle
   (d) None of the above

Chapter 7

Other Engine Types

7.1 Introduction

Computer technology has made the use of different engine types more practical. Seeking to improve fuel consumption and reduce carbon emissions, manufacturers built and fitted diesel engines to several aeroplanes. Rotary petrol engines, with fewer but larger moving parts, were made available for some aircraft. Turbine engines, previously often used in helicopters, have become more common in light aeroplanes, and the electric motors which were developed initially to assist glider pilots to return home when sources of lift failed have been developed to become primary power plants.

7.2 Diesel Engines

A diesel engine uses the same 'Otto cycle' as a traditional petrol driven piston engine. However, instead of smoothly burning a fuel/air mixture in the cylinders, it relies on the fact that continuing to compress the mixture will produce an explosive reaction, which in turn can provide the power stroke. The engine itself must be built of stronger, and therefore heavier, material to absorb the shock of this detonation. However, it only needs an ignition system, invariably an electronic one, for starting or restarting in an emergency.

Its major advantage over a petrol engine is that it uses cheaper and more accessible fuel than AVGAS. Road or agricultural diesel, or even central heating fuel, may be advertised as capable of burning in and turning most diesel engines. However, these fuels are not intended to provide power in the variable air pressures and temperatures of flight, nor to restrict corrosion in aircraft materials. JET-A1, however, has a guaranteed quality and so that is the only fuel accepted in the UK for aviation diesel engines.

Diesel engines were originally seen as less polluting than petrol engines, producing less CO_2. However, particulates in diesel exhaust are now seen as equally, or more hazardous, to the environment.

7.3 DC Electric Motors

The principle of an electric motor is relatively simple. The magneto we considered in the previous chapter is an electric generator, converting mechanical rotation into electrical energy. An electric motor effectively reverses that procedure.

The conversion of the electrical energy relies on the fact that an electric current flowing through a conductor placed in a magnetic field causes the conductor to move if it is free to do so. A simple DC motor relies on a coil of wire being placed between a North pole of a magnet and a South pole of a magnet in such a way that it can rotate between them, as in figure 7.1. A current passed along the wire generates a movement upwards where the current is flowing out of the paper and downwards where the current is flowing into the paper. As the coil rotates clockwise, the electrical connection at the end of the coil is broken, then made again so that the current flows along the wire in the reverse direction but again into the paper on the right and out of the paper on the left, so the coil continues to rotate.

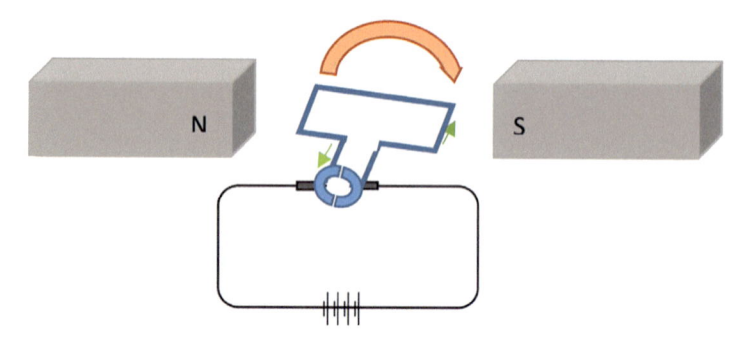

■ Figure 7.1 **Simple DC motor**

7.4 AC Electric motors

An alternating current flows first in one direction then the other, reaching peaks in each direction like a wave. By tradition we call one direction positive (+) and the other negative (-), and the shape of the wave a 'sine' wave. Figure 7.2 shows 4 'cycles' of the wave. The number of cycles occurring in a given time is the 'frequency' of the wave, usually given in cycles per second or 'Hertz'.

■ Figure 7.2 **Sine wave**

This wave of current in a coil produces a comparable wave of magnetic flux. If a ring of electromagnets is arranged in a circle, an alternating current can energise the coils in opposing pairs, in sequence, to produce a magnetic field that effectively rotates around the circle. A conducting object placed within the circle will be affected by that field and rotate if it is free to do so. Each pair of coils has a positive peak at a different time during the rotation; they are 'out of phase' with each other. Figure 7.3 shows a '3-phase motor', but each phase may be distributed to several coil pairs in the same sequence around the core. The more coil pairs, the smoother the motor rotates.

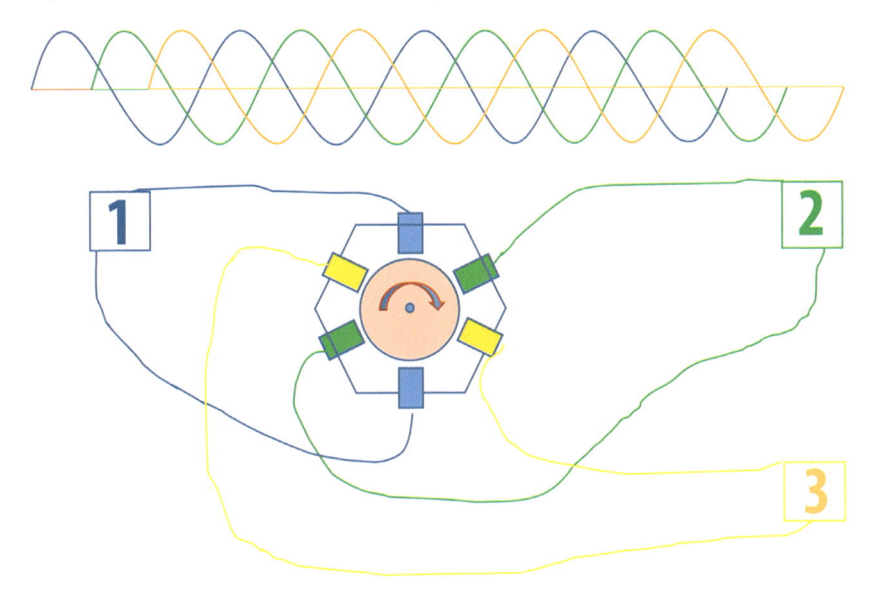

- Figure 7.3 **A 3-phase AC motor**

The circle of electromagnets is called the 'stator' and the rotating part is called the 'rotor'. The rotor is an electrical conductor, and the rotating magnetic field (sometimes referred to as RMF) induces an electric current inside it. If the conductor is a ring or a wire, as in the simple coil in figure 7.1, a current is 'induced' to flow around it in a loop. This gives the type of motor its name; an 'induction' motor. In simple induction motors the coil is a long wire very tightly wound around a conducting core. The induced current produces its own magnetic field which tries to align itself with the rotating magnetic field by rotating as well, at the same speed as the current changes. This produces torque at the rotor.

The theoretical speed of the rotor in an induction motor depends on the frequency of the AC supply and the number of coils that make up the stator and, with no load on the motor, comes close to the speed of the rotating magnetic field. However, any load on the motor tends to slow the rotor down, so in a 'synchronous' motor, a computerised control device adjusts the power and frequency of the current to maintain the rotor speed to that of the changing magnetic field.

The rotor can be connected to whatever the manufacturer wants to rotate. This may be directly to a gyroscope rotor in an artificial horizon, or in the case of the electric aircraft engine we are considering here, directly or indirectly to a propeller. Instead of being physically inside the stator, the conductor may be fashioned into a plate positioned against the face of the stator, rotating about a thin axle as the magnetic field rotates.

Different rotor designs improve the efficiency of the induction motor. Permanent magnets can be added inside an iron rotor structure, which is shaped in such a way that the iron's 'magnetic reluctance' tries to maintain alignment with the magnetic fields. This "synchronous reluctance motor" synchronises the rotor speed with the phase changes of the AC current. A separate DC motor may be needed to overcome rotor inertia during startup.

A typical aircraft electric engine is fitted with a computerised electronic speed controller (ESC) which produces a rotor speed compatible with that selected by the pilot. The ESC includes an 'inverter' to produce the required AC current from a DC supply. The power delivered depends on the propeller torque, which is adjusted by a FADEC system (see para 8.9). The rotor of an electric motor can accelerate very rapidly when electrical power is applied, although overcoming friction and the torque from the propeller reduces the rate at which the rpm can be converted into useful power.

7.5   Electric Engine Ancillaries and Problems

The portable source of electrical power in an aircraft is the battery, which produces direct current at a low voltage (see Chapter 11). The electrical energy required to power an aircraft engine can only be supplied by the most efficient batteries, which at the time of writing would be Lithium Ion. These batteries have a limited life, and power loss is rapid at the end of that life, so some form of 'battery management system' is usually provided. This should provide an indication of how much battery life remains under the present operating conditions, and may also incorporate an emergency back-up battery.

An electric engine, and especially its inverter, produces a lot of heat and requires a cooling system. As with some piston engines, a jacket around the engine is filled with liquid, usually a mix of water and glycol, pumped from its 'expansion tank' through a radiator in the airflow. A separate bottle may be included to contain any liquid overflow.

Any short-circuit in a battery or its circuits can generate considerable heat and consequent damage, so a battery temperature monitoring system, at the very minimum a gauge, is an essential feature of an electric engine. The rotating parts and gearbox require lubrication, so an electric engine has a similar oil system to that of a piston engine.

7.6 Turbojet Engines

A turbine is a rotating device which extracts kinetic energy from a fluid such as air. Air flow is deflected by vanes to drive the 'rotor' which is attached to a shaft. The rotating shaft in turn can drive another device, such as the turbocharger mentioned in Chapter 6.

Turbojet engines were first fitted to aircraft during the Second World War, and the basic principle is still used today. Fuel is mixed with air and then burnt in a combustion chamber in a continuous process. In order to produce efficient burning, especially at high altitudes where air pressure is low, the air must be compressed before mixing. The fuel must also be vapourised to produce efficient burning and to prevent the flame from being extinguished. The energy contained in the hot gases produced can be used for whatever purpose the manufacturer desires, so this part of the turbojet engine may be called the 'gas generator'.

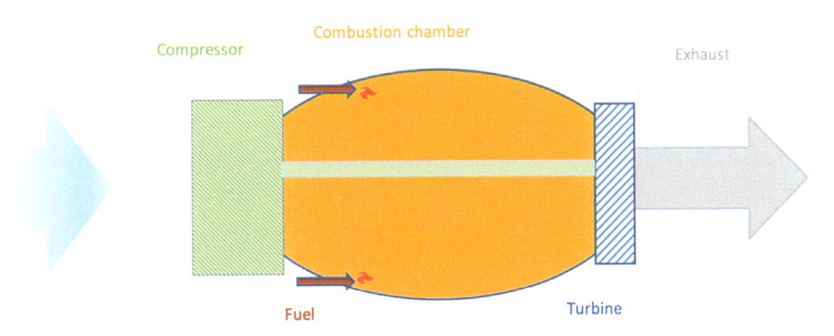

■ *Figure 7.4 **Simple turbojet engine***

Air enters the engine through an intake and onto 'guide vanes' which direct the air onto the rotating blades of the compressor. The compressor increases the temperature and pressure of the air so that the fuel injected into the combustion chamber can burn quickly and easily. Ignitors start the burning, but are not required to maintain it, although they can be easily activated in case of engine failure or 'flame-out'. The hot gases originally used Newton's third law to provide the propulsion for an aircraft, as in figure 7.4. However, some of the hot gas energy had to be used to deflect the blades of a retaining turbine, which provided the power to the compressor which increased the air pressure for combustion.

7.7 Turboprop Engines

By altering the flow of the exhaust gases, and adding a second turbine, the energy produced by the gas generator can be used to turn a propeller as well as the compressor. This turboprop engine is a more efficient method of using the output from the gas generator.

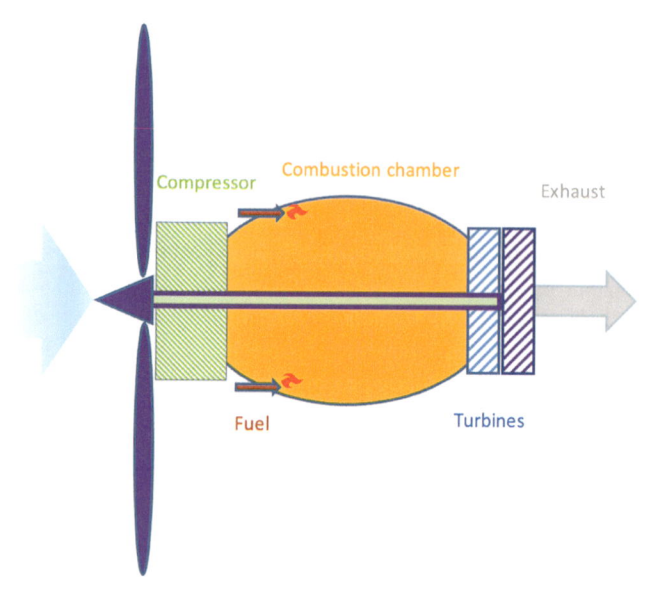

■ *Figure 7.5* **Simple turboprop engine**

Modern turboprop engines use the space available more efficiently by reversing the original flow pattern, as in the PT-6 engine shown in figure 7.6.

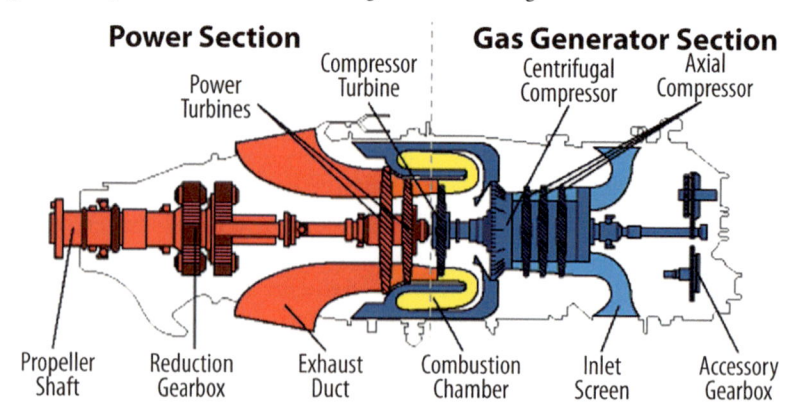

■ *Figure 7.6* **Pratt & Whitney Canada PT-6A Engine**

This engine is typical of small gas turbines fitted to aircraft below 5700 kg. Compared with the simple engine in figure 7.5, the shaft between the propeller and its driving turbine does not have to pass through the compressor drive shaft, which simplifies the engineering. A separate dedicated turbine drives the compressor, in this case a combination of centrifugal (pushed outwards) and axial (along the centreline) flow stages. The compressed air entering the combustion chamber which surrounds the turbines warmed further by the turbines and already turbulent when it is mixed with the fuel. The air enters the engine from the sides which reduces the risk of compressor damage from foreign objects, including birds.

Gas generators are much less sensitive to fuel quality than are piston engines. Although designed to run on paraffin (Jet-A1), they can burn higher quality fuels (AVGAS) without immediate failure, although less efficiently and long term damage is likely.

Carburettor icing is avoided, but airflow into the compressor can be affected by icing in the intakes and screens, and also on the compressor intake guide vanes, so some form of anti-icing system is necessary.

Intentionally Left Blank

7.8 Exercise

1. Compared to a petrol engine, a diesel engine of comparable power:
   (a) is lighter and requires no electrical power to maintain ignition
   (b) is lighter and requires more electrical power to maintain ignition
   (c) is heavier and requires no electrical power to maintain ignition
   (d) is heavier and requires more electrical power to maintain ignition

2. In a turboprop engine, what drives the compressor for the gas generator?
   (a) The turbine which also drives the propeller
   (b) A separate turbine from that which drives the propeller
   (c) The exhaust gases drive the compressor directly
   (d) The propeller drives the compressor directly

3. What electrical phenomenon is the basis for an electric engine?
   (a) Capacitance
   (b) Resistance
   (c) Generation
   (d) Inductance

4. In an engine with a synchronous motor, the output rpm is synchronised with:
   (a) The voltage of the controlling current
   (b) The number of phase changes in the controlling current
   (c) The frequency of the controlling current
   (d) The amplitude of the controlling current

5. Compared with a piston engine, what additional warning devices are required in a synchronous electric aircraft engine?
   (a) A gauge indicating the outside air temperature
   (b) An indication of the turbine inlet pressure
   (c) A system to warn of excessive battery temperature
   (d) An indication of the current provided by the DC motor

6. Compared to a petrol fuelled piston engine, which of the following are true of a synchronous electric engine?
   (a) The electric engine requires no cooling system
   (b) The electric engine requires no oil for lubrication
   (c) Both (a) and (b)
   (d) Neither (a) nor (b)

Intentionally Left Blank

CHAPTER 8

Propellers

8.1 Introduction

A piston engine converts vertical or lateral motion in the pistons to rotational motion of a crankshaft. The output from the engine as a result of burning fuel is measured by the rotational force produced - the 'torque'. A certain amount of torque is needed to move the pistons in their cylinders to compress the gas and to complete the cycle, and more is needed to overcome internal friction. The remaining torque is available to be converted into thrust.

A propeller consists of two or more blades around the central hub which is driven by the crankshaft, usually directly but sometimes through a reduction gear. Each blade is in the shape of an aerofoil, and as such generates both lift and drag as it moves through air. The torque from the engine ("engine torque") pushes the blades through the air against the drag resulting from their movement ("propeller torque"), and the blade lift produced at the same time is the thrust force needed to overcome the aircraft's total drag. A spinner is usually fitted over the hub to reduce drag.

8.2 Blade Angle

Let us first consider an aeroplane which is static (not moving). The propeller blades move through the air at 90° to the direction the aircraft is pointing (the longitudinal axis - see chapter 1), so their relative airflow arrives from a similar direction (parallel to the aircraft's lateral and normal axes - from "the beam"). The angle between the blade and the relative airflow (its angle of attack) is the same as the "blade angle", which is the angle between the blade and static relative airflow. The thrust available (roughly the equivalent of lift from a wing) and the torque produced (the equivalent of drag) depend on the blade shape and angle of attack (its C_L), its area, the air density, and the rotational speed given to the propeller by the engine.

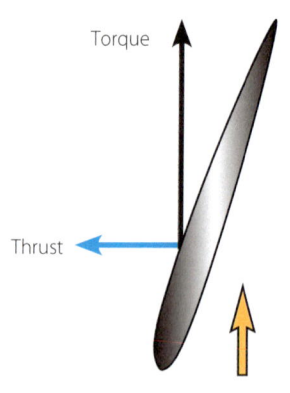

■ *Figure 8.1* **Forces on the Propeller Blade of a Static Aeroplane**

If the aeroplane starts moving forward, the relative airflow will arrive from slightly forward of the beam. The angle of attack reduces, although the blade angle remains the same. This means that propeller torque (its induced drag) reduces and as forward speed increases so does propeller (and engine) rpm. As forward speed increases, at some stage the angle of attack will reduce to zero, and depending on the blade aerofoil shape, so will thrust. At angles of attack greater than the blade's stalling angle, a lot of propeller torque would be produced but there would be little thrust available, so a blade angle of less than 15° might be advisable to produce initial aeroplane acceleration. As aircraft speed increases, the angle of attack reduces, and at some stage will reach the most efficient angle of attack of approximately 4°. Any further increase in speed will produce a reduction in efficiency to the point where the thrust has reduced to zero. That means that while the thrust from an engine/propeller combination varies with the rpm, it reaches a maximum at a certain IAS.

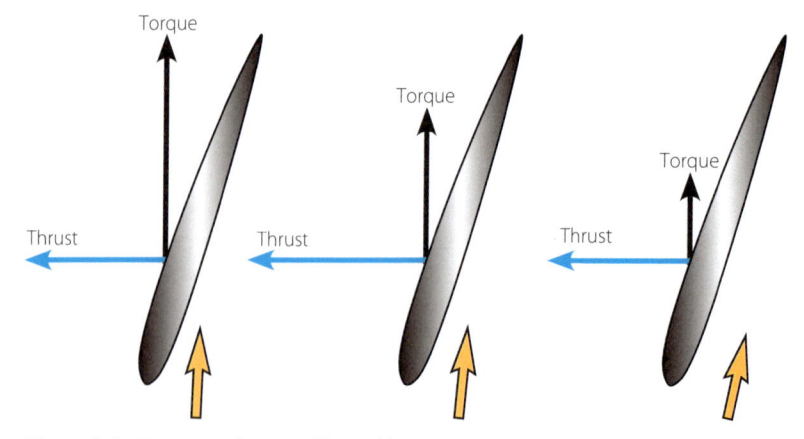

■ *Figure 8.2* **Forces as Forward Speed Increases**

If the engine stops driving the propeller, the torque causes the blades to decelerate until the airflow is actually turning the blades like a windmill. A "windmilling" propeller produces considerable drag, reducing an aircraft's gliding range and steepening its descent angle.

The path of any point on the rotating blade as it moves forward through the air while rotating is called a "helix". The angle between that actual path and the aircraft's beam is called the "helix angle", and increases as aircraft forward speed increases. The angle of attack of a forward moving propeller blade is the difference between the helix angle and the relative airflow.

8.3 Blade Twist

The helix angle depends on a combination of forward speed and rotational speed. At any given aircraft speed, the propeller tips are rotating rapidly but the root parts are rotating slowly. The helix angle at the tip is much lower than the helix angle at the root. In order to produce a reasonably constant angle of attack along the blade, the blade itself is twisted, so that the blade angle at the tip is much less than at the root. On a simple propeller, the amount of twist may be engineered to produce the ideal angle of attack all along the blade at the same rpm and aircraft speed (the aircraft's design cruising rpm and speed), but in practice the design is likely to vary from that in order to produce a fairly wide range of overall relative efficiency.

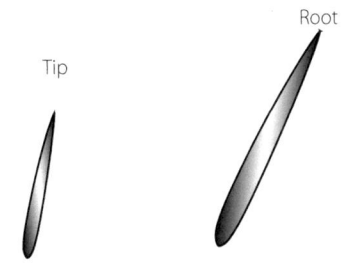

■ Figure 8.3 **Blade Angle Twist**

8.4 Variable Pitch

We have seen that there is only one speed (or speed band) at which the propeller is efficient. If we want efficient cruising, we must accept that static thrust and therefore acceleration from rest will be low at the high angles of attack. Similarly, rapid acceleration to allow use of short runways prevents us achieving high cruising speeds.

The solution lies in varying the pitch (the average blade angle) of the propeller. In its simple form, a cable may be employed to unlock and turn the blades by hand from the cockpit. The static blade angles are set low ("fine pitch"), allowing rapid acceleration and climb rates at slow speeds. For cruise, the pilot pulls the cable to unlock a latch in the propeller hub and turn the blade to a greater "coarse" pitch. To return to fine pitch for landing and possible go around, unlocking the blades again allows the natural twisting forces on the blades to turn them into the fine pitch position again. It is possible to have more than two pitch positions, and pilots of motor gliders (and many multi-engined aeroplanes) usually also have a separate but similar control which turns the blades to a fully coarse position where they lie parallel to the direction of flight ("feathered") producing maximum propeller torque but minimum aircraft drag.

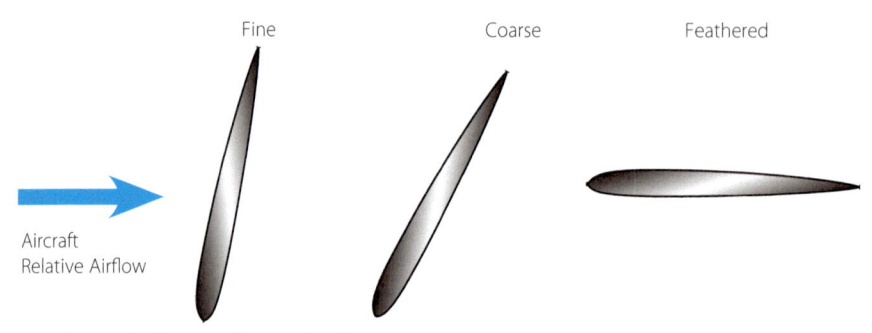

■ *Figure 8.4* **Propeller Pitch Changes**

8.5   Constant Speed Units

The simple variable pitch propeller described above has still only two efficient speeds. It is relatively not much more complicated to produce a device which varies the pitch constantly to keep the blades at their most efficient angle throughout the aircraft's speed range (or at least most of it). Such a device relies on the principle that for maximum efficiency at a given rpm, the propeller torque must be at a minimum. A spinner is usually fitted over the hub to reduce drag.

We have said that the rotational forces are constantly trying to twist the propeller to fine pitch. The simple constant speed unit employs engine oil under pressure to push a piston against that twisting force. If propeller torque increases, the propeller will slow down. To return it to efficiency, the blades must be allowed to turn to fine to allow the rpm to increase again, so oil pressure must be reduced until the correct speed is reached.

A rpm governor is controlled by weights spinning against a spring whose base is connected to the piston. As propeller speed reduces, the spring overcomes the reduced rotational inertia (commonly called centrifugal force) of the weights and allows the piston to move to allow less oil to reach the propeller hub. As the propeller speed increases, the weights move out again until the forces balance. If the propeller speeds up, the increased rotational inertia pushes the weights outward overcoming the spring force and allowing more oil to coarsen off the propeller, as indicated with the yellow flow shown in figure 8.5. The pilot is given a "rpm lever" or "pitch control", coloured usually pale blue, with which he can set the desired propeller rpm by moving the piston (and therefore the spring top) physically.

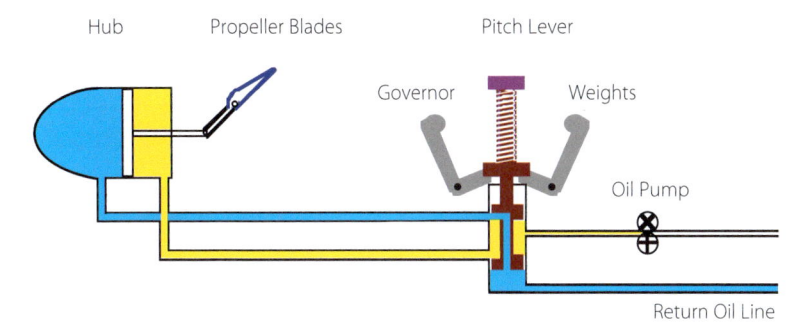

■ *Figure 7.5* **Constant Speed Unit**

The governor can only control rpm over a limited range. When engine torque is low, the blades reach a "fine pitch stop" and any further reduction in engine torque produces a reduction in rpm, so at low engine power settings the propeller behaves in a similar fashion to a simple "fixed pitch" propeller.

8.6   Use of a CSU

While it is not intended to go into detail here about operating aircraft, it is important to note the following procedure when adjusting power on a piston engine fitted with a constant speed propeller. If the pilot wishes to increase the power from his engine, he should first select the rpm required on the pitch control lever, then adjust the throttle. To reduce power, first reduce the throttle setting, then the rpm. Perhaps the expressions "prop up" and "throttle back" may assist in remembering this important technique.

8.7 Propeller Emergencies

The forces on a propeller blade are considerable. Any crack in a blade, especially on its leading edge or tip, is likely to spread very rapidly, possibly allowing parts to break off. The forces from an unbalanced blade are likely to cause severe vibration, followed by probable internal damage to the engine itself, and possibly the airframe to which it is attached.

Oil pressure failure will allow the blades of most constant speed propellers to turn to the fully fine position. While that is advantageous in that it allows safe operation at low speed, if the propeller and therefore the engine rotational speed becomes excessive, again serious damage may result. A pilot hearing the rpm increasing unexpectedly should close both throttle and rpm levers until the rpm is well within limits. If the oil pressure failure subsequently causes engine failure, the drag from the fully fine propeller may be more than that with which the pilot may have carried out practice forced landing procedures. However, many aeroplanes designed for aerobatics employ a spring to force the propeller to the fully coarse position in the event of oil pressure failure.

8.8 Reaction

The propeller produces thrust by pushing the air rearwards, and this push gives the air which has been affected by the propeller (the 'slipstream') extra energy. The effective airspeed of the aerofoil surfaces over which the slipstream passes will be greater than those without this extra energy, and the effectiveness, and associated feedback to the pilot (feel), will vary with propeller rpm. Even at low airspeed, if engine (therefore propeller) rpm is high, elevator and rudder control will be positive. However, once rpm reduces, unless airspeed increases the effectiveness will be lost. This may be noticed during landing; if the throttle is closed during the flare or hold off phase with the elevators up, the nose will pitch down unless the pilot increases the elevator deflection even more than would be required by the simultaneous reduction in airspeed.

The slipstream is also given a rotary motion. This changes the direction of the relative airflow over the rear surfaces of the airframe, creating a sideways force on the fuselage and fin. A similar force is produced by the airframe's reaction to the rotation of the crankshaft and propeller (torque). Although in most training aeroplanes the structure is shaped to compensate for these sideways forces at cruising speed and rpm, any difference in either will require the pilot to act to prevent yaw and unbalanced flight. A propeller rotating clockwise as seen from the cockpit (as in most training aeroplanes) will induce a roll and yaw to the left at low airspeed and high rpm, such as on take-off, in a climb, or during stall recovery. The pilot must use rudder to stop the yaw and keep the aircraft "in balance".

8.9 Modern Advances

Many modern engines employ some form of computer to control various operations in the engine. Fuel injection is controlled by such computers, and automatic control of such things as mixture and cowl flaps is available. Advances in computer technology now allow relatively cheap fully automatic direct engine control (FADEC) systems to be fitted to light aircraft, and propeller operation is an important part of these FADEC systems.

The pilot has only one engine control in a FADEC system, the "power lever". With this lever, which looks like a throttle but is connected to the computer not the throttle valve, he selects the amount of power he wants from the engine/propeller combination. The computer considers the air and flight conditions (and perhaps even the specification of the fuel in the tanks), and selects the most efficient combination of fuel/air mixture, ignition timing, and propeller blade angle to provide that power while maintaining other conditions such as engine temperature and (if applicable) turbine speed at their most efficient. This efficiency reduces fuel consumption and engine wear, and therefore costs, but also minimises noxious emissions into the environment. The computer may also be able to carry out all necessary pre-flight checks automatically, and diagnose faults before they significantly affect the operation of the aircraft.

Intentionally Left Blank

8.10 Exercise

1. A fixed pitch propeller blade is twisted. Which of the following statements is true?
   (a) The pitch at the tip is coarser than the pitch at the root
   (b) The angle of attack always remains relatively constant along the blade
   (c) The helix angle of the tip is greater than the helix angle of the root
   (d) None of the above are true

2. For maximum efficiency at low speeds, propeller pitch should be:
   (a) Fine?
   (b) Feathered?
   (c) Coarse?
   (d) Lean?

3. While the engine is turning the propeller, propeller torque is greatest when:
   (a) The blade angle is at a minimum
   (b) The propeller is at the fine pitch stop
   (c) The propeller is feathered
   (d) The engine is at full power

4. When applying full power with a constant speed propeller fitted, a pilot should:
   (a) Set propeller pitch fully coarse then open the throttle
   (b) Open the throttle fully then set propeller pitch fully fine
   (c) Open the throttle fully then set propeller pitch fully coarse
   (d) Set propeller pitch fully fine then open the throttle fully

5. Which of the following will happen if the latch is opened on a manually operated variable pitch propeller?
   (a) The propeller will remain at a constant pitch until the pilot selects the desired pitch
   (b) The propeller will attempt to turn to the fully fine position
   (c) The propeller will attempt to turn to the fully coarse position
   (d) The propeller will attempt to feather itself.

6. If a pilot notices a small crack in the leading edge of a fixed pitch propeller blade, what must he do?
   (a) Nothing, small cracks are not dangerous
   (b) The pilot must smooth out the area of the crack before next flight
   (c) The pilot must have the crack inspected by an engineer at the next scheduled inspection
   (d) The pilot must have the crack repaired and inspected by a licensed engineer before next flight

7. Propeller blades are best inspected by
   (a) Rubbing a hand along the leading edge and tip while holding the other blade firmly
   (b) Visually inspecting only
   (c) Running a hand lightly along the leading edge and tip while keeping one's body away from the propeller
   (d) Pushing the blades firmly backwards and forwards with both hands

8. A propeller blade is twisted towards the tip in order to:
   (a) Maintain the same blade angle from hub to tip
   (b) Increase blade angle towards the tip to create more thrust
   (c) Provide efficient angles of attack along the whole blade
   (d) Provide the optimum angle of attack at the tip

9. During takeoff in an aeroplane whose propeller turns clockwise as seen from the cockpit, torque will induce:
   (a) A pitch downwards but no roll or yaw
   (b) A roll and possibly yaw to the left
   (c) A roll and possibly yaw to the right
   (d) A pitch upwards but no roll or yaw

10. If the aircraft is fitted with a manually selected variable pitch propeller, what selection should the pilot make for takeoff and climb?
   (a) Fine pitch
   (b) Coarse pitch
   (c) Feathered pitch
   (d) Braking pitch

Chapter 9

Engine Instruments & Health

9.1 Introduction

We have considered engine and propeller operation in previous chapters. This chapter will provide some guidance into understanding and using the indications available to the pilot. We shall consider normal operations and possible actions in the event of malfunctions which may be indicated.

The first point to make is that every aeroplane is a glider. If the engine (every engine) stops, even if the propeller produces lots of drag by remaining at fine pitch, the pilot can make a glide approach onto whatever surface is available to him. We shall see later that the cockpit area is generally a very strong part of the aircraft structure. If the pilot concentrates on flying at the correct approach speed, and makes as normal a landing as possible on the available surface, maintaining control until the aircraft stops, injury to the occupants is unlikely to be very severe.

9.2 Power Indicators

Every aircraft has a tachometer, which measures the number of revolutions the crankshaft (and normally the propeller) makes every minute (rpm). In an aeroplane with a fixed pitch propeller, the rpm is a rough measure of the power being provided by the engine. The engine speed must not become excessive, or it may be damaged internally, so a red line is drawn on the tachometer to indicate the maximum permitted rpm as detailed in the Flight Manual. Sometimes a yellow arc indicates a speed range which may be used for only a short period of time every flight. The bottom of this range is the "maximum continuous rpm". Sometimes (usually in engines without cylinder head temperature gauges), a rpm limit is laid down for operating with the mixture control in anything other than the fully rich selection.

The rpm of a fixed pitch propeller will change with aircraft airspeed. If however the rpm is noticed to drop (by ear confirmed by the tachometer) at a constant airspeed, the pilot should suspect carburettor icing, and select full carburettor heat. If icing is present, the rpm may drop further and the engine run rough as the ice starts to melt and water displaces mixture in the cylinders. The engine may even stop in severe cases, so it is important to prevent ice formation.

In an aeroplane with a constant speed propeller, rpm provides no indication of engine power. Such engines are provided with inlet manifold pressure (MP or "boost") gauges. Manifold pressure is an indication of suction from the cylinders combined with forward speed (and turbo-charging). When the engine is stopped, manifold pressure is equal to the environment air pressure. However, the gauge is usually calibrated in inches of mercury rather than hectoPascals, so it may be worth mentioning that 29.92 inches of mercury equates to 1013 hPa. A normally aspirated engine (one without turbocharging) at full throttle on takeoff can be expected to indicate about 26 inches of boost, while during cruise a typical figure may be about 23 inches. Often the Flight Manual will place a minimum rpm limit at high boost settings.

Diesel or electric engines with fully automatic direct engine controls (FADEC) may have different indications. A 'load meter' indicates the percentage of the maximum power available which the engine is supplying, as determined by the propeller torque.

If an engine is operated at any time outside its published limitations, it is important to note the time spent outside them, and the actual indications. These must be noted in the technical log, and the aircraft must not be flown again until an engineer has determined its airworthiness and signed a certificate of release to service *(see chapter 13)*.

9.3 Performance Instruments

The temperature of the exhaust gases can give an indication of engine efficiency. We saw in chapter 6 that an exhaust gas temperature (EGT) gauge can be used to weaken the mixture and minimise fuel consumption in a piston engine. In fact, the absolute minimum fuel consumption for maximum endurance comes at maximum EGT, but for maximum range the mixture should be set slightly richer, to give an EGT reading 100°F or 50°C lower than maximum. Although the actual EGT reading does not relate directly to the power available, a drop in EGT when no other changes have been made can indicate a power loss, for example possible carburettor icing.

A drop in EGT could also indicate damage to the exhaust system, which has to provide free flow from the cylinders to the outside, otherwise the some of the burnt gases will remain and limit combustion. However, a damaged exhaust system may also allow carbon monoxide to enter the cockpit. This colourless, odourless gas is one result of fuel combustion, and if it enters human lungs tends to displace oxygen in the arteries carrying blood to the brain, causing dizziness, nausea and perhaps death. Fortunately, other gases in aircraft exhausts are not odourless, so if a pilot smells fumes he should immediately find a way of breathing fresh air, and land as soon as practicable. The fumes may have entered through a heater, so that should be switched off.

We also mentioned the cylinder head temperature (CHT) gauge in chapter 6. If the CHT is maintained within an optimum range as described in the Flight Manual, efficiency is maximised, fuel consumption is reduced, and power available is maximised. A pilot should open and close the cowl flaps (where fitted) as required to maintain the CHT as close to optimum as possible.

A fuel flow indicator ("flowmeter") can also be used to minimise fuel consumption. Provided the engine continues to give sufficient power (airspeed and altitude remain constant) a reduction in fuel flow may be obtained by leaning the mixture. However, fuel flow can also be a useful indicator of engine problems. A gradually increasing fuel consumption suggests wear developing in some part of the engine, and an increased indicated fuel flow may be the first positive sign of such an increased fuel consumption. Note that if actual fuel consumption increases but indicated fuel flow is normal, there may be a leak from the fuel system before the flowmeter.

9.4   Engine Health

Excessively high (or low) CHT in a piston engine may indicate a damaged baffle or blockage at some part of the air cooling system. Without cowl flaps, power and airspeed should be adjusted to maintain CHT within limits, although be aware that because the gauge normally senses at only one cylinder, a low indication at that cylinder may be a symptom of high CHT at another.

We mentioned the oil gauges in chapter 6. At normal engine operating temperature, these can provide early warning of possible problems in the lubricating system before they cause damage. Higher than normal pressure might indicate that an oil filter is blocked by particles which may find their way into more sensitive parts of the engine, spreading the damage. Higher than normal oil temperature may provide an indication, in the absence of a CHT gauge, that the engine itself is overheating. It may also provide early warning of an oil leak, as the remaining oil returns to the hot engine before it has cooled as much as usual. Lower than normal pressure might indicate a failing oil pump, or when coupled with increasing oil temperature may indicate an actual loss of oil. Engineering assistance should be sought in any case of any abnormal indications or noises from an aircraft.

Not every aircraft is fitted with a comprehensive bank of engine instruments, and in any case, an unusual noise is often the first indication of developing problems. Increased noise may only be the result of a damaged exhaust manifold or pipe, but any damage there will affect the engine's efficiency and the noise may mask more serious noises from the engine itself, in addition to the danger of carbon monoxide poisoning mentioned earlier.

When carrying out the pre-take off power checks, each magneto is switched off in turn. An excessive drop in rpm (more than 50, or perhaps 75 as detailed in the Flight Manual) may indicate one or more plug "fouled" by oil, which is often the result of long periods at low rpm. If the rpm is kept high and the mixture is leaned to its most efficient (see paragraph 6.9) for a minute or so, the fouling may be burnt away and a further check might be satisfactory.

9.5   Other Instruments

Carburettor icing has already been discussed. It is the most common cause of engine power reduction, and instruments which provide warning are available. A carburettor temperature gauge indicates the air temperature in the venturi. It may include a yellow mark covering the temperature range at which icing is most likely. However, manufacturers recommend that such gauges should be calibrated at regular intervals. Electronic or light sensitive devices may be fitted to warn of actual ice formation, but their effectiveness may deteriorate with time. Carburettor heat can dissolve carburettor ice, but hot air should not normally be applied when the throttle is already fully open, nor continuously on the ground (the unfiltered air may cause wear inside the pistons).

Outside air temperature (OAT) gauges, often measuring the air temperature at the windscreen, are of no value for warning of carburettor icing. However, they can indicate the likelihood of ice forming on the airframe, or on runways or taxiways when on the ground. If the aircraft flies into any cloud or precipitation when the OAT is below freezing, especially if the precipitation is liquid (rain or drizzle), ice will form (see the volume on Meteorology). The aircraft must be flown out of the conditions as quickly as possible. An OAT gauge may also provide a useful reminder to dress warmly, or at least carry warm clothing, as an aid to survival in the event of a forced landing!

9.6   Manufacturers' Guidance

This book provides information, suggestions and good practice, but it must be emphasised that the manufacturer's Flight Manual as described in paragraph 13.7 is the definitive guide for operating the aircraft, its engine and its systems. Before a pilot flies in conditions outside his normal experience, he should consult that Manual and follow its advice, or that of the manufacturer's Pilot's Operating Handbook if there is no Flight Manual.

9.7 Exercise

1. If the engine of a single engined aeroplane stops, what is the pilot's first priority?
   - (a) Attempt to re-start the engine
   - (b) Select a possible landing field
   - (c) Achieve and maintain gliding speed
   - (d) Call Air Traffic Control for help

2. The red line on a rpm gauge indicates:
   - (a) The rpm for most efficient engine operation
   - (b) A datum line for calibrating the instrument
   - (c) The maximum permitted continuous rpm
   - (d) The rpm which must never be exceeded

3. An increase in oil pressure may indicate;
   - (a) An oil leak
   - (b) A blocked oil filter
   - (c) Damaged cowling baffles
   - (d) Any or all of the above

4. Before taking off from an aerodrome in a mountainous area, a pilot should:
   - (a) Add 5% to his take off distance calculations
   - (b) Consult the Flight Manual and follow its recommendations
   - (c) Lean the mixture before takeoff
   - (d) Select only uphill runways for takeoff

5. In the cruise with an engine with a fixed pitch propeller, if rpm reduces in cruising flight, the pilot should;
   - (a) Select the carburettor heat control slightly open?
   - (b) Increase throttle setting until rpm recovers?
   - (c) Close the cowl flaps?
   - (d) Pull the carburettor heat out fully?

6. What indications would you expect if your aeroplane engine lost most or all of its oil?
   - (a) High oil pressure and low oil temperature
   - (b) High oil pressure and high oil temperature
   - (c) Low oil pressure and low oil temperature
   - (d) Low oil pressure and high oil temperature

7. If the engine exceeds its permitted maximum rpm in a dive at less than full throttle, you must:

   (a) Place the aircraft unserviceable in the technical log immediately after landing?
   (b) Have the engine specially inspected at the next scheduled servicing?
   (c) Report the fact to the engineer at the next C of A renewal?
   (d) No action is required because routine maintenance will discover any fault

8. Before the engine starts, a serviceable manifold pressure gauge will indicate:

   (a) Zero
   (b) Maximum deflection
   (c) The outside air pressure
   (d) Off the bottom of the scale

9. The pilot suspects a problem with the oil system in flight. He should:

   (a) Transmit MAYDAY and land immediately in a suitable field
   (b) Ignore the problem
   (c) Continue until the engine starts running roughly
   (d) Plan a landing as soon as possible and investigate the problem

10. If the earth wire in the magneto circuit becomes broken on the ground, what effect is that likely to have?

   (a) The engine will not start
   (b) The engine will run roughly when started
   (c) The engine may start unintentionally if the propeller is moved
   (d) The engine may kick back when starting

11. An increased cylinder heat temperature may indicate;

   (a) over-rich mixture?
   (b) damaged cowling baffles?
   (c) an oil leak?
   (d) any or all of the above?

12. Before starting the engine in very cold temperatures a pilot should:

   (a) Select carburettor heat fully ON
   (b) Select fully lean mixture
   (c) Turn the propeller over by hand as many times as the engine has cylinders
   (d) Consult the Flight Manual and follow its recommendations

Chapter 10

The Airframe

10.1 Introduction

An aircraft must be strong enough to fly and manoeuvre in turbulent conditions, and also to land on relatively rough surfaces without damage. The structure of the aircraft gives it that strength.

Early aeroplanes were constructed with a wood frame which provided the required structural strength. The frame was often covered with a fabric "skin" to reduce the drag from the open framework, and this fabric was stretched tight with 'dope' to provide a shaped lifting surface which was strong enough in normal use while keeping weight to a minimum. The same techniques are still used in some gliders, microlights and homebuilt aircraft today, and also in balsa wood flying models.

In fact, although metal alloy has generally taken the place of both wood and fabric, most aeroplanes still retain similarities with the traditional framework and covering. However, engineering techniques have advanced, so modern designs often use glass or carbon fibres in their construction. These and other materials can provide airframes which no longer require a full traditional framework.

10.2 The Traditional Framework

As we have seen, the complete aeroplane is composed of several parts. The wings (in fact really one continuous wing) provide the lifting surface and must be the strongest part of the airframe. The fuselage contains the pilot and every other part is attached to it. The vertical fin provides directional stability and the tailplane provides pitch stability.

Traditional wings are built around a "main spar" (construction terms were derived from ship-building), which runs continuously from wingtip to wingtip. For practical purposes the main spar may be said to lie along the aircraft's lateral axis, with any other spars which may be fitted being parallel to that, although to maintain the wing shape the spars may converge towards the wingtips. There may be a "rear spar" to prevent twisting, and perhaps spars along the leading or trailing edges.

Fixed to the spars and at 90 degrees to them are the wing "ribs" or perhaps "formers", which maintain the shape of the wing in both plan and section. The interaction between the spars and the ribs provides great strength at reasonable weight. Figure 10.1 shows these parts of a wing from above (without the necessary covering), figure 10.2 shows a rib, fitted to the spars, from the side.

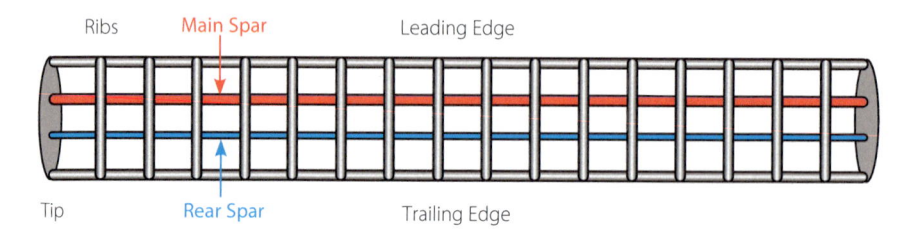

■ *Figure 10.1* **Wing Structure from above**

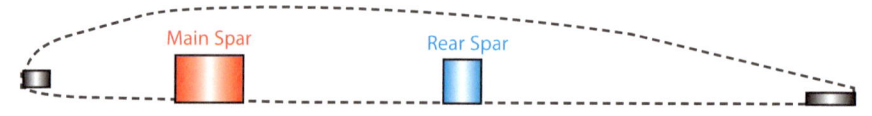

■ *Figure 10.2* **Rib with Spars included**

The 'traditional' tailplane is constructed in a similar fashion. A 'traditional' fin is also very similar, but because the fin is mounted vertically, the expression 'spar' is not used. The main vertical structural members to which the ribs are attached are referred to as "posts".

A fuselage was required to contain the pilot, passengers and freight, so had to be made hollow. The cockpit area is usually reinforced to minimise injury to the occupants in the event of a forced landing. Since most of the stresses are in the pitching or yawing planes, the strength is needed along the longitudinal axis. A group of "stringers" or "longerons" (running "along" the fuselage) provide that strength, and are separated by "frames" (also known as "formers" or "spacers"), which maintain the required fuselage shape. The longeron at the bottom of the fuselage is often referred to as the "keel". Figure 10.3 shows the side view of a 'traditional' fuselage without its covering, and figure 10.4 shows the front view of a typical frame. A solid frame is called a "bulkhead".

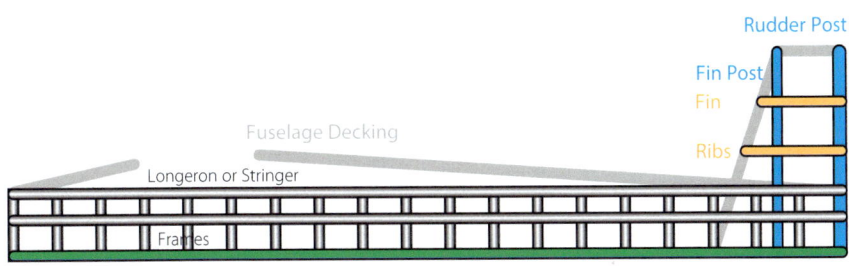

Figure 10.3 **Fuselage and Fin Structure from Port Side**

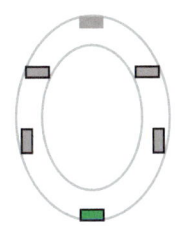

Figure 10.4 **A Frame showing Longerons**

Longerons in modern aircraft are often made of metal tubes. This may be a suitable point to mention that a circular tube is particularly strong for its weight, although that strength reduces considerably if it is damaged. In fact, a hollow rectangular box section is also strong, and spars are often constructed in that way.

10.3 Monocoque Construction

Doped fabric was easily damaged, and plywood became a common skin material on military aircraft before the Second World War. However, to manufacture the numbers of aircraft required for war, mass production techniques had to be employed. These techniques were easier to apply to metal than to wood, so metal alloys (mixtures) became the preferred material for both the skin and structure of aircraft.

The increased strength of a metal skin could take some of the load from the framework. A strong skin around the wing leading edge, forming a D shape with the main spar, allowed the removal of the leading edge spar. If the skin were made strong enough, much of the internal strengthening could be removed. This 'monocoque' or "stressed skin" construction, using no longerons, was first used in manufacturing fuselages, to leave more space for the payload. However, the need for wings to keep their integrity under large 'g' forces meant that they retained at least part of the traditional framework in the form of the main spar and some (although fewer) ribs. Nevertheless, because the skin of most aircraft is a load bearing part of the structure, any damage to it must be investigated.

Glass (and the even stronger carbon) reinforced plastic (GRP and CRP) is now used in aircraft design, and monocoque construction (although virtually always retaining the main spar in both wings and tailplane) is common. However, most aeroplanes currently used for training are of a "semi-monocoque" construction throughout, retaining a few of the traditional internal parts already described inside a strong metal skin.

10.4 Materials

All materials used in aircraft construction are more flexible, and can sustain greater loads, in one direction than another. Wood is strong along the grain (up and down the tree stem or trunk). Glass (and to an even greater extent carbon) reinforced plastic is strong along the fibres. The crystalline structure of metals gives greater strength in one direction than the other. It is important that the correctly designed and manufactured parts are used during construction and subsequent maintenance. 'Unapproved' materials or parts should not be used.

It is also important that any unintended loads placed on the structure (for example a crushing force on a spar which is designed to take a flexing load) are investigated, and any damage is repaired so that the repaired part has an equal strength to the original. If that is not possible then replacement is the only option.

The materials used in aircraft construction are easily damaged by moisture, especially acid or alkaline liquids, and must be protected from the elements (and in the case of fabric and GRP even strong sunlight). Corrosion occurs when two dissimilar metals, such as steel and aluminium, come into contact. Rotting wood, corroding metal, or softening plastic is much weaker than the original material, and corrosion or rot spreads at an exponential rate, so any such damage must be detected and repaired early. Protective coatings, such as paint, gelcoat, or even galvanisation (coating an easily corroding metal with a less corroding one), must be kept clean so that scratches can be identified and repaired correctly (usually after applying a suitable corrosion inhibitor).

Most people can recognise rust on iron and steel. Corrosion on aluminium alloy is frequently visible as a white powdery deposit on the surface as in figure 10.5. Rotting wood initially looks discoloured, but as the rot takes hold it starts to smell badly, and in extreme cases flakes of soft wood may fall away.

■   *Figure 10.5* **Dissimilar Metal Corrosion**

10.5   Joining the Parts

Traditional fabric is tightened by applying taughtening dope. Modern synthetic fabric coverings are often shrunk onto the framework by applying heat. Dope or heating will also stick the fabric onto the frame. Glue is normally used to attach wooden parts to each other, which includes forming solid structures such as propellers from layers of "laminated" wooden sheets. Although early 'casein' glue had a short life and was easily damaged by sunlight, modern synthetic glues are much longer lasting.

Glue is also used to attach certain metal parts. This is usually supplied as two separate substances, which when mixed together in the correct proportions provide a strong bond. Similar glues are used to attach GRP parts to metal parts or to each other. More common methods of attaching metal to metal are soldering, welding, riveting and bolting.

Solder is a material which when gently heated melts and when cooled becomes solid again, covering and connecting wires for example to each other. Solder conducts electricity well, but is not strong enough to fix load bearing parts together.

Welding is a much stronger process which uses high temperatures to rearrange the crystalline structure of two parts made of (usually) the same metal to fuse them together. 'Spot welding' provides small areas of connection, but is not suitable for load bearing parts. A proper aircraft weld involves treating the complete area of the join, and every weld must be inspected by a licensed engineer before a repair can be accepted.

Rivets are small metal plugs which are fitted in holes drilled in the metal. Each end of the rivet must be flattened to prevent it pulling out of its hole. Dissimilar metal corrosion may occur if the rivets are of a different metal to the plates they are joining.

Bolts placed through drilled holes are also routinely used to join aircraft parts, not only metal but also wood or GRP. Where little load has to be carried, a metal part may have a tapped hole in it into which the bolt is screwed, but more commonly a nut will be needed. Apart from the danger of dissimilar metal corrosion, the type of nut is important. Ideally, the nut should be "castellated", so that a split or other safety pin can be inserted through a small hole in the bolt and rest against the 'castellations' to prevent the nut moving. Figure 10.6 shows a bolt with the hole drilled for such a pin just visible. Other "lock-nuts" may have metal tags or nylon inserts which grip the bolt threads. If these are permitted in important positions in an aircraft, they must only be used once. As in figure 10.6, washers are usually required to spread the force between the bolt head or nut and the structure. Most bolts used in aircraft, especially those carrying loads, must be tightened to a specific torque using an appropriate tool (a 'torque wrench').

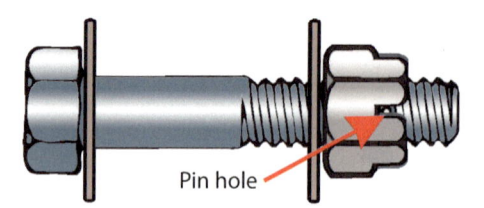

Pin hole

■ *Figure 10.6* **Bolt, nut and washers**

The major parts such as wings and tailplane may be made removable for surface transporting, as in the case of gliders. Bolts are the preferred method of holding such major parts together.

10.6 Control Runs

As described in chapter 2, each plane of aircraft movement requires control surfaces attached to some part of the structure (although the first designs actually changed the shape of some of the structure by "warping" it). Early aeroplanes used external wire cables to move the control surfaces, and many still use cables, especially to move the ailerons. Wire cables may cause serious friction damage to the airframe structure if they rub against it, so the cables must be kept away from that airframe and also from each other.

The cables, composed of many twisted strands of thin wire, are now kept mainly inside the structure, where they are guided in straight lines through "fairleads" of soft fabric or plastic material. They are guided around corners by pulleys rotating on bearings. The bearings may be metal cylinders rotating around other cylinders of different metal (steel inside bronze is common), but may also be ball or roller bearing races.

All cables must be regularly inspected, and any broken or corroded strand indicates that the cable must be replaced (repair may be possible but is usually more expensive). The amount a cable may bend is restricted (hence the pulleys), so knots are not used. To connect cables to each other or to form loops to attach to the controls themselves, the cable must be "swaged" or gripped by a metal collar which has been squeezed to the correct size around the join in a machine. A swaged loop can be attached by a bolt through the loop.

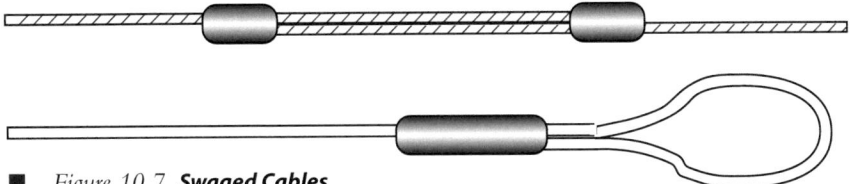

■ *Figure 10.7* **Swaged Cables**

Control cables must be kept at the correct tension. To achieve that, they are usually attached to one or more "turnbuckle" (a metal sleeve with threaded eyes at each end), which can be rotated to adjust the tension. Turnbuckles must be locked to maintain that tension, either by special nuts or by wire (which passes through both eyes and the small hole in the middle).

■ *Figure 10.8* **Turnbuckle**

The requirement to keep cables properly tensioned has led to an increased use of solid (in fact hollow) rods to connect the controls, especially for rudders and elevators. These, like the cables, must be connected by bolts with nuts held with safety pins or wires.

Control cables and rods are often fitted with "stops" to limit the amount the control can be deflected by the pilot. These should not be confused with the physical stops fitted to the aircraft structure at the control surface, which prevent the control surface itself moving further than designed.

In an aircraft where space is at premium, the control surfaces may not actually be directly connected to the cockpit controls. The surfaces may be operated by (usually electric) motors, and the pilot's control inputs are converted to electrical or perhaps light signals which are transmitted along wires or fibre optic cables. At present, however, light aircraft controls are directly connected by either cables or rods.

10.7 Engine Mounting

The engine has to transmit its power to the whole of the aircraft structure. It is therefore mounted directly on very strong parts of that structure, usually at the front of the fuselage. However, the mountings themselves have to absorb considerable vibration from the engine to prevent damage to the airframe and occupants. The mounting bolts therefore are usually fitted through large, heavy duty, thick rubber washers.

Because the hot engine is surrounded by inflammable liquids under pressure, it is advisable to separate it from the aircraft occupants. This separation is provided by a thick bulkhead, the "firewall", through which any holes drilled are carefully sealed.

10.8 Electrical Bonding

Lightning is produced in cumulonimbus clouds (see the volume on Meteorology), because water drops develop a different electrical potential (or 'charge') from each other. The result is a sudden flow of current as the objects equalise that charge, seen as a powerful spark either between different parts of the cloud or between the cloud and the ground.

Any potential difference between the cloud and an object such as an aircraft may lead to the lighting flash passing through that object. Any potential difference between different parts of the aircraft will lead to the lightning spark flashing between these parts, and considerable damage is likely. However, lightning takes the path of least resistance, and if all aircraft parts are joined together with low resistance wire, any electrical current can pass easily without internal sparking. The lightning should pass through the aircraft structure causing the minimum of damage (although some must be expected, if only at the points where the lightning entered and left the structure).

Connecting the parts is called "bonding". Although many metals conduct electricity easily, and most joints between metal and metal will provide a relatively low-resistance path for electrical charge, thick (low-resistance) wire is needed to connect any parts which do not have a satisfactory connection already. Bonding not only reduces the risk from lightning strikes, but also minimises internal interference ("noise") with radio equipment. All aircraft must be bonded, connections must be clean, and the resistance to current flow between the different aircraft parts tested during routine maintenance. The bonding connection between rudder and fin post illustrated in figure 10.9 has been disconnected for training purposes.

■ *Figure 10.9* **Rudder Bonding Disconnected**

Intentionally Left Blank

10.9 Exercise

1. In a monocoque fuselage, what material are the longerons usually made of?
   (a) Metal
   (b) Wood
   (c) Glass reinforced plastic
   (d) There are no longerons

2. A wing main spar runs parallel to which aircraft axis?
   (a) Longitudinal
   (b) Lateral
   (c) Normal
   (d) None

3. If a bolt is used to attach two load bearing surfaces, what other parts are usually required?
   (a) A nut and often one or more washers
   (b) A nut but never a washer
   (c) A washer always but no nut if the lower surface is tapped with a thread
   (d) No other parts if the lower surface is tapped with a thread

4. A turnbuckle is fitted to tension a control cable. It has no special locking nuts. Which of the following statements is true?
   (a) It must be locked in place with locking wire
   (b) It must be locked in place with a split pin
   (c) It must be locked in place with either a split pin or locking wire
   (d) Locking is not essential

5. Where control cables change direction, they are guided around:
   (a) Fairleads
   (b) Bearings
   (c) Swages
   (d) Pulleys

6. What is the purpose of the control stops fitted to the aircraft structure?
   (a) To prevent damage to the controls in strong winds
   (b) To limit control column movement
   (c) To prevent excessive control surface movement
   (d) To prevent the control surfaces moving on the ground

7. Corrosion of aluminium alloy structures is often visible as which of the following?
   (a) White powder
   (b) Reddish brown flakes
   (c) Greenish brown powder
   (d) Black flakes

8. A semi-monocoque fuselage contains:
   (a) No internal strengthening parts
   (b) A complete internal frame which bears all the load
   (c) Some internal structure which provides additional strength to the load bearing skin
   (d) An external framework which bears most of the load

9. Electrical bonding of aircraft parts is required:
   (a) At all times, only between the flying controls
   (b) Only when the aircraft is certificated to fly in cloud
   (c) At all times, between all parts
   (d) Only when the aircraft is operated for public transport

10. The pilot discovers a dent in the skin of a semi-monocoque wing. What should he do?
   (a) Have the wing inspected by an engineer before the next flight.
   (b) Attempt to pull out the dent with a proprietary puller. If it comes out, the aircraft can fly.
   (c) Nothing. The wing skin bears no loads in flight.
   (d) Only have the wing inspected if a rib has been obviously damaged.

CHAPTER 11

Aircraft Systems

11.1 Introduction

It is possible for a simple airframe and engine to fly without any additional systems beyond a pipe connecting a fuel tank to the carburettor. However, practicality (and in some cases the law) requires that certain additional items are carried and operate correctly. We have already seen that the engine itself requires a lubrication system, and fuel and electrical systems are important to the operation of even an uncomplicated training aircraft. Other systems may provide power to flight instruments.

11.2 Engine Drives

The power produced by the piston engine is shared between the propeller and other auxiliary systems which assist the pilot in operating various services. We have seen that the rotating crankshaft normally drives the propeller directly, but some of the power can be distributed to these auxiliary services by either direct gearing from the crankshaft or by belts connecting pulleys.

Gears are normally used for providing power for systems internal to the engine itself, such as the camshaft and oil pump described in chapter 6. They require continuous lubrication, as do the pulleys used in belt drives although usually to a much lesser extent. The belts themselves must not be allowed to deteriorate, so require regular and careful checking as well as any necessary adjustment of their tensioning (by moving the securing bolt in fig. 11.3).

11.3 Fuel System

Fuel for a petrol aircraft engine should be aviation gasoline. This 'AVGAS' is commonly designated '100LL', but for many engines 'UL91' is also suitable and more friendly to the environment. It is carried in the aircraft in one or more fuel tanks, and travels to the engine through pipes or 'lines'. An engine driven pump ensures that it is delivered to the carburettor or injectors. However, there must be some means of providing sufficient pressure for high power operation, and also to provide some fuel for starting the engine in the first place! If the aircraft has its fuel tank(s) above the engine, in a high wing for example, gravity can provide that initial pressure, but if the tanks are situated below the engine, as in most low wing aeroplane designs, an additional electrical "booster" pump is fitted. Often a fuel pressure gauge is fitted to confirm the booster pump's operation. In fuel injected engines, the electric fuel pump may only be needed to provide fuel boost for priming and for vapour suppression at high altitudes. To prevent over-pressurising the fuel lines, such a pump should be switched off for take-off and normal flight.

Pumps are designed to move incompressible fluids, and although liquids do not compress (change volume) much under pressure, gases do. Any gas bubbles in the liquid flowing through a pump will cause problems, sometimes called 'cavitation'. Air might be sucked from a tank which is empty, and can be easily trapped in the pump. Pilots must not allow a fuel tank to become completely empty in the air. It may take a long time for the air bubble to clear even after fuel becomes available from a tank which still contains fuel. Liquid fuel itself may also form gas bubbles under conditions of high temperature and low pressure, and such bubbles can also prevent fuel flow. Motor vehicle gasoline (MOGAS) is particularly susceptible to such "vapourisation", and its use (when permitted) in aircraft engines is restricted to conditions of low altitude (high air pressure) and low ambient temperature.

The tanks may be an integral part of the aircraft structure, or be separate structures inside it. These may be rigid GRP or metal lined with a protective coating, or collapsible plastic or rubber. They are usually filled through holes (necks) in the top, which are sealed with removable filler caps. Although the storage and distribution of aviation fuel is carefully controlled, filters are fitted in several places to minimise any risk of contamination entering the engine. Often a filter will be fitted just below the filler cap to trap external dirt, and there will always be a filter where the fuel leaves the tank, in case for example parts of the tank lining itself break away.

There will be a fuel "cock" or selector valve, situated close to the engine but on the fuselage side of the firewall, which can shut off flow from one or all of the tanks. If more than one fuel tank is fitted to the aircraft, there will usually be a 'collector tank' between the main tanks and the engine, in which the cock and probably the booster pump will be fitted. There may be valves at the tank outlets to prevent fuel flowing back into one tank from another, although that is not always the case. Fuel gauges will indicate the contents of each tank, but old ones are often unreliable, although they are required to be accurate when the tank is empty!

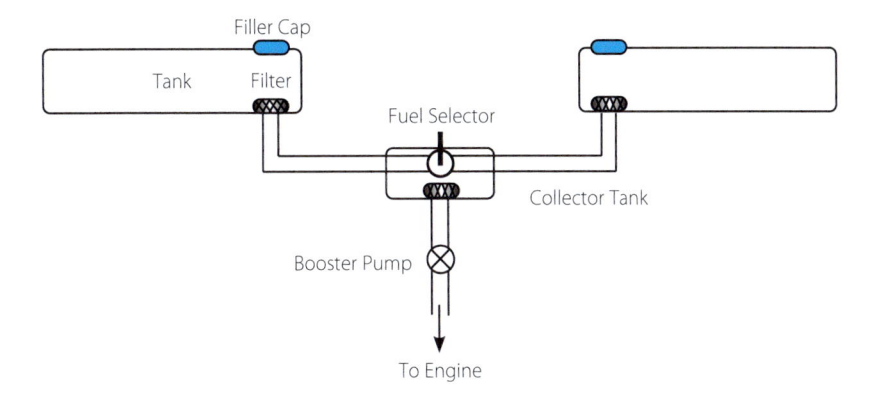

■   *Fig 11.1* **A Fuel System**

In a sealed system, the fuel being drawn into the engine would quickly reduce the pressure in the tanks, which would stop the fuel flowing. It is therefore important to have a method of equalising the pressure of the air in the fuel tanks with the air outside. This can be done by providing a series of vent pipes leading to the outside, sometimes through a pipe under the wing. However, frequently the same effect is achieved by providing a small air vent valve in one of the filler caps. The vent system must not be allowed to become jammed by dirt or insects. Another reason for fitting a vent system is to allow for fuel expansion as the tanks warm up after fuelling. The vented fuel may be mistaken for a leak, so pilots must know where their system vents to atmosphere.

Fuel may become contaminated by dirt (perhaps the lining of the fuel tank itself), or frequently water. Water will not burn so may stop the engine or at least reduce engine power and may freeze in sub-zero temperatures. It may enter the fuel through either condensation as the air inside the tank cools overnight, or directly by rain entering through an improperly fitting filler cap. Before flight (especially after refuelling), the pilot should check the fuel at all the drain valves provided by draining off a certain amount into a testing vessel and inspecting the contents for colour (AVGAS 100LL is pale blue, although UL91 is colourless), dirt particles, and any water which may be identified as bubbles or by using special water detecting papers. A small amount of water may be drained away by continuing to draw test samples until the fuel is clear, but the presence of large amounts should be investigated. Pilots should note that rubber tanks have been known to wrinkle and hold water away from the drain valve. The drains must be properly closed after testing, because a fuel drip on the ground may become a stream in the lower air pressure in flight.

Fuel in an aerodrome's storage and distribution system must also be checked regularly. AVGAS is stored in containers and transported in vehicles with red labels. Diesel or turbine engines use Jet-A1, which is labelled in black. Fatal accidents have resulted from the incorrect fuel being used in aircraft engines. Samples must be taken every day, checked for water and contaminants, and stored for future inspection in the event of an incident. In addition, there is a danger that sparks might ignite fuel vapours while fuel is being transferred between containers. Before transferring any fuel the two containers must be bonded in a similar fashion to that described in chapter 10. When refuelling from a fixed or mobile installation the bonding lead must be connected to the aircraft structure before the fuel nozzle touches the aircraft and not disconnected until the nozzle has been removed. In fact, most hoses have an individual bonding lead attached to the nozzle, which again should be connected to the filler neck before the nozzle touches it.

11.4 Electrical System

Although magnetos are totally self-contained, a source of electricity is required to power other pieces of equipment in aircraft. Lights are needed for flying at night or in bad weather, and radios are needed for flight in Controlled Airspace, where certain navigation aids are also required for IFR flight.

The primary source of electrical power is an electrical accumulator or battery. Most of these are a collection of cells, each of which produces a small "potential difference" or voltage. The cells are connected in series (one after the other) so their voltages add to each other, normally to end up as a 12 volt battery (although there are different systems). The voltage in the cells of many aircraft batteries is produced by a reaction between lead plates and the acid in which they are immersed, caused by an electric current. While the battery is being charged, electrolysis from the charging current makes one set of lead plates positively charged and another set negatively charged, as illustrated in figure 11.2. That difference in charge can be used to provide power for a finite length of time until the battery becomes 'discharged'. The capacity of a battery is measured in 'ampere hours' being the product of the amount of current it can provide and the time it can provide it. For example, a 20 ampere hour battery can provide either 20 amps for 1 hour, 10 amps for 2 hours, or 40 amps for half an hour.

■ *Fig 11.2* **Batteries**

The danger of damage from acid spillage is great, so increasingly the acid is stored in gel, rather than liquid, form. Other electrolytes are also available, and result in names such as lithium ion, or nickel cadmium, which is commonly used in self-contained equipment such as hand-held GPS or radio units. Nickel cadmium batteries are more expensive than lead acid, but have several advantages. Their power to weight ratio is greater, and they last longer. They maintain a stable output until they are almost completely discharged, and they can be recharged rapidly without damage. Lithium ion batteries last even longer, and have a high energy density (power to weight ratio), but at the time of writing their technology is regarded as not yet fully mature. They are the only practical power source for an electric engine but require special precautions, especially when being charged.

Batteries, especially lead acid ones, should be removed from the aircraft before charging from an external source. They must not be overcharged. Nor should they be allowed to become completely discharged ("flat"), as re-charging from that condition is not guaranteed, and in any case is likely to take considerable time. While external power or a boost from another battery may start the engine of an aircraft whose battery has been allowed to become flat, the battery must be allowed to recharge normally before flight.

There may be more than one similar battery fitted to an aircraft. For example, two 12 volt 20 ampere hour batteries may be connected in series (one after the other) in which case the voltages are added and the capacity remains the same (24 volts with a capacity of 20 ampere hours), or in parallel, in which case the voltage remains the same but the capacities are added (12 volts but 40 ampere hours capacity). Some aircraft have a voltmeter but most only have a 'low volts' warning light.

The battery cannot be relied on to provide all the electrical requirements in flight for long. An engine driven electrical generator is usually provided to take over the loads once the engine has started, although pilots may find a generator powered by the airflow in some older light aeroplanes. The generator is similar to a magneto described in chapter 6 in that mechanical rotation of an armature produces a magnetic field which constantly changes across a coil to produce electrical currents, which when passed through brushes and contacts within the generator produce a direct current. The output of the generator, often powered by a belt drive from the engine as in figure 11.3, is controlled by a voltage regulator to be slightly more than the battery voltage, usually 14 volts. An ammeter is often fitted, and will indicate a positive reading when the generator is supplying the electrical loads and charging the battery.

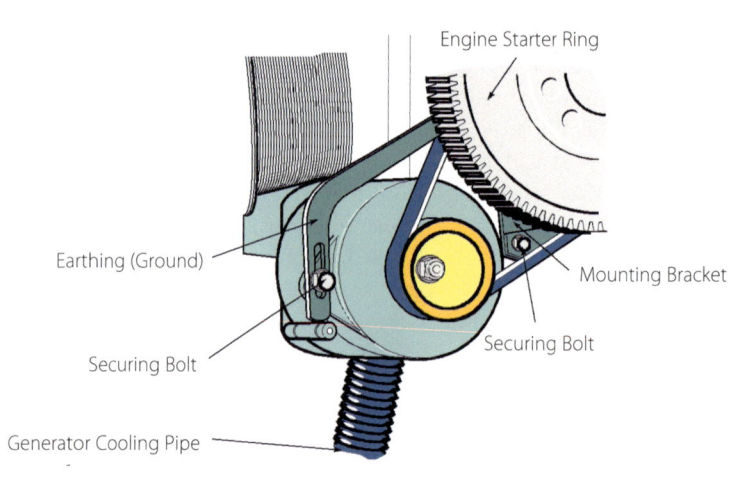

■ *Figure 11.3* **Generator**

The individual electrical loads are often connected to a central "bus bar" through a component which automatically disconnects them if the current gets too high, for example in the event of a short circuit. The danger from an excessive current is overheating and possible fire. The connections are usually either fuses which are designed to break or 'blow' if their specified rating (so many amps) is exceeded, or more commonly circuit breakers which pop out. Circuit breakers may be reset, and a fuse changed (for one of the same rating) by the pilot. However, delay any reset until the circuit has cooled. If they continue to break they may well be indicating a major problem and it is not advisable to reset circuit breakers, or replace fuses, more than once.

Figure 11.4 illustrates a typical simple electrical system in a piston engined aircraft. The ammeter indicates how much current is flowing to or from the battery, and indicates whether the battery is being discharged, as would a generator warning light if that were included. The symbol ═ indicates that the wire is connected to a common earth, in most cases the airframe but in non-metallic airframes a separate metal plate.

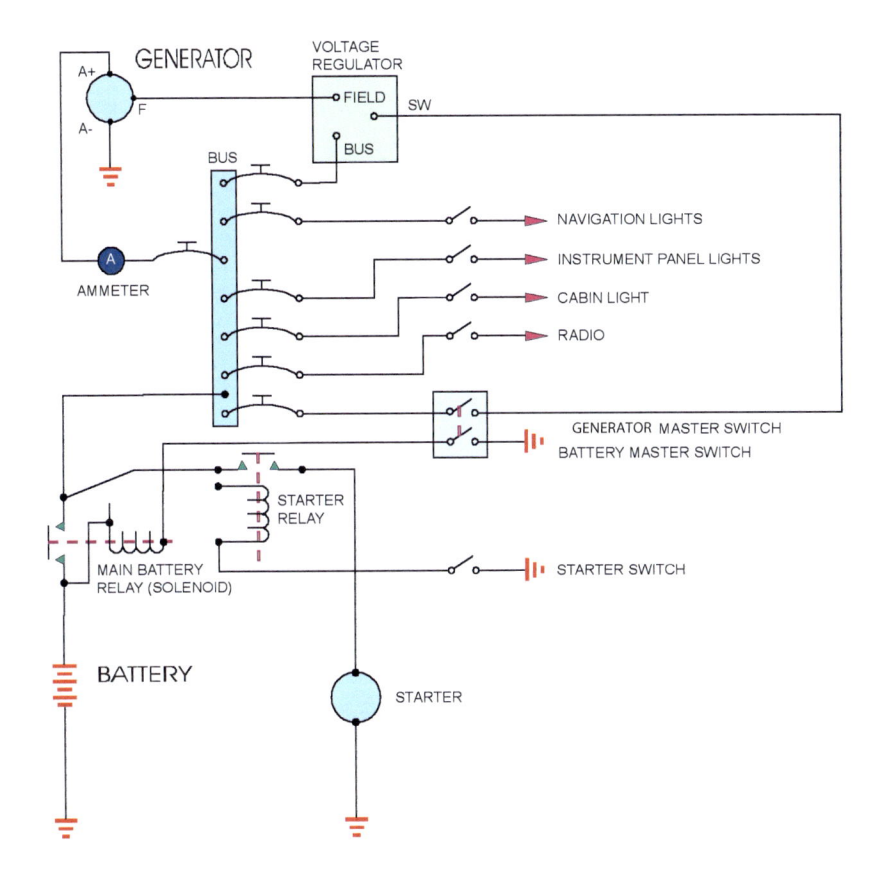

Figure 11.4 **Simple Aircraft Electrical System**

Although most connections are made by simple switches, anything which requires a lot of current, or needs to be switched off automatically, is often controlled through a "relay". A relay, such as the starter relay in figure 11.5, is held open by a spring, but when power is applied to the coil surrounding it, the magnetic field generated moves the core and the relay itself into the closed position. Anything which removes the power to the coil allows the spring to open the relay and rapidly switch off the power to the service it controls.

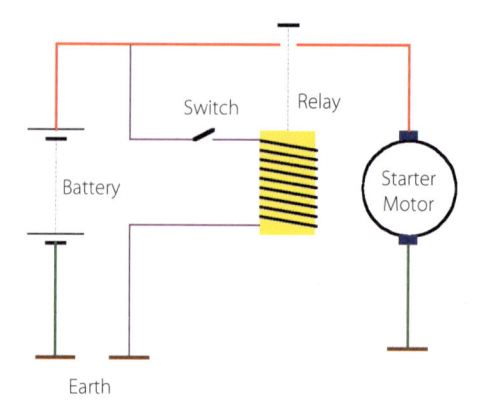

■ *Figure 11.5* **Starter Relay**

Modern aircraft, like modern cars, use an alternator to charge the battery and supply the loads in flight. An alternator, which may require power from the battery to increase the magnetic field strength, can supply alternating current to many of the loads. Only those loads requiring direct current (DC) have the current "rectified" through what may be termed a "TRU" (transformer/rectifier unit). Alternators tend to be more reliable and lighter than generators, and more efficient at low engine rpm.

In the event of the generator or alternator failing in flight (indicated by a discharge on the ammeter and/or a "low volts" warning light), the battery will continue to provide electrical power for a certain period. However, it is important to reduce the electrical load by switching off non-essential services and keeping radio transmissions to a minimum. It is advisable to land before the battery is itself exhausted. It is not advisable to reset an alternator circuit breaker in flight if it has tripped.

A flat battery may cause a high ammeter reading after starting, but a high reading in flight suggests a fault in the alternator circuit. To minimise damage to the battery, the alternator should be switched off and action taken as if it had failed.

11.5 Hydraulic System

Although the flying controls of most light aeroplanes are operated through direct linkage, operating most aircraft at some stage requires the use of more force than the pilot's muscles can reasonably be expected to exert, even if only to bring it to a stop after landing. Some form of assistance is needed, and one method is to use the incompressibility of liquids already mentioned in paragraph 11.3 in a 'hydraulic' system.

A very simple hydraulic system is illustrated in figure 11.6. A relatively small force applied to the small piston on the left will increase the pressure in the liquid by a function of the force applied divided by the area of application (pressure = force ÷ area). The increased pressure acts in all directions, including onto the large piston on the right, where the resultant pressure exerts a much greater force on the attached rod. If, for example, the pilot applies the initial force by pushing on a brake pedal attached to the piston in a small 'master cylinder', the resultant force from a larger piston in a 'slave cylinder' can be used to squeeze brake pads onto a disc to stop the individual wheel (stopping the aircraft in a straight line will require both pedals to be operated!). The aircraft parking brake is often only a mechanical catch, so if hydraulic pressure has been allowed to reduce after the engine has stopped, the brakes will not be effective until pressure has been applied by the pilot once more.

■   *Figure 11.6* **Hydraulic Theory**

In some aircraft, operating services such as the flaps, and raising and lowering undercarriage legs and doors, may require assistance which often is provided by a more complex hydraulic system. Although knowledge of such systems is not required for basic PPL exams, the information may be required for differences training. Each service is operated by a rod attached to the piston of a 'jack', which moves in the direction determined by the position of its selector valve. A reservoir is needed to replenish the fluid level, and the pressure is maintained at an appropriate high pressure by a pump. Figure 11.7 shows most of the components of a hydraulic system, although only one jack and its selector valve are shown for simplicity.

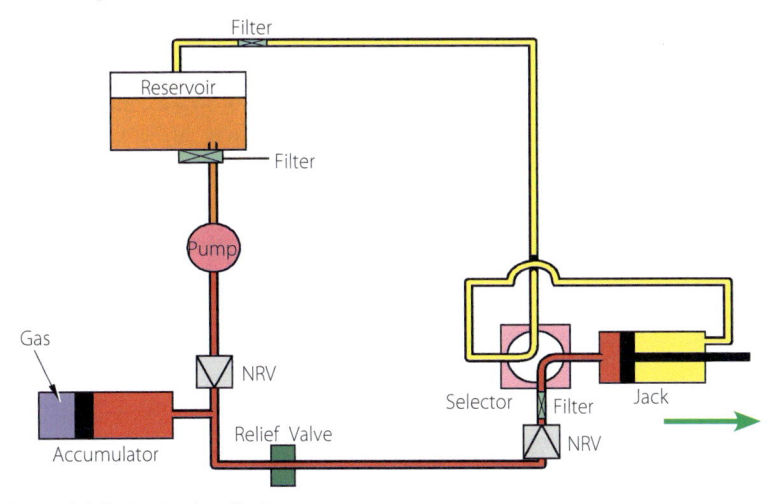

■   *Figure 11.7* **An Hydraulic System**

The red line indicates fluid under pressure, starting to move the jack towards the right. The yellow shows excess fluid being allowed to return to the reservoir through the selector valve. Pressure in the system is maintained temporarily in the event of a pump failure or leak by non-return valves (NRV). Sometimes an additional hand pump is provided for emergency back-up, but this system includes an accumulator, which not only keeps a certain amount of fluid under pressure to operate the important services (usually only once), but also makes the operation of the services smoother.

One or more relief valves prevent an overspeeding pump or high temperature from increasing the fluid pressure too much and damaging the relatively delicate seals. Note the number of filters to keep the fluid clean, also to prevent seal damage. These seals may be made of rubber or synthetic materials, and the fluid used in the system must be appropriate for that material, so it is important, whether the aircraft uses hydraulics to operate many services or just the brakes, to replenish the fluid with the correct type as specified in the Flight or Maintenance Manual.

11.6 Undercarriage

Aircraft spend more time on the ground than they do in the air. While there, the aircraft's weight is balanced by the reaction of the ground upwards through the wheels (undercarriage). The position of the wheels affects the ground movement of the aeroplane; for example, the pilot of a tailwheel aeroplane has to deliberately lower the nose to achieve the takeoff attitude, rather than raise it as in a nosewheel aeroplane. Taxying is also usually more difficult because the pilot cannot see directly in front of him, so he must weave the nose from side to side. However, tailwheel aeroplanes tend to suffer less often from nose damage resulting from bad landings.

The undercarriage has to absorb the landing forces. Most of that absorption takes place in the suspension, which in many training aeroplanes is the actual construction of the undercarriage legs. The wheels are set slightly outwards on the legs which in turn are angled outwards. As the aircraft hits the ground, the legs are forced further outwards and bend, absorbing the force.

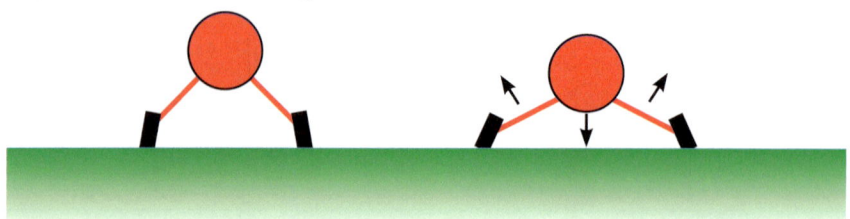

■ *Figure 11.8* **Landing Loads Absorbed**

However, although the undercarriage can cope with quite large vertical forces, there is a limit to the amount of sideways force it can absorb, for example in a crosswind landing. The 'demonstrated crosswind' given in the Flight Manual does not mean the aircraft can absorb that amount of sideways force, but does provide an indication of its strength relative to others.

Another shock absorbing mechanism is the oleo-pneumatic unit or 'oleo'. A piston connected to the wheel moves inside a cylinder connected to the airframe and compresses the air inside as a load is applied. The compressed air acts as a shock absorber, but to damp out oscillations there is also a certain amount of hydraulic fluid in the cylinder. The leg is kept straight (and connected to the aircraft) by a 'torque link' behind it, and to prevent the wheel vibrating sideways, or "shimmy", there may be a small damper fitted to the torque link.

The nosewheel oleo may also be fitted with push/pull rods (often connected to the rudder linkage by springs) which provide nosewheel steering. Severe sideways forces can be produced while taxying, especially if a steerable nosewheel is turned too tightly. Either or both the nosewheel or the main wheels can be subjected to stress. The same can happen if a towbar turns the nosewheel through an angle greater than it is designed to turn.

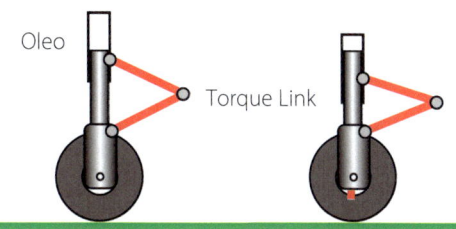

■ *Fig 11.9 **Oleo Leg***

The tyres on the aircraft wheels must be kept in good condition without cuts or excessive wear, and at or near the pressures recommended in the Flight or Maintenance Manual. Incorrect inflation can result in damage. Many tyres can be seen with painted marks on both the tyre and the wheel against it, as on the right of figure 11.9. These 'creep' marks are important if the tyre has an internal tube, because if the tyre rotates away from the mark, the valve may split from the tube. Such rotation is not so dangerous in a tubeless tyre as is fitted to most light aeroplanes, but is likely to be an indication of low tyre pressure. The continued use of an underinflated tyre can be identified by wear on the 'shoulders' of the tyre.

Some aircraft may be fitted with 'spats' which cover the axle and upper part of the wheel, in order to reduce drag from the undercarriage. If operating from grass runways or taxiways, these may become filled with mud. The spats may only be removed for flight if the Flight or Maintenance Manual specifically permits it, and pilots must remember that their performance is likely to be reduced and fuel consumption increased if the aircraft is flown without the spats.

Undercarriage legs (and often doors to reduce profile drag) may be made retractable by electric motors or hydraulic jacks (see para. 11.5). Locking systems to maintain the legs in position may also be controlled by electric relays or hydraulic jacks, and lowering systems will usually use the same power source. However, gravity is often used as a back-up means of lowering undercarriage legs if the main system fails. It is not intended to go into individual systems here. Pilots converting to a type with a retractable undercarriage must study the Flight Manual as part of their differences training.

11.7 Cabin Conditioning

The air inside the cabin of most light aircraft is very similar to the air outside. Any difference in temperature or static pressure is normally the result of flow through gaps in the doors and the occupants' bodily warmth. However, there is usually an external scoop, or 'air intake', facing forward into the airflow so that some of the dynamic pressure of the air as the aircraft moves forward can be used not only to ventilate the cabin, but more importantly to blow over the windscreen in an attempt to keep it clear of condensation from the occupants' breath as it meets the cold clear perspex. However, such flow direction usually requires the pilot to direct the air towards the windscreen by moving a selector lever.

The air used for cooling the cylinders is often used to provide a source of heating for the cabin if required. In that case, two flows of air, one from the engine compartment and one from outside, arrive in a mixer box. The proportion of hot and cold air entering is adjusted by a valve connected to a temperature selector in the cockpit. Again, the pilot can direct the flow of air to the windscreen and /or one or more outlets in the cabin by use of another selector. Some multi-engined aircraft have separate air heaters rather than taking air from the engine compartment. These burn fuel internally to heat the air around them, which is then ducted into the cockpit. The fuel used by the heater (often situated in the aircraft nose) must be taken into account when calculating overall fuel consumption.

Aircraft with turbo-chargers have a source of high pressure air (already warmed by the compression) which may be used to increase the air pressure inside the cabin if required for high altitude flight. The air pressure inside the cabin is controlled by a valve which lets the excess air out once the required pressure (in fact the pressure difference between cabin and outside air) has been reached. This pressure controller normally contains a simple barostat similar to a pressure altimeter (see chapter 4).

11.8 Radio Equipment

The most common piece of electrical equipment fitted to a light aircraft is a radio. Most aviation radio transmissions take place in the very high frequency (VHF) band, between 118 and 137 MegaHertz (MHz - millions of cycles per second), with the frequencies just below that being used for some radio navigation aids. Every radio will have a frequency selector on its control unit, perhaps similar to that in figure 11.10, on which the pilot can select the frequency on which he wishes to receive and transmit signals.

■ *Fig 11.10* **Radio Frequency Selector**

On this, as in many control units, there are two frequency displays, with a push-button (marked in fig 11.10 with the double arrow <>) to change the displays between them. The first display shows the frequency currently selected for use, and the other shows the 'standby' frequency which the pilot is able to change with the frequency change knobs (on the right in fig 11.10). In order to change the frequency in use, the pilot turn the knobs until the standby display shows the desired frequency, then press the push-button to transfer it to the main display. Once he has made contact on the new frequency he can then select the next desired frequency on the standby display, ready to be selected as required. There may be a facility to load regularly used frequencies as 'channels'. Many modern control units are integrated with navigation displays as shown in figure 12.12.

Although most aircraft have one or more loudspeakers from which the received signal may be heard after it has passed through an amplifier, cabin noise dictates that most pilots wear headsets which reduce external noise while allowing clear radio reception. Some modern headsets are able to electronically counter outside noise. If more than one person is using a headset in the aircraft, care should be taken to ensure that they are electronically 'compatible' with each other; otherwise one pilot may experience reception difficulties.

The volume control selects the level of receiver volume only. A 'squelch' control may be available to adjust the level of background noise included in the amplified signal. In order to hear the intended signal clearly, the squelch knob should be rotated until the background noise is heard, and then turned down slightly until that noise appears to have just disappeared. Some radio controls have a squelch switch rather than a rotating knob. During pre-flight checks the switch should be operated to confirm that background noise is heard when squelch is switched off. In sets similar to that in fig 11.10, squelch is adjusted automatically. However, the 'test' button may be used to bypass the squelch facility and check that the radio is receiving background noise.

Attached to most headsets will be a microphone, through which the pilot can talk, although in some aircraft a separate hand-held microphone may be fitted. In order to make a transmission to a ground station or other aircraft, the pilot should speak clearly into the microphone while pressing the spring loaded press to transmit (PTT in fig 11.13) button. The transmit button switches the receiver off during transmissions, so he must release it in order to receive a reply. If no reply is heard, it may be because the transmit button or circuit is faulty, and the radio is continuing to transmit without the pilot intending it.

There will also be an 'intercom' facility to allow pilots and passengers to talk to each other. In a simple system, if the radio is switched on, any person talking into a microphone without pressing the transmit button will be heard by others in the aircraft, using the radio's 'side tone'. More commonly in training aircraft, an additional intercom system is fitted, with its own controls for volume and possibly for a voice activated circuit to prevent background cockpit noise being amplified all the time. The intercom may either have its own dedicated control unit, or be included in a unit such as that in figure 11.11. A rotary switch selects the transmitter in use (and automatically its corresponding receiver), and the individual buttons select any additional receivers to which the pilot wishes to listen, such as a second radio, or one or more of the aircraft's radio navigation aids.

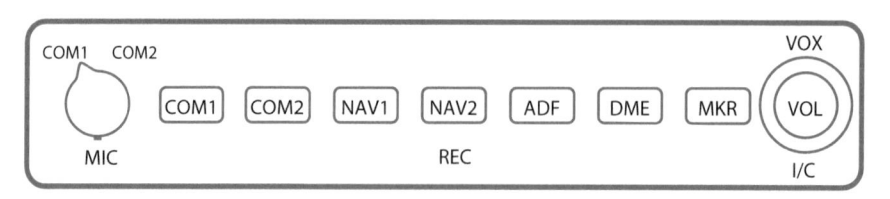

■ *Fig 11.11* **Receiver and Intercom Control Unit**

For transmission, the electrical signals at the selected frequency (the 'carrier') are modulated (changed) by a signal converted at the same frequency as the pilot's voice. They are then passed to one or more aerials (antennas), which usually project vertically from the aircraft's skin.

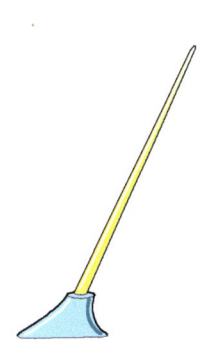

■ *Fig 11.12* **Whip aerial**

If the antenna is the correct length (half the wavelength, or if, as is normal, the aircraft skin is used as a reflector, a quarter of the wavelength), the electrical signal causes it to "vibrate" electronically and generate an electromagnetic wave which travels through the atmosphere at the speed of light (300 million metres per second). The length of that wave as it travels through the air (the 'wavelength' - approximately 2.4 metres for aviation transmissions) is inversely related to the frequency (the number of wave crests leaving the transmitter every second). VHF transmissions travel virtually in a straight line, so cannot normally be received if there is an obstruction between the transmitter and receiver, such as a hill or the curved earth's surface, although reflections may be received if the signal is strong.

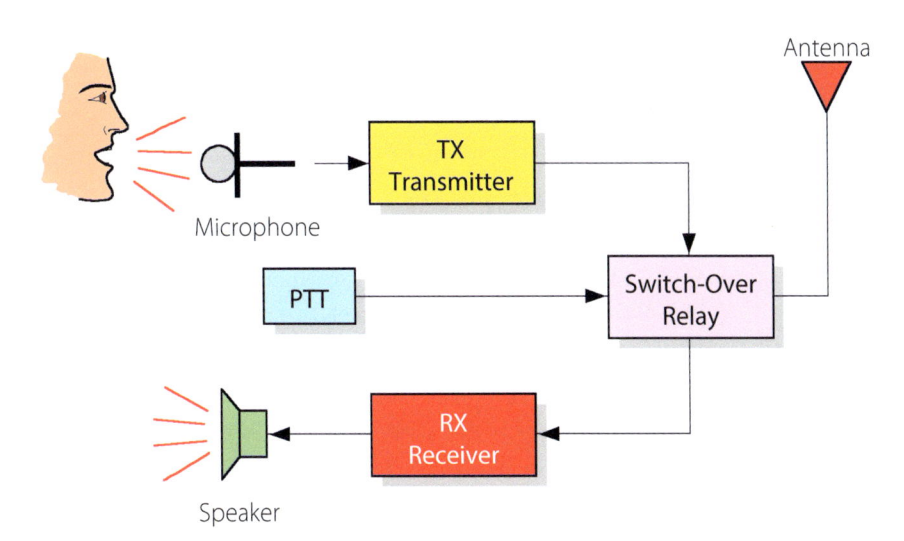

■ *Fig 11.13* **Simplified Radio Diagram**

If the receiver antenna is the correct length as described above, it 'vibrates' electronically when the wave reaches it and generates a very weak alternating electrical current exactly the same as the transmission signal. This is then amplified and demodulated in the receiver to produce the voice signal in the pilot's headphones or loudspeaker.

The actual transmitter and receiver, and their amplifiers, may be located in a separate box from the control unit. All wiring between individual units, including the aerials, must be 'screened' to prevent interference from the electrical currents. Any other wires in the aircraft which carry alternating current may have to be similarly screened, especially the ignition circuits.

Radio navigation aids are described the volume on Navigation. However, most aircraft carry a "secondary surveillance radar" (SSR) transponder, which receives radar signals from ground stations and replies automatically by broadcasting information in three modes. Mode A information can be set by the pilot by selecting four digits, each from 0 to 7, as required by air traffic control. Mode C transmits the aircraft's pressure altitude, and Mode S transmits the aircraft's individual identification. "Enhanced" Mode S can also transmit other information such as the aircraft's flightpath, but is not required for light aircraft under VFR. Figure 11.16 shows a typical transponder set to transmit Mode A code 1200 and also Mode C (ALT).

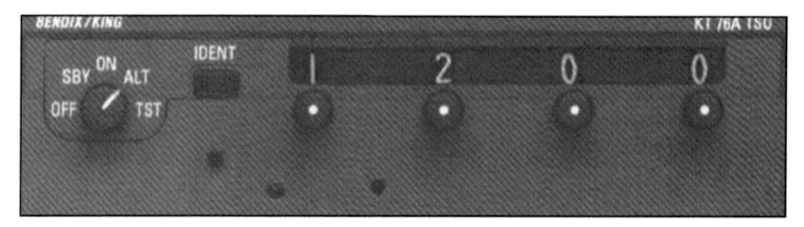

■ *Fig 11.16* **SSR Transponder (Courtesy Honeywell)**

The 'TST' position on the rotary switch tests the internal circuitry. When the IDENT button is pressed it sends a double signal to the ground radar receiver. While changing codes in Mode A the pilot should set the rotary selector to 'SBY' to prevent inadvertent selection of one of the emergency special codes (the volume on Aviation Law).

An extra benefit of a transponder is that most commercial aircraft are fitted with collision avoidance systems which can receive the signals and warn their pilots of at least the bearing of the transponding aircraft.

11.9 Exercise

1. During his pre-flight inspection, the pilot notices a small hole drilled in the top of one fuel filler cap. He should:
   (a) Ensure the hole does not become blocked
   (b) Cover the hole with tape to prevent water getting in
   (c) Replace the cap with one without a hole
   (d) Place the aircraft unserviceable

2. In an aeroplane with fuel tanks in its low wings, when should the booster pump normally be selected ON?

   i. During take-off and initial climb
   ii. During approach and landing
   iii. If the engine starts running roughly
   iv. When changing fuel tanks
   v. At all times

   (a) (i) and (ii) only
   (b) (i), (ii) and (iii) only
   (c) (i), (ii), (iii) and (iv) only
   (d) (v)

3. The pilot is unable to receive radio signals. He notices that the radio circuit breaker has popped out. Should he reset that circuit breaker in an attempt to cure the problem, and if so how many reset attempts should he make?
   (a) He should not reset the circuit breaker
   (b) He should make no more than two attempts to reset the circuit breaker
   (c) He should make as many attempts as necessary
   (d) Resetting the circuit breaker will have no effect on radio reception

4. During pre-flight inspection, the pilot notices that the tyre creep mark is not exactly lined up with the wheel creep mark, although the paint marks are touching each other. Is the aircraft airworthy?
   (a) Yes
   (b) Not unless the tyre is a tubeless type
   (c) Not unless the tyre has an internal tube
   (d) Not at all

5. An aircraft battery, fully charged, has a capacity of 15 ampere hours. The electrical services provided from the bus bar add up to 30 amps. How long will the battery be able to supply those services in the event of a generator failure?

   (a) 10 minutes
   (b) 30 minutes
   (c) 1 hour
   (d) 2 hours

6. From question 5, assume that the landing light takes 15 amps. If the pilot notices the generator failure and switches off the landing light immediately, how much extra time will the battery be able to supply the rest of the electrical loads?

   (a) 10 minutes
   (b) 30 minutes
   (c) 1 hour
   (d) 2 hours

7. An aircraft's spats are discovered full of mud at the pre-flight inspection. What should be done?

   (a) The spats must be removed and left off to prevent further accumulation
   (b) Nothing, the mud will fall out after take-off
   (c) The wheels must be removed and the spats left in position during cleaning
   (d) All mud must be removed and the spats refitted to maintain the validity of the C of A

8. AVGAS 100LL is (i) ..... in colour and is transported in containers with (ii) ..... labels.

	(i)	(ii)
(a)	straw	blue
(b)	red	black
(c)	blue	red
(d)	blue	black

9. Flying an aeroplane with a flat battery immediately after starting the engine from a ground source:

   (a) Is not recommended because the battery is needed for the ignition system in flight
   (b) Is acceptable because the battery will be fully charged before the next flight
   (c) Is acceptable because the battery is never required in flight
   (d) Is not recommended because the battery may not charge correctly during flight

10. If the ammeter reading drops to and remains at zero in flight, what is the most probable cause?
   (a) The battery has become fully charged
   (b) The electrical system is working normally
   (c) The alternator has failed
   (d) The battery is flat

11. Air Traffic Control ask the pilot to select "SSR 3632 with Charlie". Which settings should the pilot have on his SSR transponder to comply with that instruction?
   (a) Rotary switch to SBY, 3632 in the numeric display
   (b) Rotary switch to ON, 3632 in the numeric display
   (c) Rotary switch to ALT, 3632 in the numeric display
   (d) Rotary switch to TST, 3632 in the numeric display

12. A nickel cadmium battery, compared to a lead acid one of the same capacity, will be:
   (a) Lighter and maintain its rated voltage for longer
   (b) Heavier and maintain its rated voltage for longer
   (c) Heavier and maintain its rated voltage for less time
   (d) Lighter and maintain its rated voltage for longer

13. Two 12 volt 20 amp hour batteries are connected in series. What is the total rating of the combination:
   (a) 12 volts, 20 amp hour
   (b) 20 volts, 40 amp hour
   (c) 24 volts, 20 amp hour
   (d) 24 volts, 40 amp hour

14. Two 12 volt 20 amp hour batteries are connected in parallel. What is the total rating of the combination:
   (a) 12 volts, 20 amp hour
   (b) 12 volts, 40 amp hour
   (c) 24 volts, 20 amp hour
   (d) 24 volts, 40 amp hour

15. An aircraft's fuel tanks are completely filled in the morning. What is most likely to happen as the temperature increases during the day?
   (a) Fuel will drip out of the fuel vent system
   (b) Water will condense in the fuel tanks
   (c) Air bubbles may form in the fuel
   (d) The fuel gauges will indicate less than full

16. What is a probable result if the pilot leaves the parking catch ON after shut down?
   (a) The brake pressure will be correctly maintained until the engine next starts
   (b) The pressure will increase with temperature and he may have difficulty releasing the catch
   (c) The pressure will increase with temperature and may damage a seal
   (d) The pressure will bleed away and the brakes may become ineffective

17. During preflight checks, the pilot notices that the creep mark on a tubeless tyre is not exactly aligned with the creep mark on the wheel. What action should the pilot take?
   (a) Nothing, creep is not important on a tubeless tyre
   (b) Immediately place the aircraft unserviceable in the technical log
   (c) Fly as normal but ask for the mark to be repainted during the next routine maintenance
   (d) Check that the tyre pressure is adequate before flying"

18. If the ammeter indicates a maximum positive deflection in flight:
   (a) The battery has gone flat and the alternator will continue to carry the electrical load
   (b) The alternator has switched itself off, and the battery has taken on the electical load
   (c) There is a fault in the alternator circuit and the alternator should be switched off
   (d) Too much load is being carried by the alternator and the load should be reduced

19. An aircraft has two fuel tanks. What is likely to happen if the pilot allows one of them to become empty in flight?
   (a) Air from the empty tank can be trapped in the engine fuel pump and delay the fuel flowing from the other tank when selected.
   (b) The engine fuel pump will immediately draw fuel from the other tank.
   (c) The gases in the empty tank may enter the cabin and cause CO poisoning.
   (d) Dirt in the bottom of the empty tank may be drawn into the engine and cause damage.

Chapter 12

Other Flight Instruments

12.1 Introduction

We looked at the pressure instruments in chapter 4, and engine instruments in chapter 9. However, most aircraft instrument panels contain more instruments than these, especially if the pilot wishes to be able to fly without reference to the visual horizon. In this chapter we shall discuss the flight instruments commonly found in light aircraft which rely on neither dynamic nor static pressure.

12.2 Magnetic Compass

Magnetism and compasses are described in detail in another volume of this series, 'Visual and Radio Navigation'. Basically, a light aircraft compass consists of a magnet suspended in liquid, connected to a card with numbers of degrees written on that card. The liquid reduces friction, allowing the magnet to move freely, and also damps any excessive motion. The pilot reads his magnetic heading (055° in fig 12.1) from the numbers which appear under a 'lubber line' on the face of the instrument. The compass requires no external power supply to function. However, it must be remembered that it indicates the magnetic heading of the aircraft (relative to magnetic North). Variation must be applied to find the true heading (relative to true North).

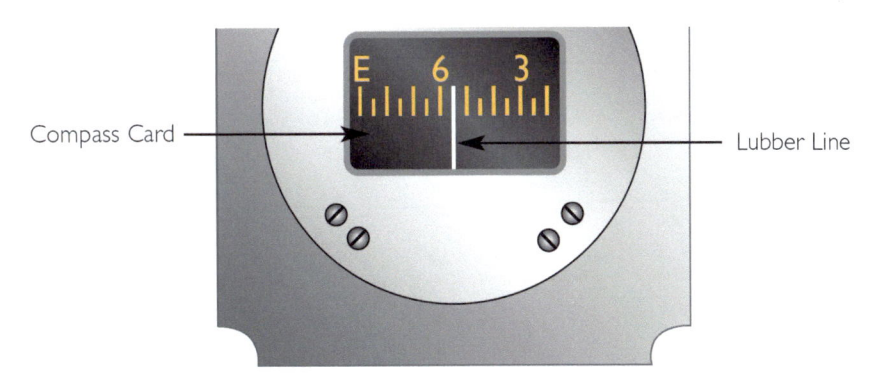

■ *Fig 12.1* **A Common Aircraft Compass**

Unfortunately, the compass only works properly when nothing interferes with it. If any ferrous metal (iron or steel) object or electrical current, either of which will alter a magnetic field, is near it, the compass needle and attached card will indicate a combination of the earth's magnetic field and the interference. There will be a 'deviation' between the magnetic heading and the compass heading. Aircraft compasses must be 'swung' (checked, adjusted and calibrated) every time new equipment is fitted to the aircraft which might alter magnetic fields. The result of a compass swing is the deviation card fitted beside all compasses, which pilots must consult if attempting to follow a specific magnetic heading.

Also, if the aircraft is banked or accelerated in any direction, magnetic dip (see the volume on Navigation) attracts the needle and attached card away from the correct heading. This is often called acceleration error (worst when accelerating East or West) or turning error (worst when turning through North or South). The compass can only be relied upon in straight, unaccelerated flight. Another instrument is needed.

12.3 Gyroscopes

Many aircraft instruments use the gyroscopic properties of a rotating mass. A small but heavy wheel is made to spin very rapidly inside the relevant instrument. One of the main properties of a gyroscope is that it attempts to keep its spin axis in a constant direction in space unless acted upon by an external force. If the wheel is allowed to move freely inside a set of 'gimbals', and set up with the spin axis vertical to the earth, for example as in figure 12.2, the aircraft can move around the gyro. If the pilot can see a line on an instrument set up at 90° to the spin axis, that line will represent the horizon, and the pilot can see the bank attitude of his aircraft in relation to that horizon. If the aircraft pitches, the same property of rigidity will apply. The gyro spin axis will again remain vertical in relation to the earth, and the pilot can deduce his pitch attitude.

Cockpit

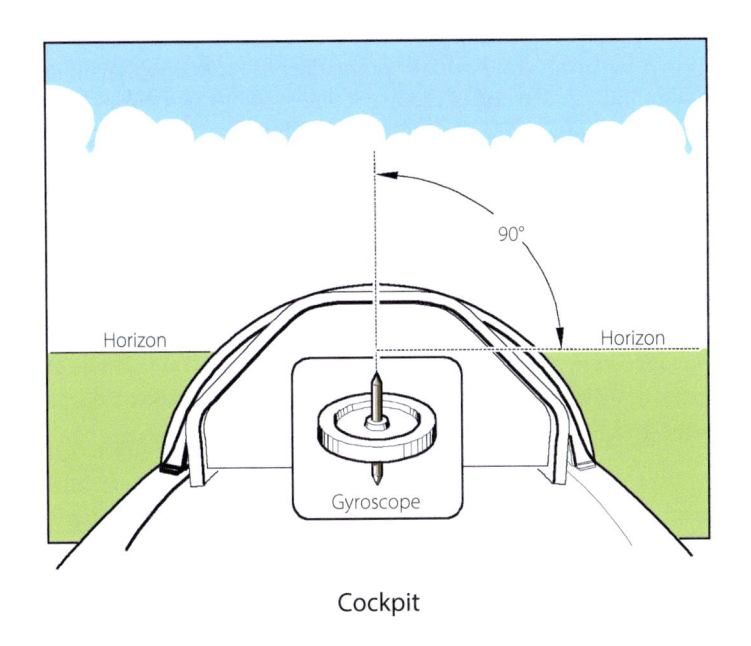

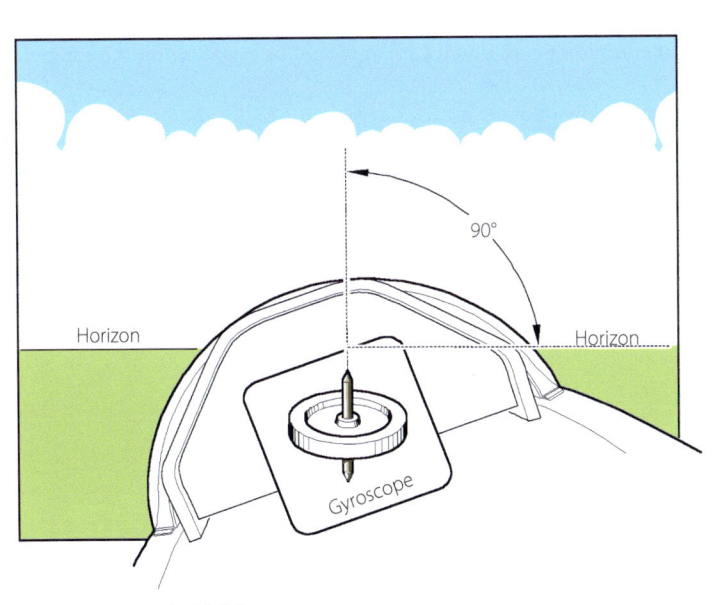

■ *Fig 12.2* **Gyroscopic Rigidity**

If a gyroscope's spin axis is horizontal instead of vertical, it can be set up or 'tied' to the earth's magnetic field; such a gyro can be used to indicate direction. If the gyro is restrained in one plane, another of the properties of a gyroscope, that of "precession", can be used to indicate the rate of change of direction in a particular plane, which in the case of the turn indicator is the aircraft's heading.

12.4 Power Supplies

Some light aircraft, mainly those of recent design, use AC electrical power for their gyroscopic instruments, using the rotor of an electric motor as the gyro rotor. High rotor speeds provide high rigidity. However, the gyro in a turn indicator requires low rigidity to function properly, so needs not spin as quickly as an attitude gyro. Most turn indicators therefore are driven by DC, and can be powered direct from the aircraft battery in the event that other systems fail.

However, most common light aircraft use a different power source for their artificial horizon and direction indicator. The gyro wheel is driven by passing air over it, pushing against little bucket shaped cut outs on the wheel rim. The air comes from a pump driven by the engine. In fact, the pump is a 'vacuum' or 'suction' pump, which reduces rather than increases the air pressure. The pressure reduction (usually regulated by a relief valve to about 5 psi) is indicated on a gauge in the cockpit. Air from outside is 'pulled' across the gyros on its way to the pump. Filters in the lines prevent damage to the instrument from dust particles, but if the filters become clogged the suction pressure reduces, as would be apparent on the gauge indication.

12.5 Attitude Indicators

We looked at the principle of indicating the aircraft's attitude using a gyroscope in paragraph 12.3. There are specific differences between an 'artificial horizon' and an 'attitude indicator' (AI), but the terms are frequently interchanged. They are both 'earth tied' gyroscopes, being set up and maintained with their spin axis at right angles to the earth's surface. The face of a typical suction powered artificial horizon for light aircraft is shown in figure 12.3. The nose of the aircraft is represented by the dot in the centre of the instrument, and the rest of the aircraft symbol indicates the wings. The horizon is a bar which moves behind the aircraft symbol, and in this case indicates that the aircraft nose is pitched down with its wings level. There is also a scale with a pointer, at the bottom in fig 12.3 but sometimes at the top, to indicate the exact amount of bank angle of the wings if the pilot wishes to know that.

There may also be a knob which moves the aircraft symbol up or down a small amount to the pilot's desired position.

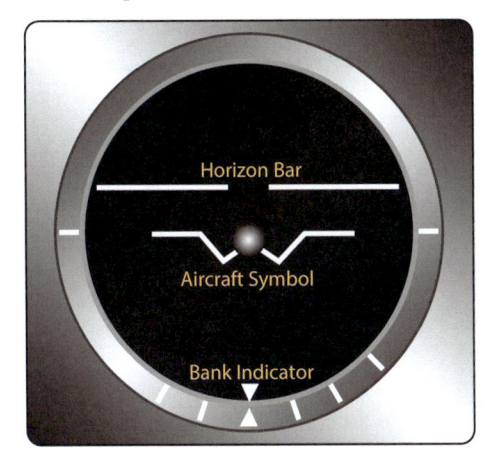

■ *Fig 12.3* **Artificial Horizon**

The horizon bar is usually free to roll right round the aircraft symbol, giving it what is called "freedom in roll". However an artificial horizon does not have "freedom in pitch". Its horizon bar moves more for a given pitch angle change when it is close to the aircraft symbol than when it is displaced a long way. If the bar is seen right at the top or bottom of the display it means the aircraft is pointing virtually straight down or up, a pitch angle of 90 degrees. Any further pitch change will make the horizon bar rotate rapidly and move from bottom to top or vice versa. The maximum freedom in pitch likely to be found is ±85 degrees in pitch, but many have less.

An attitude indicator does not change the amount of its indication as the pitch angle changes, and many do have full freedom in pitch. Figure 12.4 shows such an attitude indicator, found in military aircraft and perhaps in certain civilian aircraft. The coloured background shows the horizon as the dividing line between the blue sky and brown earth, and even has lines indicating the actual angle of aircraft pitch up (climb) or down (dive).

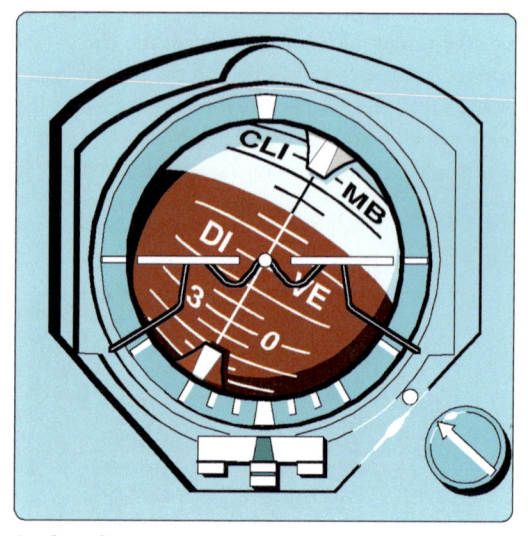

■ *Fig 12.4* **Attitude Indicator**

The basic indications and use of both instruments are for practical purposes the same. In figure 12.4 we can visualise the nose of the aircraft pointing below the horizon with the left wing low. It is banked left and pitched down. To return to level flight the pilot must roll right until the wings are level, then pitch up until the nose reaches the horizon. The greater detail from the pitch lines and bank pointer indicates that the aircraft is banked 30 degrees left and pitched 15 degrees nose down, but most private pilots would not be particularly interested in that.

If the aircraft reaches an attitude beyond the artificial horizon's degrees of freedom, for example during aerobatics, solid parts of the mechanism will touch, rub against each other and cause the indication to be incorrect. The instrument has "toppled". In most cases, flying straight and level without accelerating for a few minutes will allow the instrument to "erect" itself in the same way that it does after engine start on the ground. Electric powered instruments may be able to erect quicker by using a "fast erection" knob during the erection process.

In the event of power failure to an electrically powered attitude instrument, a small flag will appear on the face of the instrument to warn the pilot that the instrument is unreliable and must not be used. The same facility does not normally apply to suction powered instruments; the pilot must monitor the suction gauge.

After engine start and before take-off, the pilot should check the suction pressure is correct and that the instrument erects itself. It must also remain erect when the aircraft turns during taxying.

12.6 Direction Indication

In paragraph 12.3 we mentioned that if an instrument's gyro axis was horizontal, it could be used to indicate direction. Figure 12.5 shows the principle. All the pilot has to do is set up the instrument (once the gyro rotor has reached operating speed after engine start) so that the direction indicated on the instrument shown in figure 12.6, a 'direction indicator' or 'DI', is correct to start with. Provided the gyro is kept within its degrees of freedom, it should continue to indicate correctly from then on.

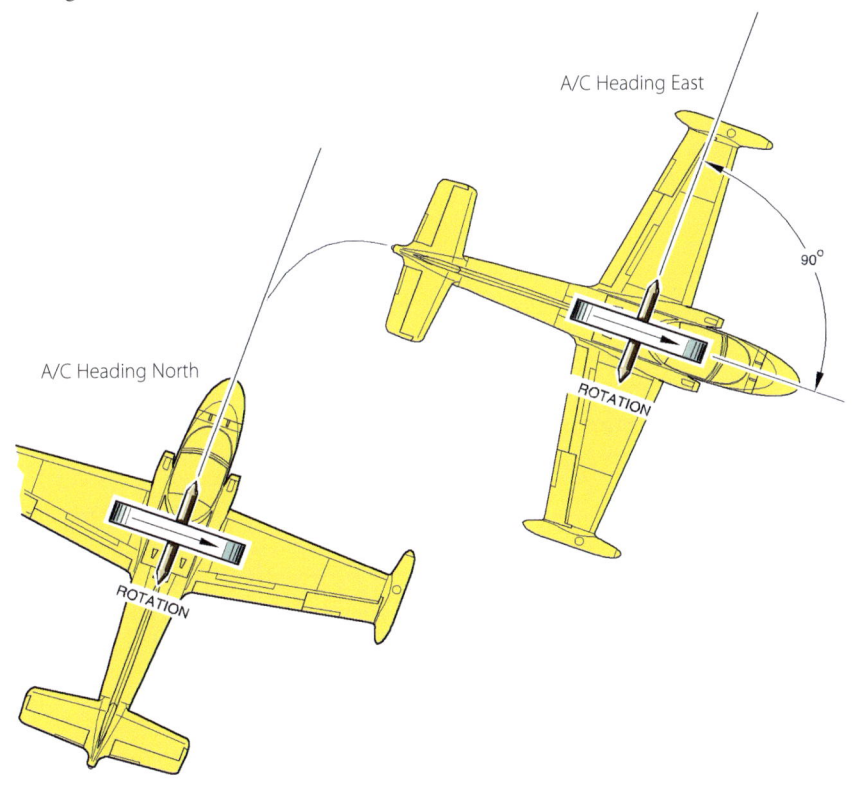

■ *Fig 12.5* ***Gyro Heading Indication***

- *Fig 12.6* **Direction Indicator**

The DI illustrated in figure 12.6 shows a heading of just over 120 degrees. The numbers are at 30 degree intervals and small lines between them are at 5 degree intervals, so the heading indicated is 125 degrees.

Unfortunately, mechanical devices are never perfect. Every gyro will 'wander' slightly, and in fact because the earth is actually spinning even a perfect gyro (which continues to point in the same direction in space) will not remain aligned with the earth which is itself moving. There are devices to reduce the problem, but in general a pilot must re-align his DI with the magnetic compass at regular and frequent intervals to overcome this 'drift' ('real' drift is caused by imperfections such as friction or wear in the gimbals and 'apparent' drift is a result of the earth's rotation). Since the compass also has limitations, this 'synchronising' the DI with the compass must be done in straight unaccelerated flight. The knob on the left of the DI in fig 12.6 usually has to be pushed in and turned to change the indicated heading for synchronisation.

After engine start and before take-off, the pilot should check the suction pressure, synchronise the instrument with the compass (confirming the setting knob is subsequently free to turn), and check that it stays synchronised during taxying turns.

More advanced instruments are available. Some indicators are automatically synchronised with devices which continually detect the earth's magnetic field. Such a 'synchro compass' usually also incorporates indicators from electronic navigation aids such as ADF or VOR (see volume on Navigation) and called a 'horizontal situation indicator' or HSI, as shown in figure 12.7. The green and yellow arrows indicate bearings to selected navigation beacons.

■ *Fig 12.7* **HSI**

12.7 Yaw indication

We mentioned a turn indicator in paragraph 12.4, and that such an instrument required low rigidity. If a gyro is "tied" to the aircraft in such a way that its spin axis is not allowed to maintain its direction, the force generated by the gyro trying do so can be used to provide an indication of how rapidly it is being moved in a particular direction. Figure 12.8 shows a instrument tied such that it indicates the aircraft's rate of yaw.

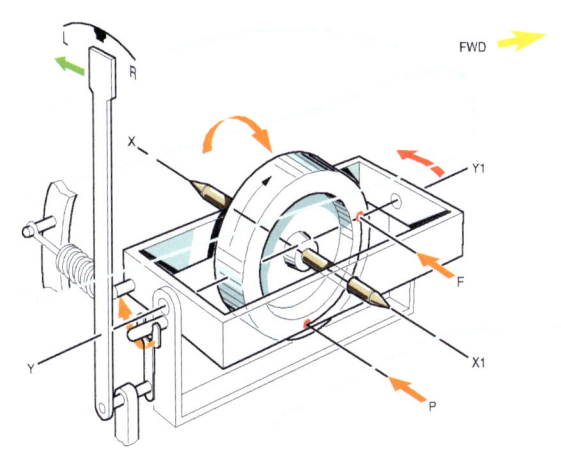

■ *Fig 12.8* **Turn Indication**

The aircraft in fig 12.8 is travelling to the right of the picture. If it yaws to its left, the gyro attempts to stay still in space, but cannot. The force from the yawing movement pushes against the right side of the front of the gyro rotor. Because the gyro is rotating, the force actually tilts the gyro rather than twists it. This 'precession' is countered by a spring, and the rate at which the yaw is taking place can be measured by the pointer moving proportionately to one side. The pointer shown in figure 12.9 is on a 'turn indicator', because every turn is in fact a yaw around the horizon.

■   *Fig 12.9* **Turn and Slip Indicator**

The left turn indicated in fig 12.9 with the pointer against the mark is called 'rate 1' or 'standard rate', because the spring is calibrated against the gyro speed to indicate a standard rate of turn of 180 degrees per minute, or 3 degrees per second. Some (usually ex-military) instruments have marks at 6 and 9 degrees per second also. It may be worth noting that the rate of turn depends on the angle of bank and the true airspeed. At 90 knots, 16 degrees of bank gives a rate 1 turn, while at 120 knots, 19 degrees of bank is required.

Under the pointer is a ball in a tube. This 'slip ball' has inertia and acts like a pendulum, against the total reaction (see chapter 1) acting on the aeroplane. It effectively indicates whether the aircraft is flying directly into the airflow or slightly sideways. Any 'unbalanced' flight will be indicated by the ball being out to one side, as in fig 12.9. The usual causes of such unbalanced flight in a single engined aeroplane are either engine torque or the pilot's foot pushing on a rudder pedal. Pushing against the ball (for example on the left pedal in fig 12.9) should return it towards the centre.

Some older turn and slip indicators may still be found powered by suction, but the vast majority are powered by DC electricity. A failure flag on the face of the instrument indicates a loss of gyro speed, not a power failure. If the gyro speed does reduce, the indicated rate of turn will also reduce even though the actual rate remains the same.

Although the turn and slip indicator is found in many aeroplanes, a more common electrical instrument is a 'turn co-ordinator' as shown in figure 12.10. This instrument (whose warning flag does indicate power failure) has a similar principle, but the pointer is replaced by a little aeroplane seen from the rear. The top of the fin is the turn pointer, but the rate marks are set against the aeroplane's wings. Note that, although the turn co-ordinator may look like an artificial horizon, it does NOT indicate the aircraft's attitude in any plane, although bank may be deduced from the rate of turn and airspeed.

■ *Fig 12.10* **Turn Co-ordinator**

After engine start and before take-off, the pilot should check that the power failure flag is not showing. He should also check during taxying turns that the instrument indicates the correct direction of turn and that the slip ball moves in the opposite direction.

12.8 The "Glass Cockpit"

Electronic flight information systems (EFIS) are generally used in airliners, and are becoming more common in light aircraft, especially those of new design. The information traditionally shown on the faces of individual instruments is displayed to the pilot on one or more liquid crystal display (LCD) screens similar to those available for home or laptop computers. The display itself is powered by the aircraft's electrical system, as is the computer which processes the information, but that information is usually obtained from the same basic sources as the traditional instruments. Figure 12.11 shows a typical electronic primary flight display.

■ *Fig 12.11* **Typical EFIS Primary Display**

Attitude and direction information comes from one or more gyroscopes. Some systems may use so-called 'solid state gyroscopes', which measure rotation rates by comparing the phases of laser light passed in opposite directions around a triangular course. Heading reference at the bottom is provided by magnetic sensors which align the directional gyro with magnetic North, as in a traditional synchro compass or HSI. Airspeed information is shown on the vertical display on the left, and altitude and vertical speed on the right, in the form of vertical strips with the data indicated digitally. These are provided from an air data computer (ADC) which receives pitot and static pressure from the pitot head, together with outside air temperature information with which it can calculate true airspeed. This can be fed to a navigation computer if required for processing with position information to calculate and show the aircraft's future track on a second display, as in figure 12.12.

As in figure 12.11, the AI display typically includes a flight director, which shows the pilot what attitude to select to achieve his intended track and in some cases the desired airspeed or altitude. The director in this particular instrument requires the pilot to align the roll arrows at the top of the display, and keep the yellow aircraft symbol lined up with the two magenta bars alongside it. The desired parameters (listed along the edges of the display) are selected either directly from a computer menu or often by selecting them from the map screen shown in figure 12.12.

■   *Figure 12.12* **Map & Engine Management Display**

The computer receives information from any or all of the aircraft's navigation aids and either displays the position in relation to those navigation aids, or as in figure 12.12 on a map background. The selected aids, and the communications frequencies selected from the 'COM' control knob, are listed along the top. If the computer contains a valid aviation database as provided with many satellite navigation receivers, the display can show controlled and restricted airspace, and also hazards such as obstructions or high ground. The information on the background to the navigation display can be selected by the pilot, and essential information can even be provided audibly.

The side of the screen shown in figure 12.12, provides engine information, in this case for two liquid cooled engines. This engine management screen may be kept out of sight, coming into view to replace the navigation display either when selected or automatically when the computer senses an engine abnormality. Indeed, one of the advantages of an EFIS is the ability to show whatever information the pilot wants at any particular time. However, the disadvantage is its reliance on the computers, and on electrical power. Faults in either can result in a loss of information displayed to the pilot, so although these two screens can control and display all the information a pilot requires, every cockpit has at least a basic set of standby flight (and usually attitude and heading) instruments which rely on more traditional methods of displaying the information.

Intentionally Left Blank

12.9 Exercise

1. If the engine vacuum pump fails, which instruments are normally affected?
   (a) ASI, Altimeter and Vertical speed indicator
   (b) Artificial horizon, Direction Indicator and Turn Co-ordinator
   (c) Attitude Indicator and Direction Indicator only
   (d) Turn and Slip Indicator only

2. When does a magnetic compass indicate most accurately?
   (a) In a turn
   (b) When slowing down
   (c) When accelerating
   (d) In straight, unaccelerated flight

3. A pilot places a metal object on the cockpit coaming. Which instrument is likely to be affected?
   (a) The compass
   (b) The artificial horizon
   (c) The direction indicator
   (d) The VSI

4. The turn co-ordinator has a warning flag. This flag will appear:
   (a) When the generator stops charging the battery
   (b) When the electrical supply drops below 12 volts
   (c) When the suction pump has failed
   (d) When the gyro rotor speed drops to an unsafe level

5. During a climb, the pilot notices the slip ball is deflected to the right. What should he do about it?
   (a) Nothing
   (b) Reduce power
   (c) Check the wings are level then push on the right rudder pedal
   (d) Check the wings are level then push on the left rudder pedal

6. How often should a pilot check the synchronisation between the compass and the Direction Indicator?
   (a) After every turn
   (b) Every ten minutes in the cruise
   (c) Before take-off
   (d) All of the above

7. A suction powered artificial horizon has a knob below it. What is its usual function?

(a) To erect the gyro after starting the engine
(b) To erect the gyro after exceeding the toppling limits
(c) Both (a) and (b)
(d) Neither (a) nor (b)

8. How does a pilot normally know that the power supply to his Direction Indicator has failed?

(a) A warning flag appears on the instrument
(b) The suction gauge has a low indication
(c) The instrument face rotates rapidly
(d) He has no way of knowing

9. The aircraft is heading 180 degrees. How long will it take to turn left onto North at the standard rate?

(a) 20 seconds
(b) 30 seconds
(c) 1 minute
(d) 2 minutes

10. If the vacuum pump fails:

(a) An adequate but unfiltered supply would power the gyro instruments from the vacuum relief valve
(b) The suction gauge would read zero
(c) An adequate but unfiltered supply would power the gyro instruments from the pitot head
(d) Residual pressure would power the instruments for a few minutes

11. If the gyroscope rpm of a turn indicator is 10% lower than it is designed for, the rate of turn indicated:

(a) Will be in the correct direction but greater than the aircraft's actual rate of turn
(b) Will be in the correct direction but less than the aircraft's actual rate of turn
(c) Will be zero
(d) Will be in the opposite direction but the same as the aircraft's actual rate of turn

12. Magnetic or metal materials placed near a magnetic compass:

(a) Will cause the indicated heading to reverse by 180°
(b) May introduce unpredictable errors in the heading indicated
(c) Will create no problem provided the DI is serviceable
(d) Will create no problem provided they are stowed securely

13. A turn and slip indicator has a warning flag. This flag will appear:
   (a) When the generator stops charging the battery
   (b) When the electrical supply drops below 12 volts
   (c) When the suction pump has failed
   (d) When the gyro rotor speed drops to an unsafe level

14. A suction powered artificial horizon has a knob below it. What is its usual function?
   (a) To erect the gyro after starting the engine
   (b) To erect the gyro after exceeding the toppling limits
   (c) To adjust the angle of bank of the aircraft symbol
   (d) To adjust the vertical position of the aircraft symbol

15. A typical electronic flight display:
   (a) Can direct the pilot to follow a desired track but relies on the aircraft's electrical system to operate
   (b) Relies on the aircraft's electrical system to operate but requires manual alignment before take-off
   (c) Contains its own electrical power supply but requires manual alignment before take-off
   (d) Can direct the pilot to any chosen waypoint and contains its own electrical power supply

16. Refer to figure 12.11. What is the aircraft's indicated altitude, and the pilot's selected altitude?
   (a) Indicated 2992 feet with 2700 feet selected
   (b) Indicated 3010 feet with 2700 feet selected
   (c) Indicated 2992 feet with 3010 feet selected
   (d) Indicated 3010 feet with 2992 feet selected

17. Refer to figure 12.11. What is the aircraft's attitude and indicated airspeed?
   (a) Nose down in a 5° left bank at 170 knots
   (b) Nose down in a 15° right bank at 100 knots
   (c) Nose down in a 15° left bank at 170 knots
   (d) Nose down in a 5° right bank at 170 knots

Intentionally Left Blank

CHAPTER 13

Other Equipment & Flight Safety

13.1 Introduction

In addition to the instruments and systems already described, most aeroplanes carry other items which do not fit into the previous chapters. Some of these have to be fitted to training aircraft for safety reasons, and others are fitted for convenience. It is neither possible nor desired to describe all of these convenience items, but a few have been included here along with the safety requirements.

13.2 Seats and Harnesses

It may seem obvious, but all passengers must have a seat provided for them, and aircraft are certificated as having that many seats (as described in the Flight Manual). Seats provided for the pilot and any other crew member who has access to the controls often move (at least fore and aft) to allow full control movement from a comfortable position from pilots of differing body sizes. The mountings of these seats are vital parts of the structure - imagine the problem if the pilot's seat slides backwards as the aeroplane rotates for take-off! Seats for passengers behind the front row are usually fixed in position, although the seat backs may fold (as probably the front seats will do also).

All seats must have at least a lap strap, in good condition and securely attached to the structure, and unless specifically permitted, the pilot's seat and other seats in the front row must also have at least a shoulder strap in addition (as must every passenger seat in modern aircraft). An alternative to the lap and shoulder straps is a full shoulder harness, which is required in any case if the aircraft is carrying out aerobatics. Lap and shoulder straps fasten at the side of the person, in a similar fashion to the passenger seats of commercial airliners as illustrated in figure 13.1.

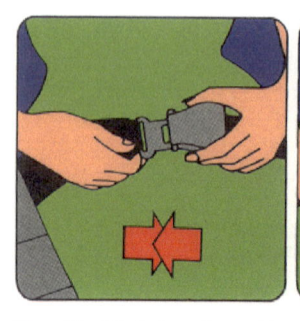

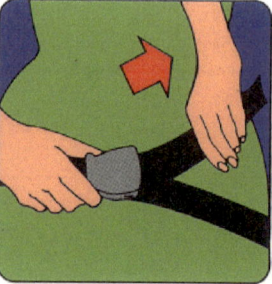

■ *Fig 13.1* **Lap Strap Fastening**

Shoulder harnesses have 4 or 5 straps fitted to a box positioned in the centre of the body. In order to fit those straps, the box is rotated slightly in one direction and the straps inserted until they click. To release a shoulder harness, the front part of the box is rotated through 90° and the straps fall out. It is sometimes possible for the shoulder straps to be released by a separate lever without releasing the lap straps.

Children under the age of 2 may be carried in addition to the normal passengers, but must be restrained by special straps attached to an adult's straps. It is recommended that children over the age of 2 be secured in a car-type safety seat attached to a normal passenger seat.

In the event of a forced landing on land or water, if a shoulder strap or harness is not provided, the 'brace' position as briefed in airliners should be adopted by all passengers. Variations of this are illustrated in figure 13.2.

■ *Fig 13.2* **Brace Positions**

13.3 Fire Extinguishers

Everywhere aviation fuel is stored must have fire extinguishing facilities in case a spark ignites the fuel vapours. The fire-fighting equipment, dispensing foam or powder (but not water which conducts electricity and can spread oil fuelled fires) is often used as a general aerodrome fire-fighting facility. Every licensed aerodrome must keep a trained mobile rescue and fire-fighting team at readiness in case of emergency during its operating hours.

Although fire extinguishers are generally red, they carry additional colours to indicate their contents. Dry powder is pale blue, carbon dioxide black, and foam cream. Halon is green. Foam can provide a smothering blanket over a fuel fire, and carbon dioxide can displace a fire's vital oxygen supply in an enclosed space such as an engine cowling. Powder is a useful and safe general 'extinguishant', which can be used on brake fires for example.

A fire in an aircraft in flight could have serious consequences for the occupants. It is not possible to stop, get out, and run away. For that reason, although fire seldom occurs, every aircraft with a Certificate of Airworthiness has to carry an extinguisher accessible to the pilot and passengers. Its primary purpose is to counter any fire which starts inside the cockpit, and for that reason it contains an extinguishant which is effective against most types of fire but will not cause further damage if it comes into contact with electricity. Although certain gases are extremely effective extinguishants, some of the best, including the common Halon, can be poisonous when heated. For that reason, not only should as much electrical equipment as possible be switched off before using a fire extinguisher (with the aim of isolating any source of further ignition), but the cockpit must be immediately ventilated after it is used.

Cockpit extinguishers normally have a gauge fitted which is visible during pre-flight checks. A safe level of extinguishant will often be indicated by a green arc, but the extinguishers should be thoroughly inspected during routine maintenance.

13.4 First Aid

As with fire extinguishers, every aircraft with a Certificate of Airworthiness must carry a first aid kit. The kit should be easily accessible in the event of a forced landing, and its contents should include large bandages and adhesive plaster, gauze and cotton wool, burn dressings, safety pins, tourniquets, scissors, antiseptic, analgesic and stimulant drugs and a handbook on first aid.

13.5 Oxygen

If an aircraft flies above 13000 feet pressure altitude (FL130) it must carry sufficient supplies of oxygen with apparatus for its use. The apparatus may be either fixed or portable, but it must be of an approved type, and the crew must use it, as they must if remaining above FL100 for more than 30 minutes. Knowledge of oxygen systems is not a PPL requirement, but included here for possible future reference.

Emergency oxygen is supplied to passengers in airliners with pressurised cabins by chemical reactions in individual devices above their seats. However, in most systems required for regular use, and many crew systems including portable ones, oxygen gas is kept in cylinders (bottles), at a pressure of about 1800 psi. The cylinders are strengthened to prevent them from breaking or exploding because of the high pressure. Figure 13.3 shows a typical regular use oxygen gas storage and supply system, using two bottles.

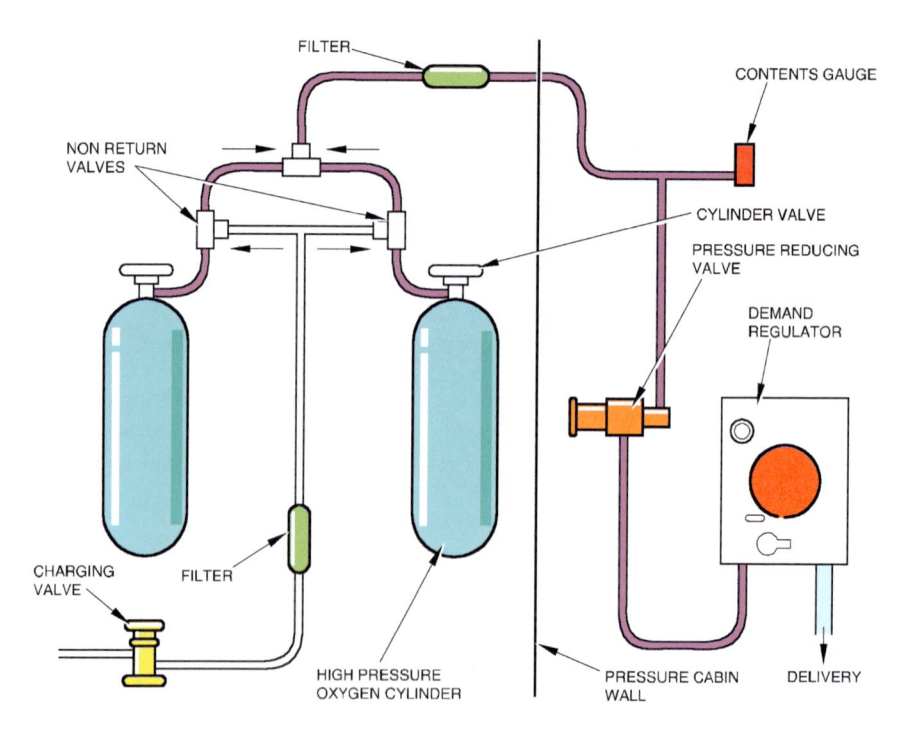

■ *Fig 13.3* **Gas Oxygen System**

Oxygen is delivered to a crew member through a regulator, hoses, and a mask. The regulator reduces the gas pressure from 1800 psi (although as in figure 13.3 the pressure may have been reduced a certain amount beforehand) to that of the cabin. The regulator may also draw in air from the cabin when only a small amount of extra oxygen is needed. At sea level a little extra oxygen is mixed with cabin air. As altitude increases, the mixture includes more oxygen and less air, until at about 30,000 ft the gas being delivered is 100% oxygen.

In the cockpit there is usually a "flow indicator" to show when oxygen is flowing through the regulator and a pressure gauge to indicate system pressure (proportional to the amount of oxygen remaining in the storage tanks). Because of the danger of hypoxia, if any problem arises in an oxygen system the pilot should immediately descent to below 10,000 feet.

13.6 Carbon Monoxide Detection

As mentioned in chapter 9, carbon monoxide (CO), one of the results of combustion, is extremely hazardous. It may enter the cockpit as the result of a leak from the exhaust system of either the engine or of a separate heater, such as is often fitted to multi-engined aircraft.

Few aircraft are fitted with detectors for CO. However, there are various devices commercially available which can be carried in the cockpit. Some are simple cardboard indicators which turn dark when CO is detected, but these have a short life and are easily contaminated by other fumes. Electronic devices are also available, and these can display the level of CO in the surrounding air any any times, and set off an alarm if a present concentration of CO is reached.

If a device indicates the presence of a dangerous level of CO, as stated in chapter 9 a pilot should immediately find a way of breathing fresh air. He should ventilate the cockpit and land as soon as practicable.

13.7 Ground Handling Equipment

An aircraft tow-bar is often supplied. It may fit over the nose wheel or tailwheel axle, but in any case should be a snug fit and easy to fit and remove. As mentioned in chapter 11, there may be a limit to the angle which the nosewheel is allowed to turn. Remembering that an airframe is designed to be strong when subjected to airflow stresses and as light as possible, the trailing edges of aerofoils should be avoided when ground handling. Consult the Flight Manual.

13.8 Covers and Plugs

To prevent insects making homes inside pitot tubes, a cover for the pitot head should be fitted after flight and removed before the next flight. Plugs for the static vents may also be available, and some aircraft may have covers for air intakes to prevent birds or small mammals finding their way inside. None of these plugs or covers should remain in place during flight, and large red streamers are useful reminders to the pilot to remove them.

13.9 Ditching Precautions

Commanders must ensure that appropriate survival equipment is carried on every flight. For flights over water out of gliding range from land, inflatable life preservers (lifejackets) must be carried and easily accessible to the occupants, indeed the CAA strongly recommends all occupants of single engined aircraft to wear suitable ones. The inflation gas is compressed carbon dioxide, carried in a bottle on the jacket. These life preservers must be inspected regularly.

Liferafts (dinghies), again inflated by compressed carbon dioxide, with sufficient capacity for all the aircraft occupants are also advised when flying over water especially if more than 100 nm from shore. These should be readily available and attached to the aircraft structure in such a way that they can be easily released once inflated. Neither dinghies nor life preservers should ever be inflated inside the cabin, which means that marine lifejackets or liferafts with automatic inflation systems must not be used in aircraft.

Part-NCO requires aeroplanes to carry Emergency Location Transmitters (ELTs). Some older ELTs found in foreign registered aircraft have been found to be unreliable and are not permitted in Europe. However, the modern generation of ELTs transmit their individual identification codes on dual frequencies (406 MHz for satellite location and 121.5 MHz for homing), and can be checked easily for false alarms. As an alternative, aeroplanes with 6 seats or fewer need only carry either an aircraft or a Personal Locator Beacon (PLB) which can transmit on both frequencies.

Ditching procedures and further advice on the subject can be found in the CAA's Safety Sense leaflet 21 "Ditching" (see below).

13.10   Other Safety Advice

The CAA publishes SafetySense leaflets on the CAA web site **www.caa.co.uk**, together with other publications. The first of these Safety Sense leaflets covers general airmanship, and others cover many of the situations in which light aircraft pilots may find themselves, such as flight into farm strips, and should be consulted as appropriate.

Aeronautical information circulars (AICs) published on pink paper cover safety-related information. These are published by the CAA in conjunction with the UK AIP and may be accessed through the AIS web site **www.ais.org.uk**.

Other sources of aviation safety material include the UK General Aviation Safety Council (GASCo), and EASA's GA Safety Promotion section which also publishes the European GA Safety Team (EGAST)'s leaflets.

Intentionally Left Blank

13.11 Exercise

1. What colour on a fire extinguisher indicates that it contains dry powder?
   - (a) Red
   - (b) Blue
   - (c) Cream
   - (d) Black

2. Before using a Halon fire extinguisher in the cockpit, which of these precautions should be taken?
   - (a) The cockpit windows must be opened before the extinguisher is used
   - (b) All electrical services should be switched off
   - (c) The pilot should engage the autopilot
   - (d) The engine should be shut down

3. If an aircraft has to ditch, when should life preservers be inflated?
   - (a) During the descent
   - (b) As soon as the aircraft touches the water
   - (c) As soon as the aircraft comes to rest in the water
   - (d) After the occupants have left the cabin

4. Under Part-NCO, when must an aircraft carry an Emergency Locator Transmitter, and on which frequency(ies) must it be capable of transmitting?
   - (a) At all times, on 121.5 and 406 MHz
   - (b) When over water more than 10 minutes flying time from the shore, on 121.5 MHz only
   - (c) When over water out of gliding range of the shore, on 406 MHz only
   - (d) When over water out of gliding range of the shore for more than 10 minutes, on 121.5 and 406 MHz

5. How can a pilot normally check a cockpit fire extinguisher for serviceability?
   - (a) By noting the reading on the extinguisher gauge
   - (b) By feeling the extinguisher's weight
   - (c) By pressing the operating handle and feeling the diaphragm is intact
   - (d) He cannot check it

6. A Halon fire extinguisher:
   - (a) Gives off highly toxic fumes and should never be used in an enclosed cockpit
   - (b) Is quite safe to use in an enclosed cockpit at any time
   - (c) Is quite safe to use in an enclosed cockpit if the cockpit is subsequently ventilated
   - (d) Is only suitable for wood or fabric fires and is therefore no use in a cockpit

7. What gas is used to inflate life preservers and liferafts?
   (a) Oxygen
   (b) Carbon Monoxide
   (c) Carbon Dioxide
   (d) Nitrogen

8. UK aeronautical information circulars giving safety information are published on what colour paper?
   (a) Green
   (b) Pink
   (c) Mauve
   (d) White

9. If carbon monoxide detector indicates that CO has entered the cockpit, what should the pilot do?
   (a) Turn the heating system off, ventilate the cabin, land as soon as possible
   (b) Shut down the engine immediately and land in the most suitable area
   (c) Apply full power and land at the nearest aerodrome as soon as possible
   (d) Close all cockpit ventilating inlets to prevent fumes entering the cockpit, land as soon as practicable

10. When must an aircraft carry a serviceable oxygen system?
   (a) At all times when flying more than 13,000 feet above ground
   (b) At all times when flying more than 10,000 feet above sea level
   (c) At all times when flying more than 13,000 feet pressure altitude
   (d) At all times when flying more than 10,000 feet pressure altitude

11. When must a pilot use supplementary oxygen in flight?
   (a) When flying for more than 30 minutes at more than 10,000 feet pressure altitude
   (b) At all times when flying more than 13,000 feet above ground
   (c) At all times when flying more than 10,000 feet pressure altitude
   (d) When flying for more than 30 minutes at more than 13,000 feet pressure altitude

12. If a pilot wishes to find advice on flying into and out of grass strips, where could he find it?
   (a) On the NATS web site
   (b) In the aircraft log book
   (c) In a CAA Safety Sense leaflet
   (d) On the back of a CAA 1:500,000 chart

13. Pilots and passengers must have safety belts available at all times. What is the normal minimum restraint which must be available for pilots and front seat passengers?
   (a) A lap strap
   (b) A shoulder strap
   (c) A lap strap and a shoulder strap
   (d) A full 4-point harness

Intentionally Left Blank

Chapter 14

Airworthiness

14.1 Introduction

A car must be roadworthy to be allowed on public roads, and an aircraft must be airworthy to be allowed to fly in UK airspace. It must not only be designed and built to be safe, but it must be maintained to stay that way. The aircraft's owner is responsible for its overall airworthiness, but the pilot must always satisfy himself to the best of his ability that the aircraft he intends to fly is fit for the purpose.

UK law differentiates between aircraft designed and built to what were European regulations and those which were never subject to those regulations. Details such as regulation and publication numbers are not required for PPL studies, but are included here for reference.

14.2 Design

For an aircraft to be allowed to fly, it must be designed and built to a recognised standard. The modern European design standards are laid down in EU regulations which have been transferred directly to UK law, and applicable aircraft may be referred to as 'Part-21' aircraft. UK designed aircraft must comply with British Civil Aircraft Requirements (BCARs).

After the first aircraft have been built and a test programme completed satisfactorily, the design organisation is given a Type Certificate (TC). The Type Certificate Data Sheet lists the conditions and limitations under which the aircraft may be operated. It also describes the equipment which must be fitted, and any permitted optional changes to that equipment (such as alternative propellers). The Type Certificate Holder (who in the case of older aircraft may have inherited it from the design organisation) is then responsible for issuing 'Service Bulletins' to ensure the type continues to be safe for flight, and must also sponsor any modifications, which must be in accordance with the design standard.

Any changes to the TC Data Sheet will be included in either a required official modification or a "Supplementary Type Certificate (STC)", proposed by the Type Certificate Holder, although EASA or the State of Design (or the State within Europe which has been given oversight of particular foreign designed aircraft) may impose mandatory "Airworthiness Directives (ADs)", as can the UK CAA. Suggestions for modifications may be proposed by any approved maintenance organisation, but they cannot be used unless they are contained in a STC issued by the Type Certificate Holder.

14.3 Additional Equipment

In addition to the equipment required by the Design Standard and the TC, PART-OPS (NCO, NCC, or SPO as appropriate) of the transferred European regulations contains regulations which apply to aircraft used for specific purposes. Schedule 5 to the ANO lists the necessary radio equipment, and Schedule 4 the other equipment, which must be carried and serviceable by UK aircraft which are not 'Part-21'. Specific 'Directions' from Parliament, listed in what is called the 'Official Record Series 4' may add to these requirements.

For a private aeroplane flight, the ANO (or a 'Direction') requires the following equipment to be carried. Helicopters have slightly different rules.

- *Spares for all electrical fuses which can be replaced in flight (minimum 3 of each rating)*
- *Maps, charts and other documents and navigation equipment for the route and possible diversion*
- *Safety belts for every seat in use, with shoulder harnesses except for rear seats of old aircraft*
- *A cockpit fire extinguisher*
- *A first aid kit*

For night flight, the following must also be carried:
- *Aircraft navigation lights as described in chapter 4 of the Aviation Law volume*
- *A landing light*
- *Lighting for reading the instruments and safety, and for the passenger compartment*
- *Torches for all crew members*
- *Signalling light if no radio is fitted*
- *A sensitive altimeter adjustable for pressure datums*
- *A Turn & slip indicator or gyroscopic attitude and direction indicators*

For aerobatics:
- *A safety harness for every seat, whether in use or not*

For flight under IFR outside controlled airspace:
- *A radio to allow communication with appropriate Air Traffic Control Units*
- *A sensitive altimeter adjustable for pressure datums*
- *A Turn & slip indicator or gyroscopic attitude and direction indicators*

14.4   The Certificate of Airworthiness

If an aircraft has been built by an approved manufacturing organisation, it will be inspected to ensure it has been built to the required standard in accordance with the relevant Type Certificate. It can then be issued with a Certificate of Airworthiness (C of A) by the State of Registry (in the UK, the CAA) which is valid for as long as the aircraft is registered in the State which has issued it. Nevertheless, the C of A becomes invalid if the aircraft is repaired or modified in other than the approved manner, and that includes any failure to carry out the required maintenance inspections.

The C of A will state the purpose for which the aircraft has been designed, such as 'normal', 'utility' or 'aerobatic', as described on the TC. An aircraft with a C of A may be flown in any ICAO State, unless specific restrictions are placed on the Certificate, and used for any purpose for which it was designed provided it is adequately equipped and complies with any requirements relating to the intended operation.

It may be necessary for an aircraft to fly without a valid C of A, in which case it needs a "Permit to Fly", which contains a description of exactly what the aircraft may do and for how long it will remain valid. EASA may authorise the issue of such a Permit if for example the aircraft is damaged, or its scheduled maintenance is delayed and it needs to fly to its approved maintenance organisation. An aircraft of a type which has no nominated Type Certificate Holder also requires a Permit to Fly. A Permit to Fly does not automatically allow operations outside the boundaries of the State issuing it.

14.5   Maintenance

Repairs and routine servicing both come under the heading of maintenance. The CAA has issued CAP 520 to provide guidance to aircraft owners, although Part-M (for maintenance) of the transferred EC EU regulations is the definitive document. To maintain the validity of the C of A, all the inspections and routine servicing laid down in the aircraft's maintenance schedule, as well as any others required by the manufacturer, must be carried out at the required intervals. The maintenance schedule must be approved by the CAA.

Maintenance inspections must be carried out within specific periods, described both as a certain number of flying hours and a calendar period since the previous inspection. Neither the hours nor the calendar period may be exceeded without the appropriate inspection being carried out. Individual components may also have specific periods after which they must be inspected or replaced, and these must also be adhered to. The 'Daily Check', sometimes called the 'Check A' must be carried out before the first flight each day, and is valid for the rest of that day.

Routine refuelling and oil replenishment may be carried out by a licensed crew member, as can tyre inflation and the Check A. Any other work on an aircraft must normally be carried out by an authorised organisation and supervised by a person licensed under Part 66 of the transferred regulation. Major work such as maintenance on large commercial aircraft must be carried out at organisations holding an authorisation under Part 145, but most work on aeroplanes with a maximum take-off mass authorised (MTMA) below 5700 kg may be carried out at smaller organisations, authorised under Part-M subpart F. These may even be individual licensed engineers, but they must hold the appropriate authorisations for the work.

Provided the aircraft has a MTMA (maximum take-off mass) below 2730 kg and is only used for private purposes, the owner if he also holds a pilot's licence may carry out certain work himself. An Annex to Part-M lists the repairs which may be carried out by a pilot owner of an aircraft used purely for private purposes. These are limited to those which do not affect the aircraft's primary structure or controls; for example, replacing tyres, spark plugs, or removable parts such as cowlings or wheel spats. In addition, he may also carry out the routine maintenance inspection required at 50 hour (or 6 monthly) intervals. These permitted tasks are also listed in the UK's Air Navigation (General) Regulations.

Aircraft, engines and variable pitch propellers all have their own separate log books in which hours operated are recorded and any work carried out must be signed for (and dated) by whoever has carried it out. Work which cannot be carried out by the pilot owner must be inspected and given a 'Certificate of Release to Service' by a licensed engineer. Any repairs or disturbance to flight or engine controls must be not only certified by a licensed engineer, but must have a duplicate inspection carried out and certified by another licensed engineer. However, a licensed pilot may carry out and certify the duplicate inspection in the case of minor disturbance when the aircraft is away from the maintenance organisation.

14.6 Continued Airworthiness

From time to time, the Type Certificate Holder may issue Service Bulletins containing mandatory modifications or inspections. The CAA or the State of Design may also impose mandatory "Airworthiness Directives (ADs)". These usually require work to be carried out in the form of modifications to or inspections of certain parts of the aircraft, and the timescale within which the work must be completed (and recorded in the relevant log book) will be included in the AD. "Emergency ADs" require quick action, possibly before the next flight. Copies of new ADs applicable to UK registered aircraft are sent to registered owners, and are then listed with previously issued ones in CAP 747. However the definitive lists are available on the web sites of each State of Design's Airworthiness Authorities.

Other information which does not affect the validity of the C of A may be issued in the form of "Letters to Owners/Operators (LTOs)" by the CAA from time to time.

The owner is responsible for the airworthiness of his aircraft, and therefore for complying with any ADs or mandatory modifications. He must also ensure that all routine servicing tasks are carried out at the correct intervals, including any tasks involving individual items (batteries for example) at times different to that of the rest of the aircraft. However, the regulation appreciates that he is unlikely to have the expertise to manage his airworthiness without serious help. Part-M suggests that the continued airworthiness of a Part-21 aircraft should be managed by an organisation with the expertise to continually review airworthiness directives and advise the owner of their applicability, as well as that of any "out-of-phase" maintenance work required on individual items. Organisations may be authorised (under subpart G) to manage continued airworthiness for owners.

No matter how much maintenance work has been carried out during the year, the aircraft must be issued with an 'Airworthiness Review Certificate (ARC)' every 12 months to maintain the validity of a C of A. An organisation authorised under Part-M subpart I must satisfy itself that the aircraft continues to be airworthy before such a certificate can be issued. This will normally involve a full review of all the aircraft's records to check that all necessary maintenance has been carried out.

If the owner has entered into a contract with a maintenance organisation authorised under subpart F to maintain his aircraft, and has his airworthiness managed by a subpart G organisation, this is considered a 'controlled environment'. If the subpart I organisation is satisfied that the aircraft has been maintained in a controlled environment, it may issue the ARC itself without carrying out a full review. However, if the aircraft has not been maintained in such a controlled environment, the full airworthiness review is required, and the subpart I organisation can only recommend that an ARC should be issued after that has been completed.

The CAA itself will then issue the ARC. In any case, a full review is required at least every 3 years.

14.7 The Flight Manual

Handbooks for aircraft are sometimes referred to as the 'pilot's operating handbook' or similar, but the official Flight Manual is produced by the manufacturer and approved by the State of Design with the Type Certificate. The CAA, or in some cases the State of Registry, may require changes or additions to the Flight Manual to comply with their own regulations. These are published in the form of "supplements" and are often related to the published performance figures. Pilots must ensure that they use the appropriate supplement figures where these differ from those in the original document.

The Flight Manual, and any handbooks which contain extracts from it, are traditionally divided into standard sections.

Section 1 is usually General Information
Section 2 contains the Aircraft Limitations, which are repeated on cockpit placards
Section 3 contains Emergency Procedures
Section 4 describes Normal Operating Procedures
Section 5 gives Performance Data
Section 6 gives Weight and Balance Information
and Section 7 includes description of the Aircraft Systems

14.8 Noise Certificate

UK registered aircraft must possess a valid noise certificate, issued with the C of A. If such a certificate contains specific requirements, these must be complied with. The UK noise requirements for the issue of such a certificate are laid down in the Air Navigation (Noise Certification) Order 1990.

14.9 Insurance

Although not actually part of formal aviation regulation, all aircraft operated within European airspace must have third party and passenger liability insurance, including war and terrorism risks. The level of cover required depends on the MTMA, and the operator must be able to produce evidence of cover in an appropriate certificate when asked.

14.10 Documentation for International Flight

As described in the volume on aviation law, certain documents must be carried by all aircraft, including private flights, when flying internationally. These are:

- *The crew's licences*
- *The Certificate of Airworthiness*
- *The Certificate of Registration*
- *The licence for the aircraft radio*
- *The insurance certificate covering passenger and third party risks*
- *A copy of the international rules for intercepting and intercepted aircraft*

In addition, it is often advisable to carry the noise certificate.

14.11 Non-Part-21 Aircraft

The design, maintenance and continued airworthiness requirements for a Non-Part-21 UK registered aircraft with a C of A are covered by national regulations. In addition to the design standards mentioned in paragraph 13.2, BCARs also contain the UK standards for maintenance and continued airworthiness of these aircraft.

Apart from the maintenance which can be carried out by pilot owners, these aircraft must be repaired by licensed engineers, or by technicians in organisations with 'M3' authorisation from the CAA whose work is supervised by these licensed engineers. To maintain the validity of a UK C of A, a licensed engineer must issue a 'Certificate of Maintenance Review' at each scheduled inspection.

14.12 Uncertificated Aircraft

Aircraft without a type certificate may be issued with a 'Permit to Fly' by EASA or a national authority. In the UK, the CAA issues Permits to Fly to home-built aircraft and to certain ex-military aircraft, and delegates to the British Microlight Aircraft Association the responsibility of issuing Permits to those aeroplanes below 400 kg MTMA (450 kg for two-seaters and 600 kg for certain factory-build aircraft). CAP 733 gives guidance regarding the requirements for the issue of a Permit to Fly, and CAP 632 specifically concerns ex-military aircraft.

The Permit lays down the conditions under which the aircraft may be operated. For example, a UK Permit will normally restrict it to flight in sight of the surface and clear of congested areas. In the case of ex-military aircraft, the maintenance requirements are similar to a certificated aircraft, but for home-built and microlight aeroplanes they are much less strict, allowing owners to carry out much of the necessary maintenance. However, the basic principles remain the same. For example, duplicate inspections are required after controls have been disturbed, and inspections from authorised inspectors are required after repair and at routine intervals.

Instead of Airworthiness Directives, the CAA issues Mandatory Permit Directives (MPDs) for Permit to Fly aircraft which fulfil the same purpose, and these are contained in CAP 661. It is unlikely that examination questions will require knowledge of specific CAP numbers, but they have been given here for reference, and all CAPs are available on the CAA's web site.

14.13 Aircraft General Exercise

1. A Certificate of Airworthiness of an aircraft used for private purposes is not valid:
   (a) If the pilot pumps up the tyres
   (b) If the owner changes the wheel
   (c) If the aircraft is repaired or modified except in the approved manner
   (d) In all the above cases

2. All light aircraft used for private purposes must carry certain items at all times. Which are these?
   (a) Spare fuses, life jackets for all occupants and charts for the route
   (b) Navigation lights, charts for the route and safety belts for all occupants
   (c) Charts for the route, spare fuses and safety belts for all occupants
   (d) Navigation lights, charts for the route, safety belts and lifejackets for all occupants

3. In addition to the items at question 2, which of the following must be carried by a UK registered light aircraft on an international private flight?
   (a) The Certificate of Airworthiness and Certificate of Registration only
   (b) The C of A, Certificate of Registration and the crew's licences
   (c) The C of A, Certificate of Registration, crew's licences and radio licence
   (d) The C of A, Certificate of Registration, crew's & radio licences and interception procedures.

4. Where would a pilot find the flight limitations which apply to his aircraft?
   (a) In the Maintenance Schedule only
   (b) In the Flight Manual only
   (c) In the Maintenance Schedule and the technical log
   (d) In the Flight Manual and on cockpit placards

5. Who may carry out a Daily Check and for how long is it valid?
   (a) Any flying club member, and it is valid for 24 hours
   (b) Only a licensed engineer, and it is valid until midnight of the day it is carried out
   (c) Any pilot with a valid licence for the type, and it is valid until midnight of the day it is carried out
   (d) Only a licensed engineer, and it is valid for 24 hours

6. If the flight controls of a private light aeroplane are disturbed for minor maintenance away from base, who may carry out the required duplicate inspection?
   (a) Only the owner
   (b) Only a licensed engineer
   (c) A licensed engineer or the aircraft commander only
   (d) A licensed engineer or any pilot with a licence valid for the type

7. A non-Part-21 UK registered aircraft may be used for any purpose in UK airspace provided it is appropriately equipped and complies with any requirements relating to the intended operation and possesses:

   (a) a UK Permit to Fly
   (b) a valid UK "standard category" C of A
   (c) an EASA C of A
   (d) any of the above

8. An aircraft with a UK Permit to Fly may fly without specific authorisation from the state over which the pilot intends to fly:

   (a) Only over UK airspace
   (b) Only over European Union airspace
   (c) Only over airspace of states signatory to the CAA
   (d) Over any ICAO contracting state

9. A Daily Check for an aircraft with a C of A was signed at 1200 hours. A pilot wishes to take off on a private flight at 0800 the following day for an estimated 4 hour flight. Which of the following is correct?

   (a) The Daily Check must be carried out again before any intended flight at 0800
   (b) The Daily Check is valid for the whole of the intended flight, even if the aircraft lands after 1200
   (c) The aircraft must land before 1200 unless the Daily Check has been carried out again
   (d) The Daily Check is not a requirement for a private flight

10. What does a Certificate of Release to Service certify?

   (a) All required maintenance work has been completed, and when the next routine maintenance is due.
   (b) The aircraft meets the design standard approved by the Competent Authority
   (c) The aircraft was serviceable at the end of the flight and no maintenance is due within 24 hours
   (d) The aircraft may only be flown by a qualified test pilot in order to obtain a C of A

11. A certificated aircraft may be modified as the owner desires:

   (a) Only if a Supplementary Type Certificate has been issued by the Type Certificate Holder
   (b) Only if the modification does not affect the flight controls
   (c) Only if the modification has previously been approved by a licensed engineer
   (d) At any time

12. What does a camshaft do in an aircraft's piston engine?

   (a) It controls the opening and closing of the inlet and exhaust valves
   (b) It ensures that the engine and propeller rotate at the same speed
   (c) It controls the timing of the spark from the spark plugs
   (d) It controls the fuel/air mixture in the inlet manifold

13. What is the purpose of the control stops fitted to the control cables?
   (a) To prevent damage to the controls in strong winds
   (b) To limit control column movement
   (c) To prevent excessive control surface movement
   (d) To prevent the control surfaces moving on the ground

14. A fixed pitch propeller blade is twisted. Which of the following statements is true?
   (a) The pitch at the tip is coarser than the pitch at the root
   (b) The helix angle of the tip is greater than the helix angle of the root
   (c) The angle of attack always remains relatively constant along the blade
   (d) None of the above are true

15. If an aeroplane accelerates while maintaining a constant altitude, what would happen to the dynamic and static forces affecting the airspeed indicator?
   (a) Dynamic pressure will stay the same, static pressure will reduce
   (b) Dynamic pressure will stay the same, static pressure will increase
   (c) Dynamic pressure will increase, static pressure will reduce
   (d) Dynamic pressure will increase, static pressure will remain the same

16. The wiring to a magneto switch is broken. Which of the following is likely?
   (a) The engine will start if the propeller is moved on the ground
   (b) The engine will not start when the starter switch is selected ON
   (c) The engine will run roughly in flight
   (d) The engine will continue to run but the ammeter will indicate a discharge

17. For how long is an Airworthiness Review Certificate valid?
   (a) Until the next scheduled maintenance is due
   (b) 12 months
   (c) 3 years
   (d) Until it is revoked

18. The landing light has failed. The pilot notices that the relevant circuit breaker has popped out. How many times should he attempt to reset the circuit breaker?
   (a) He should not reset the circuit breaker
   (b) He should make no more than two attempts to reset the circuit breaker
   (c) He should make as many attempts as necessary
   (d) Resetting the circuit breaker will have no effect on the light

19. For how long is a Certificate of Airworthiness valid?
   (a) Until the next scheduled maintenance is due
   (b) 12 months
   (c) 3 years
   (d) Until it is revoked

20. If the generator or alternator fails during flight in a piston engine aircraft:
   (a) You should switch off both master switches and continue without electrical power
   (b) You should reduce electrical loads and land as soon as practicable
   (c) You can continue as planned because the battery will supply all electrical loads
   (d) The engine will stop when the battery power reduces below its rating

21. Where will a pilot find the correct method of operating his aircraft in conditions which he has not experienced before?
   (a) In the Certificate of Airworthiness
   (b) In the aircraft Technical Log
   (c) In the aircraft log books
   (d) In the manufacturer's POH or AFM

22. In an aircraft with a fixed pitch propeller, if the airspeed is increased without moving the throttle control, what indications should the pilot expect?
   (a) The oil pressure will increase
   (b) The oil pressure will reduce
   (c) The engine rpm will increase
   (d) The engine rpm will reduce

23. Referring to the picture below, which of the following statements is true?

   (a) The TAS is 120 knots and VNO is 150 knots
   (b) VNE is 150 knots and the stalling speed with flap extended at MTMA is 35 knots
   (c) The IAS is 120 knots and VFE is 110 knots
   (d) The IAS is 120 knots and the clean stalling speed at MTMA is 35 knots

24. On a non-stressed skin wing, which components take up the twisting moments?
   (a) The ribs
   (b) The skin
   (c) The spars
   (d) The longerons

25. Refer to the picture below. What is the aircraft doing?

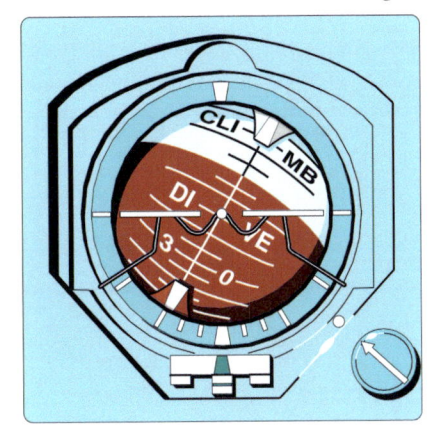

- (a) It is banked right at 30 degrees, pitched down at 15 degrees
- (b) It is banked right at 15 degrees, pitched down at 30 degrees
- (c) It is banked left at 15 degrees, pitched down at 10 degrees
- (d) It is banked left at 30 degrees, pitched down at 15 degrees

26. If the suction gauge indicates a lower pressure than normal, what effect will this have on flight instruments?

- (a) The Altimeter and Airspeed Indicator will be unreliable
- (b) The Attitude Indicator and Direction Indicator will be unreliable
- (c) The Turn co-ordinator will indicate a lower rate of turn than is being achieved
- (d) The Direction Indicator and Compass will be unreliable

27. During pre-flight inspection, the pilot notices that the tyre creep mark is not lined up with the wheel creep mark. What does this indicate?

- (a) The tyre is flat
- (b) The tyre has moved round the wheel rim
- (c) The landing gear oleo needs pumping up
- (d) The wheel needs replacing

28. What is the primary method of cooling the cylinders of a traditional aircraft piston engine?

- (a) By directing air to flow around the cylinders with cowlings and baffles
- (b) By circulating oil around the outside of the cylinders
- (c) By circulating oil around the inside of the cylinders
- (d) By circulating water around the outside of the cylinders

Intentionally Left Blank

Answers to Exercises

Chapter 1

1. b
2. c
3. d
4. c
5. c
6. a
7. d
8. b
9. b
10. d
11. a
12. a
13. c
14. c
15. d
16. d
17. b
18. b
19. d
20. d
21. c
22. d
23. a
24. c
25. b
26. a
27. a
28. d
29. b

Chapter 2

1. b
2. c
3. d
4. b
5. a
6. c
7. b
8. d
9. b
10. c
11. b
12. c
13. a
14. a
15. c
16. c
17. a
18. b
19. b
20. d
21. a
22. a
23. b
24. d

Chapter 3

1. a
2. d
3. b
4. b
5. c
6. c
7. d
8. b
9. d
10. c
11. b
12. d
13. b
14. b
15. b
16. d
17. c

Chapter 4

1. a
2. c
3. c
4. a
5. b
6. d
7. a
8. c
9. b
10. c
11. c
12. b
13. b
14. d
15. d
16. d

Chapter 5

1. c
2. d
3. c
4. c
5. b
6. d
7. a
8. d
9. a (airspeed remains relatively constant in a typical training aeroplane)
10. b
11. b
12. d
13. c
14. b
15. d
16. b
17. b
18. b
19. c
20. a
21. b
22. c
23. b
24. a
25. d
26. b
27. a
28. b
29. d

Chapter 6

1. c
2. a
3. b
4. d
5. b
6. d
7. d
8. b
9. c
10. a
11. a
12. b
13. b
14. b
15. c
16. a
17. d
18. c
19. d
20. a
21. b
22. d
23. d
24. d
25. a
26. b
27. b
28. c
29. b
30. b
31. d
32. a
33. b
34. a
35. a
36. b
37. c
38. a
39. d (not slamming the throttle)

Chapter 7

1. c
2. b
3. d
4. b
5. c
6. d

Chapter 8

1. b
2. a
3. c (not a normal condition)
4. d
5. b
6. d
7. c
8. c
9. b
10. a

Chapter 9

1. c
2. d
3. b
4. b
5. d
6. d
7. a
8. c
9. d
10. c
11. b
12. d

Chapter 10

1. d
2. b
3. a
4. a
5. d
6. c
7. a
8. c
9. c
10. a

Chapter 11

1. a
2. c
3. b
4. c
5. b
6. b
7. d
8. c
9. d
10. c
11. c
12. a
13. c
14. b
15. a
16. d
17. d
18. c
19. a

Chapter 12

1. c
2. d
3. a
4. b
5. c
6. d
7. d
8. b
9. c
10. b
11. b
(underspeed = underread)
12. b
13. d
14. d
15. a
16. b
17. d

Chapter 13

1. b
2. b
3. d
4. a
5. a
6. c
7. c
8. b
9. a
10. c
11. a
12. c
13. c

Chapter 14

1. c
2. c
3. d
4. d
5. c
6. d
7. b
8. a
9. a
10. a
11. a
12. b
13. b
14. c
15. d
16. a
17. b
18. b
19. d
20. b
21. d
22. c
23. b
24. a
25. d
26. b
27. b
28. a

Index

A
acceleration error, 164
accumulator, 146
AD, 194, 197
additional equipment, 194
adverse yaw, 25, 41
aerial, 156
aerobatics, 45, 47
aerodynamic balance, 28
aeronautical information circular, 187
AIC, 12
aileron drag, 25
ailerons, 23
air, 4
air data computer, 174
air/fuel ratio, 83
airspeed indicator, 59, 62
airworthiness, 193
airworthiness directive, 194, 197
Airworthiness Review Certificate, 197
alternate static, 54
alternator, 150
altimeter, 54, 62
altimeter errors, 56
altitude, 55
ammeter, 147, 150
angle of attack, 2, 12, 41, 67
antenna, 156
appropriate equipment, 194
ARC, 197
artificial horizon, 167
ASI, 59
aspect ratio, 11
atmosphere, 4
attitude indicator, 167
autorotation, 69, 73
AVGAS, 111, 143, 146
axis, 13

B
baffles, 90
balance, 198
barometric error, 57
battery, 108, 146
battery charging, 146
battery management system, 108
bearing, 91, 137
Bernouilli's Theory, 9
blade angle, 115
blade twist, 117
blockage, 61
bonding, 139, 146
boost, 126
booster pump, 144
boundary layer, 5
brace position, 182
brake, 151
bulkhead, 132

C
C of A, 195
CAA publications, 187
cabin conditioning, 154
cabin heater, 154
cable, 137
cam, 85
camber, 5, 10
camshaft, 85
capacity, 146
carbon monoxide, 126, 185
carburettor, 88
carburettor heat, 93
carburettor icing, 93, 95, 111, 125, 128
cavitation, 144
centre of gravity, 7, 28, 45, 48
centre of lift, 7
Certificate of Airworthiness, 47, 195
Certificate of Maintenance Review, 199
certificate of release to service, 126, 196

Check A, 196
chord line, 3
CHT gauge, 127
circuit breaker, 148
climb, 42
coarse pitch, 118
coil, 106, 107
collector tank, 144
compass, 163
compression ratio, 85
compressor, 109, 111
constant speed unit, 118
control balance, 28
control linkage, 21
control run, 137
control stops, 138
control surfaces, 21
controlled environment, 197
cooling, 90
corrosion, 134
couple, 7
cowl flap, 90
cowl flaps, 127
cowling, 90
critical angle, 2, 10, 42, 46, 67, 68, 71
cycles, 106
cylinder head temperature, 127
cylinders, 83
density, 4

D

descent, 44
design, 193
detonation, 92
deviation, 164
DI, 169
diesel engine, 105
differential ailerons, 26
dihedral, 14
dip, 164
direction indicator, 169
directional stability, 13, 24, 31, 40
ditching, 186
ditching precautions, 186
documents to be carried, 199
downwash, 11

drag, 3, 5
drift, 170
duplicate inspection, 196
dynamic pressure, 5, 59
dynamic stability, 9, 41

E

EFIS, 173
EGT, 93
EGT gauge, 126
electric engine, 106
electric motor, 106
electrical bonding, 139, 146
electrical system, 146
electronic speed controller, 108
elevator, 22
emergency location transmitter, 186
engine drives, 143
engine mounting, 138
engine starting, 96
equipment, 194
exhaust gas temperature, 126

F

FADEC, 121, 126
fairlead, 137
filter, 144, 152
fine pitch, 118
fire extinguisher, 183
first aid, 183
flap, 29, 45
flap limiting speed, 47
flight director, 174
flight envelope, 47, 72
flight level, 55
Flight Manual, 47, 56, 70, 74, 90, 93, 185, 198
flowmeter, 93, 95, 127
flutter, 28, 46, 47
forces, 1
form drag, 6
formers, 132
four stroke cycle, 84
frame, 132
frequency, 106
frise ailerons, 26

fuel, 93
fuel check, 145
fuel injection, 95
fuel pump, 143
fuel storage, 146, 183
fuel system, 143
fuse, 148, 194
fuselage, 1, 132

G

gas generator, 109
generator, 86, 147
glass cockpit, 173
glide, 44
governor, 119
ground effect, 12
ground handling, 185
guide vanes, 109
gyroscope, 164

H

harness, 181
headset, 155
height, 55
helix angle, 117
HSI, 170
humidity, 4, 93
hydraulic system, 151
IAS, 59

I

ice, 93
ICO, 93
ignition, 86
ignition switch, 87
incidence, 69
incipient spin recovery, 76
indicated airspeed, 59
induced drag, 3, 6, 9, 11, 42
induction, 84, 107
inset hinge, 28
instrument error, 56
insurance, 198
intercom, 156
interference drag, 6

international flight, 199
International Standard Atmosphere, 4
inverter, 108
ISA, 4

J

jack, 151, 154
Jet-A1, 111, 146
JET-A1, 105
joining the parts, 135

L

landing, 12, 48
lateral stability, 14
LCD, 173
leak, 62
level flight, 5
life preserver, 186
liferaft, 186
lift, 9, 44
lift coefficient, 5, 10
lift formula, 5
lights, 194
liquid cooling system, 108
load factor, 46, 47, 70
load meter, 126
log book, 196
longeron, 132
low volts, 150
lubrication, 91

M

magnetic compass, 163
magnetic field, 106, 107
magnetic flux, 107
magnetic reluctance, 108
magneto, 86, 96
maintenance, 195
manifold pressure, 126
manoeuvre, 39
manoeuvre envelope, 47
mass balance, 28
materials, 134
maximum manoeuvring speed, 46
minimum drag speed, 6, 30, 43, 45

minimum power speed, 43
mixture, 83, 89
mixture control, 92
modification, 193
MOGAS, 144
monocoque, 133

N
never exceed speed, 46
Newton's first law, 21
Newton's third law, 21
noise, 127, 139
noise certificate, 198

O
OAT gauge, 128
oil, 91
oil pressure, 92, 127
oil pressure failure, 120
oil temperature, 92, 127
oleo, 153
Otto cycle, 84
oxygen, 184

P
parasite drag, 3, 5
Permit to Fly, 47, 195, 199
pitching moment, 7
pitot, 186
pitot cover, 186
pitot head, 59, 61
pitot pressure, 59
pitot/static system, 60
position error, 56
post, 132
power, 93
pressure altitude, 54
pressure error, 56
pressure head, 61
primary effects of controls, 24
priming, 89
profile drag, 3, 5
propeller emergencies, 120
propeller torque, 115
pulley, 137

Q
QFE, 55
QNH, 55

R
radio equipment, 155, 194
rate of turn, 42
RCDI, 58
relative airflow, 2
relay, 149
repairs, 196
ribs, 132
rivet, 136
roll, 39, 45
rotor inertia, 108
rpm, 125
rpm gauge, 125
rpm lever, 119
rudder, 24

S
seat, 181
secondary effect, 39
semi-monococque, 134
separation, 68
Service Bulletins, 193
servo, 27
short-circuit, 109
skin friction, 5
slat, 31
slip ball, 172
slipstream, 120
slot, 29, 31
solder, 135
solid state gyroscope, 174
spacer, 132
spar, 131
spats, 153
speed stability, 45
spin, 48, 69, 74
spin prevention, 75
spin recovery actions, 74
spinning, 74
spiral dive, 42
spoiler, 26
squelch, 155

SSR, 158
stabilator, 22
stability, 8, 41
stability in direction, 13
stability in speed, 30
stability of airspeed, 7
stall, 5, 48, 68
stall prevention, 72
stall warning, 72
stalling, 67
stalling speed, 70
standard stall recovery, 71
starting, 87
static pressure, 53, 54, 59
static stability, 8
static vent, 53, 61
STC, 194
stops, 138
strap, 181
streamlining, 6
stressed skin, 133
stringer, 132
supplement, 198
symptoms of the stall, 71
synchro compass, 170
synchronous reluctance motor, 108

T

tab, 26
tachometer, 125
tailplane, 7
technical log, 126
temperature, 95
temperature error, 56
throttle, 89
topple, 168
torque, 84, 107, 108, 115, 136
total drag, 6
total reaction, 3
transponder, 158
trim, 45
trim drag, 8
trim tab, 27
trimming, 26
true airspeed, 59
turbine, 109
turbo-charging, 96
turbojet, 109
turboprop, 110
turn, 42, 45, 46, 70
turn co-ordinator, 173
turn indicator, 172
turnbuckle, 137
turning error, 164
Type Certificate, 193
tyre, 153

U

uncertificated aircraft, 199
undercarriage, 152

V

valve timing, 85
valves, 85
vapourisation, 144
variable pitch, 118
vent, 145
ventilation, 154
venturi, 89
vertical speed indicator, 58
VHF, 155
viscosity, 91
voltage regulator, 147
voltmeter, 147
vortex, 9, 11, 12

W

wake vortex, 12
wander, 170
washout, 10, 69
water, 93
water detecting, 145
water in fuel, 145
weight, 1, 198
welding, 136
wheel, 152
windmilling, 117
wing, 1, 131
wing section, 2, 10

Y
yaw, 39, 69
yaw indication, 171

Notes

Notes